MW00426117

The God Revealed in Jesus Christ

An Introduction to Trinitarian Theology

By Grace Communion International

Compiling selected articles by Terry Akers, Gary Deddo, Neil Earle,
J. Michael Feazell, Sheila Graham, John Halford, Paul Kroll,
Michael D. Morrison, Ralph Orr, Dan Rogers, and Joseph Tkach

CONTENTS

THE GOD REVEALED IN JESUS CHRIST

If we want the most accurate picture of God, we don't need to look any further than Jesus Christ. In Jesus we meet God as God really is. "Anyone who has seen me," Jesus said, "has seen the Father" (John 14:9).

Jesus Christ is the perfect revelation of the Father. "No one has ever seen God, but the one and only Son [Jesus]…has made him known" (John 1:18).

Through Jesus' words and actions, we hear and see what matters most to every human being—that God the Father loves us unconditionally. "God so loved the world that he gave his one and only Son, that whoever believes in him shall not perish but have eternal life" (John 3:16).

Even at our worst, God loves us. John continues, "For God did not send his Son into the world to condemn the world, but in order that the world might be saved through him" (verse 17). The Father sent Jesus out of his love and his commitment to save us.

Trinitarian-based

Jesus is God's self-revelation to the world. God has broken through to us by sending his eternal Son into our world. Jesus upheld the understanding that the one God is the object of our love and worship (Mark 12:29-31).

Jesus emphasized that God (Father, Son and Holy Spirit) was reconciling humanity to himself. That is why he instructed his followers to welcome people into right relationship with God by baptizing them in the name of the Father, and of the Son and of the Holy Spirit (Matthew 28:19).

The God we worship through Jesus Christ is the Triune God. The doctrine of the Trinity is central to how we understand the Bible and all points of theology that flow from it. That theology begins with an essential "who" question: "Who is the God made known in Jesus Christ, and who are we in relation to him?"

Trinitarian faith is based on a belief in the doctrine of the Trinity (the biblical teaching that there is one God, who is eternally Father, Son and Holy Spirit). Furthermore, it refers to a Christ-centered understanding of who God is.

Christ-centered

Christians recognize Jesus as the center of our faith and our devotion to God. Jesus reveals to us what God is like (John 6:37). "No one knows the Father except the Son and those to whom the Son chooses to reveal him" (Matthew 11:27). Trinitarian theology is first and foremost Christ-centered. Jesus is the unique Word of God to humanity and the unique Word of humanity to God (John 1:1-14). As the representative of all humanity, Jesus responded to God perfectly.

Jesus indicates that he is the key to understanding Scripture. He said to a group of Jewish religious leaders in John 5:39-40: "You diligently study the Scriptures because you think that by them you possess eternal life. These are the Scriptures that testify about me, yet you refuse to come to me to have life." Jesus, who is the focus of Scripture, is our source of salvation.

So we seek to understand the Bible through the lens of who Jesus is. He is the basis and logic of our faith—for he alone is the self-revelation of God.

Relationship-focused

Trinitarian faith is relational. Even before creation, there was a relationship of love between the Father and the Son (John 17:24). And in Jesus, that relationship of love is extended to all humanity. Jesus Christ, the only Son of God, has become one with us in our humanity to represent us as his brothers and sisters in the very presence of the Father (see John 1:14; Ephesians 1:9-10, 20-23; Hebrews 2:11, 14).

Human beings have turned away from God and broken the bonds of communion with God. But because of Jesus, God has reconciled us and renewed our relationship with him!

Not only that, as we respond to his call to us to share in that restored relationship, he comes to live in us by the Holy Spirit (Romans 8:9-11). In Jesus and through the Holy Spirit, we become God's treasured children, adopted by grace (Romans 8:15-16).

This means that Christian life and faith are primarily about four kinds of personal relationship:

1. the relationship of perfect love shared by the Father, the Son

and the Holy Spirit from all eternity,

2. the relationship of the eternal Son with humanity, established when the Son became human in the person of Jesus,

3. the relationship of humanity with the Father through the Son and by the Spirit, and,

4. the relationship of humans with one another, in the Spirit, as children of the Father.

Who is Jesus?

"Who are you, Lord?" was Paul's anguished question on the Damascus Road, where he was confronted by the resurrected Jesus (Acts 9:5). He spent the rest of his life answering this question and then sharing the answer with all who would listen. The answer, revealed to us in his writings and elsewhere in Scripture, is the heart of the gospel and the focus of Trinitarian theology.

The Son of God, who is united from eternity to the Father and the Spirit, is now also joined to humanity because of his incarnation—his becoming a real flesh-and-blood human being (John 1:14). We summarize this by saying that Jesus is both fully God and fully human. That fact will never change, because he remains, in his divine nature and his human nature, the one mediator between God and humanity for all time (1 Timothy 2:5). His Incarnation did not end with his death or with his ascension. It continues forever. He was resurrected bodily and he ascended bodily. He will return bodily, the same as he departed. So when we say Jesus Christ, we are referring to God, and we are also referring to humanity.

As the One who is uniquely God (Creator and Sustainer of all) and also fully human, Jesus is the unique meeting place of God and humanity. Through the life, death, resurrection and ascension of Jesus, God and humanity were reconciled and human nature was regenerated—made new (2 Corinthians 5:17-18). In Jesus Christ all humans are reconciled to God. As the Lord and Savior of all humanity he has opened up the way for all to enter into an eternal union and communion with God.

Incarnation for salvation

The miracle of the Incarnation is not something that happened "once upon a time," now long past and simply affecting one person, Jesus. What he accomplished changed human nature itself, changed history, changed how the entire cosmos is "wired"—it is a new creation (2 Corinthians 5:17). The spiritual reality is, for now, hidden in Christ, and we still experience the effects of evil that still occur in this world. The Incarnation of the eternal Son of

God, entering time and space and taking on our human nature to change everything forever, reaching back through all human history, and reaching forward to encompass all time. He has now become our Lord and Savior, not as an external agent, but from the inside, in his humanity.

As Paul teaches, God was, in Christ, reconciling the world to himself (2 Corinthians 5:19). Paul speaks of this transformation in Romans 7:4, where he says that even while we are alive, we are already dead to the law by the body of Christ. Jesus' death in human flesh for us, though a historical event, is a present reality that applies to all humanity (past, present and future). "You died," Paul says to the Colossians, "and your life is now hidden with Christ in God" (Colossians 3:3). Even before we die physically, we are given new life—made alive with Jesus in his resurrection.

Christ's incarnation and atoning work accomplished the renewal of our human nature. In him, God has reconciled to himself every human being, even those who lived before Jesus came.

In Ephesians 2:5-6 we read that those who trust in Christ share in his life, death, resurrection and ascension. Here Paul asserts that just as we are dead already in Jesus' substitutionary death, we have also already been "made alive together with him" and we are "raised up together with him" and "seated together with him in the heavenly realms." All this comes from God's grace and is experienced through faith—the faith of Jesus that he shares with us by the Spirit.

Jesus, the second Adam

In Romans 5, Paul addresses believers, but he also explains what Christ accomplished on behalf of all humanity even before anyone came to faith in God through Christ. Jesus Christ died for people who were still:

- "powerless" and "ungodly" (verse 6).
- "sinners" (verse 8).
- "God's enemies" (verse 10).

God accomplished his great work for us out of his "love for us" even while "we were still sinners" (verse 8). The result was that even "while we were God's enemies, we were reconciled to him through the death of his Son" (verse 10).

Paul goes on to explain that what Jesus Christ accomplished as the second Adam counteracts what the first Adam did. Through Christ, as the new head of all humanity, "God's grace and the gift that came by the grace of that one man Jesus Christ abounded for the many" (verse 15). Paul continues:

- The gift "brought justification" rather than condemnation (verse 16).

- "Those who receive God's abundant provision of grace and of the gift of righteousness reign in life through the one man, Jesus Christ" (verse 17).
- "One righteous act resulted in justification and life for all people" (verse 18).
- "Through the obedience of the one man the many will be made righteous" (verse 19).
- "Grace increased all the more" so that "grace might reign through righteousness to bring eternal life through Jesus Christ our Lord" (verses 20-21).

God did all this for us before we were even born. The benefit of what Jesus did so long ago extends to the past, to the present and into the future. Paul says, "how much more, having been reconciled, shall we be saved through his life!" (verse 10). This shows that salvation is not a one-time event, but an enduring relationship that God has with all humanity—a relationship formed within the person of Jesus Christ, who has brought God and humanity together in peace.

Jesus has not simply done something for us, he has done something *with* us by including us in his life, death, resurrection and ascension. Paul explains this in Ephesians 2:4-6:

- When Jesus died, we, in our sinful human nature, died with him.
- When Jesus rose, we, in our reconciled human nature, rose with him.
- When Jesus ascended, we, in our redeemed human nature, ascended and became seated with him at the Father's side.

Everything God has done in Christ shows us the mind, heart and character of the Father, the Son and the Holy Spirit. God is on the side of his people and all his creation. God is for us, even before we respond to him (verse 5). He has provided reconciliation and eternal life in communion with himself for every human being.

For all humanity

As Jesus made his way into Jerusalem for his final Passover with his disciples, the crowds shouted: "Hosanna! Blessed is he who comes in the name of the Lord! Blessed is the king of Israel!" (John 12:13).

Shortly thereafter, he proclaimed his impending death to those who went up to the Temple to worship. Jesus called to the Father: "Father, glorify your name!" A voice then thundered to the crowd: "I have glorified it, and will glorify it again" (verse 29).

Jesus told them the voice was for their benefit and that God's judgment on evil had come so that the prince of this world would be driven out (verses 30-31). He also said, "And I, when I am lifted up from the earth, will draw all people to myself" (verse 32). Jesus conquered evil in order to attract all people to himself. The apostles believed that Jesus died to redeem us all:

- 2 Corinthians 5:14: "Christ's love compels us, because we are convinced that one died for all, and therefore all died."
- Colossians 1:19-20: "God was pleased to have all his fullness dwell in him, and through him to reconcile to himself all things, whether things on earth or things in heaven, by making peace through his blood, shed on the cross."
- 1 Timothy 2:3-6: "This is good, and pleases God our Savior, who wants all people to be saved and to come to a knowledge of the truth. For there is one God and one mediator between God and mankind, the man Christ Jesus, who gave himself as a ransom for all people."
- 1 Timothy 4:9-10: "This is a trustworthy saying that deserves full acceptance… we have put our hope in the living God, who is the Savior of all people, and especially of those who believe."
- Hebrews 2:9: "We do see Jesus, who…suffered death, so that by the grace of God he might taste death for everyone."
- 1 John 2:2: "[Jesus is] the atoning sacrifice for our sins, and not only for ours but also for the sins of the whole world."

These passages show that Jesus died for all humanity, that is, in their place and on their behalf. Jesus did for us, as one of us, what we could never do for ourselves. This is what is meant by the vicarious humanity of Jesus (the word *vicarious* refers to a representative substitute).

In our place and on our behalf

Throughout the book of Hebrews, Jesus is depicted as our great High Priest, representing all humanity, providing on our behalf a perfect response to God. He is presented as the one who stands among us, in the midst of the congregation, and who leads us in worship (Hebrews 2:12-13). He represents us as our older brother. He has become one of us, sharing our very nature, learning obedience, being tempted as we are, but overcoming that temptation perfectly (Hebrews 2:14-18; 4:15).

Theologian Thomas Torrance explained it this way:

Jesus steps into the actual situation where we are summoned to have faith in God, to believe and trust in him, and he acts in our place and in our stead from within the depths of our unfaithfulness and provides us freely with a faithfulness in which we may share…. That is to say, if we think of belief, trust or faith as forms of human activity before God, then we must think of Jesus Christ as believing, trusting, or having faith in God the Father on our behalf and in our place. (*The Mediation of Christ*, p. 82)

Jesus is the one who, as we respond, perfects our faith and makes us holy (Hebrews 12:2; 2:11; 10:10, 14). He acted as one of us "in our place" or "on our behalf" (Hebrews 2:9; 5:1; 6:20; 7:25, 27; 9:7).

The response of faith

So how do we personally share in all that Christ has graciously done for us? How can we personally participate and be in communion with God who has, already, reconciled us to himself? We do so by trusting in him—by having faith that he, by grace, has accomplished for us all that is needed for our salvation. In short, we say we are saved by grace through faith (Ephesians 2:8).

Does this mean that we are saved by a faith that we work up? Does our salvation depend upon how great and sincere our repentance or our faith is? No, for salvation would then be dependent on something we do rather than dependent upon grace alone.

The good news is that our salvation does not depend on what we do—it does not depend on the strength of our faith or our repentance. It depends on the strength of our Savior, it depends on his faithfulness. He died for us. The gift has been given; our repentance and faith are simply responses to what God has given us. They are the way we accept and receive the free gift. Jesus has done everything necessary for our salvation from start to finish, so even our responses of repentance and faith are gifts of sharing in Jesus' perfect responses for us as our faithful mediator.

As Thomas Torrance explained, if we want to think of faith as a human activity, then we must think of Jesus as having done that for us as well. Just as he died for us, he lived righteously for us. As our representative, he presents to God a perfect response on behalf of all humanity. We are saved by his obedience (Romans 5:19)—and that includes his faith. Our salvation rests on Jesus—the perfect foundation.

As our High Priest, Jesus takes our responses, perfects them and gives them to the Father, all in the Spirit. As our mediator (1 Timothy 2:5), he ministers both from God to us and represents us in our relationship to God.

So we join him in his response.

The role of human choice

What God has done in Christ to reconcile us to himself calls for a response. We are urged to accept him, to welcome and receive him. We do so by trusting in him and what he has accomplished for us. The Holy Spirit enables us to freely welcome the truth and walk in it. But God does not force us to accept the truth of his love for us. A love that forced a responding love would not be loving. God's love then calls for our decision to freely receive and freely love God in return.

Our choice is to either affirm or deny the reality that God loves us and has made every provision for us to be his children. Denial of this truth has consequences, but it will not change the reality of what God has done for us in Christ and thus who we are in Christ. Human beings choose to accept who Christ is or attempt to live in denial of who he is.

Real freedom is found in God, as theologian Karl Barth reminds us:

> The real freedom of man is decided by the fact that God is his God. In freedom he can only choose to be the man of God, i.e., to be thankful to God. With any other choice he would simply be groping in the void, betraying and destroying his true humanity. Instead of choosing freedom, he would be choosing enslavement. (*Church Dogmatics* IV.1, p. 43)

So what is our place in all of this? We choose to accept Jesus and all he has to offer or to reject him. Through the Spirit, God the Father is calling all people to place their trust in Jesus with a thankful and hopeful heart, and to share with other believers in the Body of Christ, which is the church. As we celebrate together in communities of faith and worship, our lives are transformed.

Personal response

Jesus called people to repent and believe (Mark 1:15). The early church continued this message, calling people to repent and be baptized (Acts 2:38) and to be changed (3:19).

Our response is important. The apostle Paul writes in Romans 5:17 that "those who *receive* God's abundant provision of grace and of the free gift of righteousness [will] reign in life." Abundant and freely given grace calls for us to *receive* it in faith. In Romans 5 Paul weaves together 1) elements of the reality accomplished by Christ on behalf of all humanity and 2) our response and participation in that relationship and reality. We must take care not to confuse what is true in Jesus for all humanity with each person's response to that truth.

God's gift is offered to all in order to be received by all. It is received by having faith in what God in Christ through the Holy Spirit has done for us. It is by faith in the grace of God that we begin participating in the relationship Jesus has restored, and start receiving the benefits included in that relationship.

We do not "decide for Christ" in the sense that our personal decision causes our salvation. Rather, we accept what is ours already in Christ, placing our trust in Jesus, who has already perfectly trusted for us in our place. When we accept the grace of Jesus Christ, we begin to participate in God's love for us. We begin to live according to who we really are, as the new creation that God, prior to our ever believing, made us to be in Christ.

Some people find it helpful to explain this using the terms *objective* and *subjective*. An objective truth is a reality, whereas our understanding of and response to that reality is subjective. There is a universal, or objective, truth about all humanity in Jesus, based on the fact that he has joined himself to our human nature and turned it around. But there is also the personal, or subjective, experience of this truth that comes as we surrender to the promptings of the Holy Spirit and join with Jesus Christ.

These categories of objective (universal) and subjective (personal) truth are found in Scripture. For one example, in 2 Corinthians, Paul starts with the objective nature of salvation: "All this is from God, who reconciled [past tense] us to himself through Christ and gave us the ministry of reconciliation: that God was reconciling the world to himself in Christ, not counting people's sins against them. And he has committed to us the message of reconciliation" (verses 18-19).

Here we find an objective truth that applies to all—God has already reconciled all to himself through Jesus, the incarnate Son of God. Paul then goes on in verses 20-21 to address the subjective truth: "We are therefore Christ's ambassadors, as though God were making his appeal through us. We implore you on Christ's behalf: Be reconciled to God."

How can all be "reconciled" already and yet some need to "be reconciled"? The answer is that both are true. All are already reconciled in Christ—this is the universal/objective truth—but yet not all embrace and therefore personally experience their reconciliation with God—that is the personal/subjective truth. God has a gracious attitude toward all people, but not everyone has responded to his grace. No one benefits even from a freely given gift if that gift is refused, especially the gift of coming under the grace of God in Jesus Christ in the power of the Spirit.

A second example of objective/subjective truth is found in the book of Hebrews where the author states in a straightforward manner, "For good news came to us just as to them, but the message they heard did not benefit them, because they were not united by faith with those who listened" (Hebrews 4:2) The benefits of a relational reality such as salvation can only be subjectively (personally) experienced when received by faith.

So while Christ is Lord and Savior of all, has died for all, and has reconciled all to God, not all will necessarily be saved. Not all will necessarily receive Christ who is their salvation. Not all will necessarily enter into their salvation, which is eternal union and communion with God as his beloved children. Some may somehow "deny the Savior who bought them" (2 Peter 2:1). While Scripture teaches the unlimited scope of Christ's atoning work, taking away the sins of the whole cosmos, it does not offer us a guarantee that all will necessarily receive the free gift of grace.

No explanation is given as to why or how this rejection of grace could happen. But rejection is presented as a real possibility, one that God has done everything needed to prevent. If there are those who reject Christ and their salvation, it will not be due to any lack or limit of God's grace. So we, sharing in the very heart of God, can also be those "not wanting any to perish, but all to come to repentance" (2 Peter 3:9).

What is our Christian mission?

Jesus' life and ministry provides the motivation for every aspect of our life, including our participation in mission and ministry with Jesus. The love of Christ compels us to take part in what Jesus is doing in the world through the Spirit. Out of love we declare the gospel and invite all people to receive and embrace it. In doing so, we hope what is true of them already in Christ will be experienced by them personally in faith. Like Jesus, we desire all to participate and receive all the benefits of Christ now. Then they, too, can join in Jesus' ongoing mission to draw others into a living relationship with their Lord and Savior. What greater joy and privilege could there be?

Our participation now in Jesus' love and life bears good fruit and personal joy that stretch into eternity. As we welcome the truth of the gospel, we can't help but worship our Lord and Savior!

Key Points of Trinitarian Theology

Following are some basic precepts of this theology:.

1. The Triune God created all people through the Son of God, who also is known as the Word of God.

2. We were created so that we could participate in the love relationship enjoyed by the Father, the Son and the Holy Spirit.

3. We are enabled and qualified to participate in this relationship of love through Jesus Christ.

4. The Son became human, the man Jesus Christ, taking on our human nature.

5. He did this to reconcile all humanity to God through his birth, life, death, resurrection and ascension.

6. The crucified, resurrected and glorified Jesus is the representative and the substitute for all humanity.

7. As Savior and Lord of all humanity, Jesus now sits at the right hand of the Father, and he draws all people to himself by the power of the Holy Spirit.

8. In Christ, humanity is loved and accepted by the Father.

9. Jesus Christ paid for all our sins—past, present and future—and there is no longer any debt to pay.

10. The Father has in Christ forgiven all our sins, and he eagerly desires that we receive his forgiveness.

11. We can enjoy his love only as we believe/trust that he loves us. We can enjoy his forgiveness only when we believe/trust he has forgiven us.

12. When we respond to the Spirit by turning to God, believing the good news and picking up our cross and following Jesus, the Spirit leads us into the transformed life of the kingdom of God.

Recommended Resources for Further Study

To study Trinitarian theology in greater depth, we recommend the following resources:

GCI articles

Grace Communion International has hundreds of helpful articles that address Christian belief and practice. Some of them are included in this book. See our website for more.

GCI video programs

You're Included is an online program presenting interviews with Trinitarian theologians and authors. View or download these interviews at https://learn.gcs.edu/course/view.php?id=58.

Books

Michael Jinkins, *Invitation to Theology* (InterVarsity, 2001; 278 pages)

Darrell Johnson, *Experiencing the Trinity* (Regent College, 2002; 112 pages)

C. S. Lewis, *Mere Christianity* (HarperCollins, often reprinted; 225 pages)

Fred Sanders, *The Deep Things of God: How the Trinity Changes Everything* (Crossway, 2010; 256 pages)

James B. Torrance, *Worship, Community and the Triune God of Grace* (InterVarsity, 1996; 130 pages)

Thomas F. Torrance, *The Mediation of Christ* (Helmers & Howard, 1992; 144 pages)

AN INTRODUCTION
TO TRINITARIAN THEOLOGY

I. Introduction

A. Stating the topic

We say that we have a "Trinitarian theology." However, most churches accept the doctrine of the Trinity, and their theology is at least somewhat Trinitarian, but we emphasize the Trinity more than most churches do. Sometimes we say that we have an Incarnational Trinitarian theology, or a Trinitarian Christ-centered theology. None of these are completely distinctive terms, but they do mention some of the emphases that we have.

We call our theology Trinitarian because the doctrine of the Trinity is not a side point, or just one of many other doctrines. We are trying to be more consistent with it, to let it be the organizing principle for other doctrines. Whether we are talking about sin or salvation or the church, we want to ask, how does the doctrine of the Trinity help us understand this particular doctrine? How is it connected with the nature of God, and of who God is in his innermost being?

We are trying to understand a little better some points about God's relationship with humanity: his purpose in creating humanity, the way in which he saves us, and how we should respond to him. We believe that our theology is true to the Bible, and that it helps make sense of what we are doing on the earth and in the church. It helps tie different doctrines together.

B. Not trying to criticize others

In the process of explaining our theology, we find that our beliefs are sometimes a little different from other theological traditions, and in some points of doctrine, we conclude that those other Christians are mistaken. This does not mean that we think they are non-Christian, or that those people won't be saved. We all make mistakes, and we have no doubt made a few of our own.

We all believe that we are saved through the life, death and resurrection of Jesus – and it is good for us to have that in common with many other Christians around the world.

Thankfully, we are saved not by having absolutely perfect theology, but we are saved by Christ, by grace, by trusting in Jesus to do for us what we cannot do for ourselves. Other Christians are doing the best they can, and we are doing the best that we can, to understand the Bible, and to understand the meaning of life and how it all fits together. Our purpose here is not to criticize other people and other theologies, but simply to do the best that we can in explaining what we believe, and how we think it is true to the Bible, and how we think it helps us understand what our life is all about.

C. A desire to understand as much as we can

This is what the early church called "faith seeking understanding." We already understand some things about God, and we believe them, but we are convinced that this is something we'd like to know more about, and so we try to understand as much as we can. We have fallen in love with Jesus, and we'd like to learn more about who he is, and the relationship he has with us, and what he has in mind for our future.

We could also describe our goal as an act of worship: we want to praise God for who he is and what he has done and what he has promised to do in the future – and in order to praise God for these things, we need to understand what they are. The goal is to explain things as best as we can, based on the Bible and the way that God has revealed himself to us ultimately and personally in Jesus Christ.

D. Practical significance

We will not try to cover all the biblical or historical evidence for the doctrine of the Trinity. We have published other articles about that. What we would like to focus on here is the practical significance of the doctrine.

At first, it seems like the doctrine of the Trinity is just information about God: God is three Persons in one Being. It's about him. But what does that have to do with us? Does it make any difference to us here on earth?

Yes. That is because persons have relationships with one another, and relationships are important for all of us. God created us to have relationships similar to the relationships that exist for all eternity within the Triune God. The divine Persons in the Godhead have relationships, and persons here on earth have relationships, too, and there is supposed to be some similarity in the kind of relationships we have.

The Bible tells us that "God is love" (1 John 4:8). Not that he has love, but that he IS love. That is descriptive of who he is and how he lives in eternity, how he interacts with other persons. Even before God created the universe, even before God created angelic beings, he was love. When God was the only thing there is, God was love—love among the triune Persons.

Before God created anything, what would God be like? If there is only one person in God, there would be no one to love, because love means caring for and caring about someone else. But if God were somehow loving but alone, that would mean that God would be unable to fully be or express some of his internal nature. God would be deficient. The statement that "God is love" would be meaningless before creation, if God were only one Person, because the love could not be expressed.

The doctrine of the Trinity tells us that even before God created anything, he could be love, because the Father loved the Son, and the Son loved the Holy Spirit, and the Spirit loves the Father, and so forth. There was love within the Triune God, even before anything had been created (John 17:24). The three Persons were distinguishable from one another, but united to one another in love. This is important for who God is, and it's important for who we are, as well.

II. Centered on Jesus Christ

As mentioned above, we sometimes say that we have a Trinitarian, *Christ-centered* theology. Some people wonder, if all three Persons in the Godhead are fully divine, and *equal* in being divine, why should we center our theology on *one* of them in particular?

A. Jesus is fully divine

God is revealed to us *most clearly* in the Person of Jesus Christ. Jesus is where God has chosen to make himself *visible* to us (Colossians 1:15). Jesus is the <u>Word</u> made flesh—God the Son become human. He has revealed himself in a way that we could see him, touch him, hear him and see how he lives. Jesus is the way that God has chosen to reveal himself to us.

In John 14:8, Philip asked Jesus: "Lord, show us the Father and that will be enough for us." Jesus responded in verse 9: "Don't you know me, Philip, even after I have been among you such a long time? Anyone who has seen me has seen the Father."

Jesus is not saying that God the Father is 5 foot 8 inches tall, with brown hair and Middle Eastern features. Rather, he is saying that in his most important respects (his character, purposes, heart, and mind), *God the Father is like Jesus Christ* in terms of the way he interacts with others. The compassion that Jesus had shows us what God is like. The zeal for righteousness, that's what God is like. The willingness to sacrifice for others, God is like that, too. Jesus helps us see what God the Father is like – and the Holy Spirit is like that, too.

When Jesus became a flesh-and-blood human being, he was showing us in a tangible and visible way what the Triune God is like. The apostle Paul says, "The Son is the image of the invisible God" (Colossians 1:15). Even though we cannot see God directly, Jesus shows us what he's like, in a way that we *can* see and hear.

Colossians 2:9 says, "In Christ all the fullness of the Deity lives in bodily form." Jesus is the summary that we are given of what we need to know about God. We can never know God completely – he is much bigger than our minds are capable of comprehending – but we are able to have an accurate understanding of at least *some* things about God, because Jesus embodies all that any human being can know of God, and he came to reveal God to us. He does not reveal everything, but what he does reveal is accurate. John 1:18 says, "No one has ever seen God, but the one and only Son, who is himself God and is in closest relationship with the Father, *has made him known.*"

B. Jesus is fully human

All orthodox Christian theology includes the teaching that Jesus is fully human. That might seem obvious to many people – he was born as a baby, grew as a boy, and he died. As the Bible says, in John 1:14, "The Word *became flesh* and made his dwelling among us." He didn't just put on a costume that made him *look* human – no, he was a real human being. He ate ordinary food, breathed air like an ordinary person, his fingernails grew and he got thirsty and tired. When he scraped his knee, he bled, and when they crucified him, he died just like other people would have.

He was fully God and fully human – both at the same time. We have never seen that combination before, but with God, all things are possible, and so if that's what he did, then we have to make room in our theology for it. God can do one-of-a-kind things that aren't comparable to anything else. He is able to be in his own creation. The Incarnation of the Son of God is that unique kind of thing.

There are a number of reasons as to why a divine Person might want to become a human being. He came to communicate to us on a level we could understand; he came to die for us; he came to experience life as a human so that we could know for sure that he understood what it's like for us to be human. But just as Jesus shows us what God is like, he also shows us what *humanity* is really like. He is the perfect human.

C. Connecting human beings to God

Jesus has a unique role. He has been part of the circle of God's triune life, and he's been part of the human circle of life, and because of that, he provides a unique connection between humanity and God. In a sense, he is a bridge between the two, a bridge God uses to bring us into the divine fellowship. Not that we are part of the Trinity, but in and through his humanity, we do share in God's life.

2 Peter 1:4 says, "He has given us his very great and precious promises, so that through them you may *participate* in the divine nature." So in some way we participate in what God is. We are in the family of God, or the kingdom of God. We are in fellowship with God, in a *relationship* with God – and this is all made possible by Jesus.

1 Timothy 2:5 says, "There is one God and one mediator between God and mankind, the man Christ Jesus." A mediator is a person in the middle – in this case, a person serving to connect humanity with God. God initiated this; he is the one who sent Jesus to earth to become a human being, and to be resurrected back into heaven to make this connection work. Jesus is the key link or connector between humanity and God.

The doctrine of the Trinity is important for this understanding. For our connection with God, for our future with God, it is essential that our mediator be fully God in his own right. No human being is good enough to *earn* a connection with God, who is infinitely far above us in power, glory, wisdom and righteousness. No created human being could rise up to God's level as Creator, but God is able to put himself at *our* level.

Jesus is perfect in righteousness and holiness, and yet one of us. He is the pathway by which other human beings are brought *into* the presence of the holy and perfect God. The doctrine of the Trinity says that Jesus is fully God, and the doctrine of the Incarnation says that Jesus became fully human, and he continues to be both divine and human, and with that combination, now we are ready to talk about a relationship between God and humanity.

III. Humanity in the image of God

A. Created in his image

Jesus shows us what God is like, and he also shows us what humanity is supposed to be like, and this implies that there is some important *similarity* between God and humans. This is not because humans are good enough to rise up to the level of God. No, it all comes from God as a gift given to us. He is the one who created us this way in the first place. We find it stated in the first chapter of the Bible:

> God said, "Let us make mankind in our image, in our likeness, so that they may rule over the fish in the sea and the birds in the sky, over the livestock and all the wild animals, and over all the creatures that move along the ground." [27] So God created mankind in his own image, in the image of God he created them; male and female he created them. (Genesis 1:26-27)

God did it, and he said it was good. Humanity was created "in the image

21

of God," to somehow look like God and to represent God here on earth. Again, we are not supposed to think of skin color, hair color or the number of fingers on our hands. Those things are incidentals that only apply to creatures. What is important is that humanity should be like God in a *spiritual* sense, and we see that emphasis in Galatians 5:22, where the apostle Paul describes the results of the working of the Holy Spirit in us: "love, joy, peace, forbearance, kindness, goodness, faithfulness, gentleness and self-control." Humans are supposed to be like God in *these* ways.

Now we can ask the Trinitarian question: In what way does the doctrine of the Trinity help us understand what humanity is? The answer is, that just as the Persons in the Trinity interact with one another in love, so also we as persons ought to interact with all other human persons *in love*. That's the first fruit of the Spirit, and the way that we were made to be like God. Love should be the basis for our lives and our societies.

Just as the Triune God is essentially relational, with the Persons defined in reference to one another, so humans are also essentially *relational,* and our identity as persons depends on our relationships with other people. "Who we are" depends on the relationships we have with others. No one is a solitary individual; the meaning of life is not in *self*-existence, but it is to be found in our relationships with each other, in the way we live and think about other people. We were created to be in right relationship with the Triune God and also to be in right relationship with each other in a way that mirrors Jesus' relationship with the Father and the Spirit.

B. Sin defaces the image

Genesis tells us that humans didn't want life on the terms that God had given them. They wanted to define their own life, doing their own thing, instead of having to do God's things. So instead of love, joy and peace, they choose selfishness, and they got strife and unhappiness.

What does the doctrine of the Trinity reveal about the nature of *sin?* How does it help us better understand what sin is? If good is defined as humanity being in the image of God, then sin is doing things that are <u>un</u>like God. If God is a relational being, and humans were created to be in relationships of love, then sin is a disruption in our relationships – problems in our relationships with God, and problems in our relationships with one another.

As a practical matter, we have rules that describe what a good relationship is. In a good relationship, we don't lie to each other, we don't steal from one another, we don't dishonor or disrespect the other, and so forth. Avoiding these problems doesn't necessarily *create* a good relationship, but breaking these rules *hurts* our relationships. Rules do not exist for their own sake, but in order to serve something more important, and that is relationships based on love.

When humanity rejected God, we also rejected him as the source of the *love* that we need. We were created to be like God in that respect, but we went in a wrong direction.

C. God restores the image – in himself

The Old Testament doesn't say much more about the image of God, but the New Testament picks up the phrase "image of God" and applies it to Jesus Christ. We have already looked at Colossians 1:15: "He is *the image of the invisible God.*" He is the image that Adam failed to be. He shows us in a *visible* way what God is like in the invisible, spiritual world.

Hebrews 1:3 tells us something similar: "The Son is the radiance of God's glory and *the exact representation of his being.*" When we see Jesus, we see what the Father is like in relationship to Jesus. So we expect God to be like Jesus, in his compassion and mercy and love.

D. We are in the image of Christ

This concept becomes directly relevant to us when we see that the Bible talks about us being formed in the image *of Christ.* We can see this in 2 Corinthians 3:18: "We, who with unveiled faces all reflect the Lord's glory, are being transformed *into his likeness* with ever-increasing glory, which comes from the Lord, who is the Spirit." That is, we look more and more like him – and again, that's not talking about his physical shape, size and color – it's talking about the way he is spiritually, in relationship to the Father and the Spirit from all eternity.

- Galatians 4:19 talks about how "Christ is formed in you."
- Ephesians 4:13 talks about how "we all reach unity in the faith and in the knowledge of the Son of God and become mature, attaining to the whole *measure of the fullness of Christ.*"
- Colossians 3:10 says we "have put on the new self, which is being renewed in knowledge *in the image of its Creator"* – and that is Jesus Christ.

Since Christ is the image of God, when we become more like Christ, we are being brought back toward the image of God that we are supposed to be. Right now, it is a spiritual transformation, a *mental* and ethical or relational transformation, and eventually, it will be a physical transformation as well, all based on God's original plan.

This concept is seen in a different way in Romans 5. In that chapter, Paul is comparing Adam with Jesus Christ. Verse 14 says that Adam was a type, or a model, "a pattern of the one to come." Just as the first Adam brought in sin and death, the second Adam brought in righteousness and life. Just as we shared in the results of the first Adam, so also we share in the benefits of the second Adam. Paul summarizes it in verses 18-19:

> Just as one trespass [Adam's sin] resulted in condemnation for all people, so also one righteous act [that of Jesus] resulted in justification and life *for all people*. For just as through the disobedience of the one man [Adam] the many were made sinners, so also through the obedience of the one man [Jesus] the many will be made righteous.

All humanity was included in the results of the first Adam, and all humanity is included in the results of the second Adam, Jesus. It's not just a few people that God chose ahead of time, and it's not just one particular nation, or one particular social class – God's plan is for everyone he has created. Jesus is Lord of all.

Adam messed it up, but Jesus did it right—and in Christ, all humanity has a fresh start on being "the image of God." Jesus is the key to our transformation – not only is he the model that we copy, but he is also the engine that drives the whole process. He supplies the power and the direction.

IV. The covenant relationship

A. The covenant formula

Even though the Old Testament does not use the phrase "image of God" very often, it does talk about the relationship we have with God, and the term it uses for that most of the time is *covenant*. We can see the basic idea in Exodus 6:7: "I will take you as my own people, and I will be your God." And we see it in

- Leviticus 26:12: "I will walk among you and be your God, and you will be my people."
- Jeremiah 7:23: "I will be your God and you will be my people."
- Ezekiel 36:28: "You will be my people, and I will be your God."

Old Testament scholars call this the "covenant formula." It's found more than 20 times in the Bible. It is an adaptation of words that people in the ancient Middle East used for marriages, and adoptions, and for political treaties. In a marriage, it would go something like this: "I will be your husband, and you will be my wife." In an adoption, it would be "I will be your father, and you will be my son." In a political treaty, it would be adapted: "I will be your king and you will be my people." It is declaring a relationship that the people intend to be permanent, a relationship that now defines who they are in relation to the other.

In the Law and in the Prophets, God repeatedly talks about covenants between God and humanity. He made covenants with Abraham, Isaac, Jacob, Aaron and David. In each covenant, he says, in effect, I have made with you a covenant relationship, and as you live according to it, then our relationship will be a good one. *The goal* is to have an ongoing relationship.

B. A new covenant promised

The people of Israel broke the covenant time and time again. Eventually through the prophets God promised that there would be a *new* covenant, made in the hearts of the people, and God's Spirit would be in them. This is not something that the people could achieve for themselves – it would be something that God would have to do *for* them. He would *give* them a new heart, a new Spirit.

- Jeremiah 31:33: "This is the covenant I will make with the people of Israel after that time," declares the Lord. "I will put my law in their minds and write it on their hearts. I will be their God, and they will be my people."
- Ezekiel 36:26-27: "I will give you a new heart and put a new spirit in you; I will remove from you your heart of stone and give you a heart of flesh. I will put my Spirit in you and move you to follow my decrees and be careful to keep my laws."

In Isaiah 42:6, God promises to make his servant "to be a covenant for the people and a light for the Gentiles." The covenant relationship between God and humanity would be focused and embodied in one person – who we now know as Jesus Christ. The covenant that we have with God is found in him; he is the covenant for all the people; our connection to God depends 100 percent on him.

C. Relationship terms in the New Testament

The New Testament says that we have this new covenant in Christ. The Lord's Supper reminds us that we have a new covenant in the blood of Christ. But this is not the only relationship term in the New Testament. For example, it calls us children of God; we are *adopted* into the family of God.

- Romans 8:15 says, "The Spirit you received does not make you slaves, so that you live in fear again; rather, the Spirit you received brought about your adoption to sonship."
- Ephesians 1:5 says, "He predestined us for adoption to sonship through Jesus Christ."

This means we become part of God's family, with rights and privileges that are part of being in the royal family. We are in a new social class.

Paul uses a different relationship term in 2 Corinthians 11:2: "I promised you to one husband, to Christ, so that I might present you as a pure virgin to him." This marriage concept is used in the book of Revelation, too: "Let us rejoice and be glad and give him glory! For the wedding of the Lamb has come, and his bride has made herself ready" (Revelation 19:7).

> I saw the Holy City, the new Jerusalem, coming down out of heaven from God, prepared *as a bride* beautifully dressed for her husband. And I heard a loud voice from the throne saying, "Look! God's dwelling place is now among the people, and he will dwell with them. *They will be his people,* and God himself will be with them *and be their God."* (Revelation 21:2-3)

Here the covenant formula is used again, this time in the context of a wedding. God will live with us, and we will live with him. We will be his children, adopted as siblings of Jesus Christ, part of the royal family forever. Through Jesus, we are brought into fellowship with the Triune God, sharing in his status as Son.

Another way to describe this is "the kingdom of God." That biblical phrase means being part of the universe in which life is lived in the way that God lives. We become part of the ruling family, with the privileges and responsibilities of that.

It means that eternal life is *not just living for a really long time* – it means that we live *with each other, and with God,* forever and ever. It is social, not solitary, because that is *the way that God made us to be.* We were made in his image, and he is social, and not solitary. The doctrine of the Trinity helps us understand who we are, what life is all about, and how God is bringing it about for us. The Triune God who began a good work in us is sure to finish the job, creating humanity to be a reflection of what God is: Persons in perfect community and harmony.

V. Salvation is more than a verdict

Understanding where we started, and where we will end up, can help us understand a little more about what *salvation* is. Some people think that salvation is just a matter of going to heaven when you die. But when it comes to salvation, there's a lot more to it than just a change in location.

Some people think that salvation is just a matter of getting a favorable verdict on the day of judgment. There's going to be a day of judgment, they warn, and everybody is guilty and deserves to be thrown into hell. But if you believe in Jesus, that guilty verdict will be changed to "innocent." It is *true* that there will be a day of judgment, and that everyone is guilty of sin, and that Jesus allows us to escape the verdict we deserve, and he allows us to enter a heavenly paradise.

But doesn't salvation have anything to do with life right now? Yes, it does. There's more to salvation than just a change in our future verdict.

A. Restoring us to God's image

Salvation means that we are rescued from *sin,* not just guilt, and we are rescued from the results of sin. It means that God's original plan gets back on track – and the original plan is that we were made in the image of God and we were to live in that covenant relationship. It is a *spiritual* likeness that God wants us to have, and that can be summed up in the word *love.* We are to love God with everything we have, and we are love other people in the way that we love ourselves.

Just changing our location isn't going to restore us to being like God. Just changing the final verdict isn't going to make us the people we were meant to be. The goal in salvation is to change *us* – so that we are spiritually like God, so that we are his children in a way that mirrors Jesus' own sonship. That's the original plan, and God hasn't given up on it. He sent Jesus to show us the way and to <u>be</u> the way, for all humanity to be brought back into fellowship with the Triune God. The Father initiated the plan, the Son of God carried out key steps in the plan, and the Holy Spirit also has *an ongoing role* in the transformation, the change that we all need. We will briefly look at each of those.

B. The role of the Father

Some people describe the gospel as the Father setting the rules, and getting angry at us because we have broken the rules. He says that we deserve to die, but then the Son has compassion on us and volunteers to pay the penalty for us. So the Father pours out his anger on his Son, and then he says, "Justice has been done. Those sinners can come into my kingdom, because the penalty has been paid." We have an angry Father and a compassionate Son who is able to get his Father to change his mind.

Maybe that's the way it works in some human families, but that's not the way it works in the Triune God. It's not true to the Bible, and not true in any system of theology, whether it's Trinitarian or Calvinist or Catholic or Eastern Orthodox.

Trinitarian theology reminds us that Jesus is fully God. He is just like God the Father. He is just as angry as the Father is, and just as *loving* as the Father is. He didn't change the Father's mind about anything. Rather, he *reveals* the

Father's mind – the Father wants us to be saved just as much as Jesus does. Let's look at a couple of scriptures that show that.

- John 3:16 says it well: "*God* so loved the world that he gave his one and only Son, that whoever believes in him shall not perish but have eternal life." God the Father loves humanity and he wants us to be saved, not to be condemned or punished.
- Romans 5:8: "God demonstrates *his own love* for us in this: While we were still sinners, Christ died for us." God did not demonstrate his love for us by sending *somebody else* to die. It is only because Christ is God, that *his* death could demonstrate the love of God. They have equal love for us, equal compassion for us. The Triune God is in *full agreement* on our salvation. Father, Son and Spirit created us for a purpose, and they are working together to bring us to completion.

C. The role of the Son

Even though the Father initiated the plan, we often forget that, and usually think of Jesus as the Savior, the one who carried it out. He has the more visible role. How did Christ save us? Christians usually think that we were saved by Jesus' death on the cross. That is an important part of the picture, but it is only *part* of the picture.

1. The first step in our salvation was the Incarnation, when Jesus was made a flesh-and-blood human being. He took our nature as his own. That is when he became the second Adam, the new *leader* of all humanity. Just as we were all guilty because of the sin of Adam, so also we are made righteous in the righteousness of Jesus, because Jesus came to give all humanity a new beginning (Romans 5). This is not a matter of genetics – it is a *spiritual* reality, that the Incarnation includes all of us in the salvation that Jesus brings. In himself, Jesus reconnects all humanity to God.

2. The next step in our salvation is that Jesus had to live a righteous life, without any sin – because if he sinned, then he would simply be like one of us, needing to be saved. He would not even be able to save himself, and not anyone else. He lived without sin – he had a perfect relationship with the Father and the Spirit and, as much as could be done from his side, with all humans. Since he is our Creator, he represented us, and we are allowed to share in his righteousness.

3. Third, Jesus had to *die* for us. The wages of sin is death, the Bible says, and death is the result we would *expect*, if we try to live independent from the creator and sustainer of the universe. Jesus, as

a mortal human being, experienced death, the result of our sins. He took our sins upon himself, so that we might share in his righteousness. Since the Creator of all humanity became a human, he had an essential unity with all of us. As our Creator, he was able to accept responsibility and the consequences for all of our sins, and to die for the sins of all humanity.

4. Fourth, Jesus had to be resurrected. Romans 5:10 says that we are "saved by his life." Jesus is able to save us from death because he has overcome death. He has been there, done that, and now he can do it for us, too.

5. Last, Jesus had to ascend into heaven as one of us, fully human, and be restored to complete fellowship with the Father and Spirit. The Bible says he ascended bodily into heaven, as a glorified human being, and he is now at the Father's right hand, which is a figure of speech meaning the most honored position. His is eternally, even now, our mediator, our intercessor, praying for us, and *transforming* us to become more like he is. By the Spirit he is sharing with us his regenerated and perfected humanity.

Our salvation is not complete with just the forgiveness of sins. We *need* that, but if that's all we got, we'd still have a big problem, because we all have a tendency to sin again, and we want to be *freed* from that tendency. Paul calls it a slavery to sin, and we want to be liberated from that slavery. So, by sending us his Spirit, all that Jesus had done for us on earth and completed for us in heaven is now being worked out in us. Jesus by his Spirit is continuing to work for our transformation.

We can rightly say that we are saved by the death of Jesus, but that is only part of the picture. A more complete statement is that we are saved by the incarnation, life, death, resurrection and ascension of Jesus. If that's too much to say at one time, then just say that we are saved *by Jesus*. We are saved by who he is, and what he has done.

How did Jesus save us?

Let's focus on the death of Jesus for a few minutes, because it is an important part of the picture, and perhaps the most distinctive part of Christian theology. How can the death of Jesus do anything for our salvation?

One common explanation is that our sin requires a penalty, and Jesus serves as a substitute to pay the penalty on our behalf. This is called the penal substitutionary theory of the atonement, and it is so common that some people think that it's the only explanation. But there is a danger in this theory, and the Bible gives us other ways to explain it, as well.

1) Not focused on punishment

First, the danger. A problem can arise if we focus on the "penalty" part of the theory, by suggesting that God had to *punish* Jesus for all the sins that we committed. This suggests that one Person in the Godhead is inflicting pain on another Person in the Godhead; this suggests separation rather than unity in the Triune God. This does not seem like a very righteous thing for God to do; our penal codes and systems of justice do not allow one person to be punished in place of another.

This theory acts as if the primary problem with sin is the punishment, as if the primary problem with crime is that our prisons are full. But this is focusing on the results, not the real problem. It focuses on the verdict, and it still leaves people with a problem: we all have a tendency to sin, and the death of Jesus does not address that problem. The problem is not just in the things that we do, but in the kind of people that we are.

What has happened here is that people have let a legal metaphor, a figure of speech, become the controlling description of what God is doing. All our words are based on human experiences, and the meaning of our words depends on how they are used in human affairs. But our experiences are not the measure of what such words mean in the divine realm. When God uses courtroom terminology to describe sin and salvation, we should not let *our* concepts of legal procedure to be the final description of what God is doing. When we say that the penalty of sin is death, we should not think that "penalty" is an exact description of what is going on, as if God is obligated to inflict punishment for every transgression of his law.

"Consequence" would probably be a more appropriate term. The result of sin is death, even without God having to step in to inflict it. When Jesus died for us, he experienced the consequence of our sin, the result of the way of life human beings chose, but God did not have to perform additional pain and suffering so that Jesus could pay the penalty we deserved. No, he suffered and died without any need for extra punishments coming from God.

God does pronounce a judgment on sin. He says, "If you sin, you're going to die." He does not say, "If you sin, I'm going to kill you." Death is a *natural* result of us turning our backs on the One who gave us life. God doesn't have to do anything extra to us in order for us to suffer from the results of sin and to die from the results of sin. We experience the judgment, the result he warned us about, without him having to do anything extra to punish us. Similarly, he didn't have to do anything extra to Jesus for Jesus to die for our sins. When God *did* intervene, he gave Jesus life instead of death.

That's what he does for us, too. God is angry about sin, but as Ezekiel says, he takes no pleasure in the death of the wicked (18:23, 32). Death does not serve his purpose. His goal is salvation, not punishment. The reason that he sent Jesus to us is so that we could *escape* the consequences of sin. He wants to *rescue* us, not punish us. We should not force God into our legal metaphor.

Trinitarian theologians accept the idea that Jesus' death was substitutionary, that Jesus died as a substitute for us. But we generally avoid the word "penal," because that word suggests that God the Father punished his one and only Son, and did something to increase his pain. It puts legal requirements and demands as putting requirements on what God has to do, as if law and punishment is the most important description of what good relationships ought to be. When we bring the doctrine of the Trinity into the picture, it helps us see that *punishment* is not the best way to think about it.

2) Biblical descriptions of salvation

If the Bible does not describe the death of Jesus as a punishment required by some law that God had to obey, how does it describe it? In several ways. Articles could be written about each one, but here we will give only a summary:

1. Jesus said that he would die as a ransom: "The Son of Man did not come to be served, but to serve, and to give his life as a ransom for many" (Mark 10:45). The word "ransom" suggests a payment that we might give to a kidnapper. Some people in the early church made elaborate theories of how Jesus paid a price to Satan, as if Satan had some legitimate claims over us. But they were making the mistake of letting a figure of speech turn into an exact description of what was going on.

2. We see a similar figure of speech in the word "redemption." That word describes people getting friends and relatives out of slavery. They bought them back; that is the original meaning of "redeem." Jesus bought us with a price, Paul says, but we should not think that anyone actually *received* that payment. It is a figure of speech. The Old Testament says that God redeemed the Israelites out of slavery in Egypt, but he did not pay anyone in order to do it. We should not let the figure of speech dictate to us what happened in spiritual reality.

3. The Bible describes Jesus as a sacrificial lamb. John the Baptist called him the "the Lamb of God, who takes away the sin of the world!"

(John 1:29). The apostle Paul says that "Christ our Passover has been sacrificed" (1 Corinthians 5:7). But again, the picture is not exact. Passover lambs were not designed as payments for sin, but they were associated with escaping slavery and death.

4. Jesus is called "an offering and a sacrifice to God" (Ephesians 5:2). In the Old Testament, there were a wide variety of sacrifices – some of animals, some of flour and oil, some for sin, some for purity rituals, some for thanksgiving, and so forth, and Jesus fulfilled the symbolism of all of them.

5. Jesus is our place of atonement. Romans 3:25 says, "God presented Christ as a sacrifice of atonement." Some translations say *propitiation,* and some say *expiation,* and scholars have argued about that for a long time. The Greek word meant one thing in a pagan context, and another thing in a Jewish context, but the Greek word is also the word used for the mercy seat on top of the ark of the covenant, the place where the high priest sprinkled blood on the day of atonement. So the NIV quoted above calls it the "sacrifice of atonement." But the sacrifice was never done at the mercy seat; a better translation might be "the place of atonement," without trying to be more precise than the word actually is. Jesus is the place, or the way that our sins are atoned, so there is nothing between us and God, so that we are restored to fellowship with God.

6. Reconciliation is a similar term; it refers to people who were once enemies or alienated, but are now on good terms with each other. Romans 5:10 says, "While we were enemies we were reconciled to God by the death of his Son." Colossians 1:20 says that "God was pleased…to reconcile to himself all things, whether things on earth or things in heaven, by making peace through [the Son's] blood, shed on the cross."

7. Justification is another important term. Some say it is the most important term of all, the one that makes sense out of all the others. Romans 5:9 says that we are "justified by his blood," or by his death on the cross. Justification means to make something right. The word could be used for making a relationship right, or it could be used for making something legally right. In a trial, a person could either be found guilty – condemned – or found righteous (cf. 2 Corinthians 3:9). When the judge declared a person to be in the right, this was justification. This can be a helpful way of looking at salvation, but it misses out on the fact that God wants more from us than to be

declared legally innocent – he also wants us to be in fellowship with him forever. Yes, we are guilty of a crime, but the solution is not just to let us out of jail, but it is to transform who we are, so that we are more like Christ.

8. In Colossians, Paul gives us another interesting way to look at the death of Jesus: "Having disarmed the powers and authorities, he made a public spectacle of them, triumphing over them by the cross" (2:15). By his death on the cross, Jesus won a victory! He defeated spiritual powers that were fighting against us. Paul does not explain the logic in how that works, but he says that it does.

The Bible uses a few additional figures of speech, but the point is clear, that there are several ways to look at it, and we should use all of these ways.

Trinitarian theology says that the meaning of human life is to be found in relationships, and relationships cannot be put into precise formulas. But we can state some basic facts about it. First, Jesus became a real human, and he was mortal. Even if the Jews and the Romans didn't kill him, he had a mortal body that would eventually get old and he would die. He was part of the Godhead, but he became part of humanity, and he accepted all of the negative consequences of that. Why did he do it? Out of love. God loved us so much that he sent his only Son to die for us, and the Son loved us so much that he did it.

So Jesus has connected the world of heaven and earth, divine and human. In his death, Jesus demonstrated that he was a real human, completely in union with humanity. He completed his identification with us, sharing in everything that it means to be human. By doing that, he reversed the curse that was against us (Genesis 3:19; Galatians 3:13). He was able, on behalf of all humanity, to suffer the consequences of sin, and yet since he was personally without any sin, death did not have a legitimate claim on him. He had to be resurrected, and as the new Adam, the new head of humanity, he sets the pattern for what will happen to all of us, and that's resurrection – not just a life that lasts forever, but a life that is in fellowship with the Triune God.

D. Role of the Spirit in our salvation

The Father sent the Son to save us, and the Son did his work. Does that mean that there's nothing left to do until the Last Judgment? Certainly not! Trinitarian theology reminds us that we should expect the Spirit to have an important role in our salvation.

Shortly before Jesus died, he told his disciples:

> It is for your good that I am going away. Unless I go away, the Advocate will not come to you; but if I go, I will send him to you…. When he, the Spirit of truth, comes, he will guide you into all the truth…. He will tell you what is yet to come. (John 16:7, 13-14)

So, even though Jesus completed *his* earthly job, part of the work must be completed after Jesus goes away – and that work is done by the Holy Spirit, the Advocate, the Comforter, who is sent by Jesus. What does the Holy Spirit do in our salvation? We don't need to present a complete theology of the Spirit here, but let's mention a few points:

1. The Spirit gives us new birth. In John 3, Jesus told Nicodemus, "No one can enter the kingdom of God unless they are born of water *and the Spirit*…. You must be born again" (verses 5, 7). We need a *new start in life,* and in one sense, Jesus gave all humanity that when he became "the second Adam." But for individuals, this is done by the Holy Spirit.

2. The Spirit helps us realize that we *are* born again, that we are children of God. Romans 8:15 says, "The Spirit you received brought about your adoption to sonship. And by him we cry, 'Abba, Father.'"

3. The Spirit also enables us to understand the gospel. In 1 Corinthians 2:14, Paul writes, "The person without the Spirit does not accept the things that come from the Spirit of God but considers them foolishness, and cannot understand them because they are discerned only through the Spirit." Unbelievers might understand what the words of Scripture mean, but people don't accept those words as *true* without the Spirit leading them. The Spirit helps us see truth about God and truth about ourselves, and helps us continue growing in the truth. As John 16 says, the Spirit teaches us and guides into the truth. No one has all the truth *yet,* so this is still a work in progress.

4. The Holy Spirit *sanctifies* us, or sets us apart for God's use. 2 Thessalonians 2:13 supports this: "God chose you as firstfruits to be *saved* through the sanctifying work of the Spirit and through belief in the truth."

5. The Spirit gives us power over sin. "If you live according to the flesh, you will die; but *if by the Spirit* you put to death the misdeeds of the body, you will live" (Romans 8:13). As the Spirit leads us, helps us understand, and gives us strength, we are to stop doing bad things and start doing more godly things. This does not mean that we stop all sin (even though we wish we could), but that our basic orientation

in life is now toward the good. Christian life and good behavior are part of the process of sanctification. The Spirit sets us apart for God's use, and God wants to use us for good.

6. The Spirit produces results in our lives: love, joy, peace, and other good qualities. These are the results God wants to see in us. This is a transformation in our attitudes as well as our actions – we are being changed from the inside out.

More could be said on each of these points – and more points could be added. Our main purpose here is just to make the larger point that the Spirit has a vital role in our salvation – we cannot be saved without the work of the Spirit in our lives. Salvation is a Trinitarian work, involving the Father, Son, and Spirit working in harmony to bring us to the kind of persons we are supposed to be.

VI. How do we respond?

We have seen some of the ways that God is working in our lives: He is restoring in us the divine image, so that we are living representatives of who he is and what he is like. It is a *spiritual* image, started when God said, "Let *us* make mankind in our image, in our likeness." We were made to be like God, and since Jesus is the perfect image of God, we are being conformed into *his* image, changed so that we are more like he is. The Spirit is doing that work in us, producing in us the fruit of the Spirit: love, joy, peace, and other attitudes and actions that help us have better relationships. This is part of the ongoing work of salvation that God is doing within us.

But a time is coming when we will be transformed into God's image in additional ways, too. Romans 6:5 says, "If we have been united with him in a death like his, we will certainly also be united with him in a *resurrection* like his." Our physical nature will be changed, and we will share in the glory of Jesus Christ. In 1 Corinthians 15, Paul describes the resurrection, and he says in verse 49, "just as we have borne the likeness of the earthly man [Adam], so shall we bear the *likeness* of the man from heaven [Jesus]." We will have the image of Christ in a more glorious way.

1 John 3:1-2 gives us a similar picture:

How great is the love the Father has lavished on us, that we should be called children of God! And that is what we are! The reason the world does not know us is that it did not know him. Dear friends, now we *are* children of God, and what we *will be* has not yet been made known. But we know that when he appears, we shall be like him, for we shall see him as he is.

We will be like he is; we will be even more fully made in his image.

All humanity has been created in the image of God, made for this purpose. We are already his children, already "in his image" in one sense, but there is more to come. As we are transformed into his image in this life in the way we live and think, we will be transformed *more completely* into his image when we are resurrected into glory and given immortality and incorruptibility. This is the wonderful future God has prepared for us.

What conclusion does John draw from this wonderful promise? He says it in the very next verse: "Everyone who has this hope in him purifies himself, just as he is pure" (verse 3). When we want to be like God is, then we want to be *like him in our thoughts and actions.* The glory that God has designed for us is that we should be like he is.

There's a lot more to eternal life than just living forever. A never-ending life of suffering would *not* be good, and that is not what God wants us to have. Rather, he wants us to have a never-ending life of love and joy, of good relationships – relationships with millions and billions of other people who *love* one another. The good news of the gospel, the good news of the Bible, the good news of salvation, is that not only do we live forever, but that we will live *with God.* That's the best part: God wants us to live with him. We can see this in the last book of the Bible, Revelation 21:1-4:

> Then I saw "a new heaven and a new earth," for the first heaven and the first earth had passed away…. I heard a loud voice from the throne saying, "Look! God's dwelling place is now among the people, and he will dwell with them. They will be his people, and God himself will be with them and be their God. He will wipe every tear from their eyes. There will be no more death or mourning or crying or pain, for the old order of things has passed away."

God will live with us, and we will live with him. We will be his children, adopted as brothers and sisters of Jesus Christ, part of the royal family forever. We are *already* his children. We already have a relationship with the Father, Son and Spirit.

How can our vision of *future* life affect the way we live now? Here's another thought that many Christians struggle with: If salvation is by grace, why does the New Testament have so many commands about what we are supposed to do? Is it grace for how we get in, but works *after* we get in? No.

It is because God is not just giving us existence that lasts forever – he is giving us life of a certain *quality,* life that is based on love rather than selfishness and competition. That's the kind of life we will enjoy in eternity, and that's the kind of life that is *good,* not just in the future but also right now.

When the New Testament gives us commands, it is *describing* for us the kind of life that God is giving us, the life of the age to come. Grace says: I am giving you a never-ending life of joy. The commands say: This is what it looks like. This is the way that will help you have joy and express love.

In a parable, we might say that God is at the gateway to his kingdom, and he invites us in. You are welcome to come in, he says, where there is no more pain or sorrow, or lying or cheating or selfishness. Some people may say, "I would like to have 'no more pain,' but can't I keep my selfishness?" God replies, "No, they are two sides of the same coin. Selfishness causes pain. If you go through this gate, I will scrub all the selfishness out of you, so that you don't cause pain either for yourself or for anyone else." It's possible that some people will cherish their selfishness so much that they will refuse to go in.

We do not want to be in love with our selfishness. Rather, we need to see selfishness as one of our enemies, an attitude that can rob us of joy and peace. It is part of the sin that so easily besets us – it is an enemy that keeps us in slavery – it is an enemy we need to be liberated from. It is an enemy that Christ has already defeated on the cross, and he wants us to share in that victory, and it is done though the Holy Spirit living in us.

A Trinitarian understanding of our purpose in life helps us see the purpose of salvation, and the purpose of the commands we see in the Bible. Once we see where we are going, it is easier to see how God is bringing us there. Love is central to the whole picture, because love is the life of the Father, Son and Spirit, and we are participating in the divine nature, sharing in the life and love of the Triune God.

As images of God, we want our life to be characteristic of *the age to come,* patterned after the life that God himself has. We are images of God and representatives of God, and we should want to live in the way that he does, the way that we will all live in eternity. This life is representative of God himself, a fulfillment of the image that we are supposed to be. In the age to come, we will forever be images of God, children of God, completely and perfectly.

VII. Conclusion

The doctrine of the Trinity has enriched our understanding of many other doctrines, and we will continue to learn more about it as we grow in grace and knowledge. It makes sense that God's nature is reflected in everything that God does, and that means it affects all other doctrines, because our doctrines are based on what God is doing in the people he has created.

We see God's *love* throughout the story, from before creation and in the cross of Christ, and on into eternity in the future. We see the Father, Son and Spirit in creation, in salvation, and in eternity. God wants to live with us, and us to live with him, in love, forever and ever. In his love and grace, he has *given* this to us – and in our love for him, we enjoy learning about it. But we know that this is only the beginning of our understanding.

In 1 Corinthians 13:12, the apostle Paul says that now, "we see only a reflection as in a mirror; then we shall see face to face. Now I know in part; then I shall know fully, even as I am fully known." We have knowledge, but our knowledge is *partial,* and we look forward to learning more. We rejoice that God knows us fully, and we can be confident that he will continue to draw us toward himself, so that on some future day, we will see him face to face and know him fully, sharing in his life and love forever and ever.

Michael Morrison

WHAT'S SO SPECIAL
ABOUT TRINITARIAN THEOLOGY?

Learning more about the nature of God has dominated my Bible study for the last decade. I find it to be more and more fascinating. Having the correct perspective of who God is cannot be overestimated. Viewing his sovereignty over eternity and the nature of his being orders all of our doctrinal understandings.

I love the following quote from Charles Haddon Spurgeon, England's best-known preacher for most of the second half of the 19th century:

> The highest science, the loftiest speculation, the mightiest philosophy, which can ever engage the attention of a child of God, is the name, the nature, the person, the work, the doings, and the existence of the great God whom he calls his Father. There is something exceedingly improving to the mind in a contemplation of the Divinity. It is a subject so vast, that all our thoughts are lost in its immensity; so deep, that our pride is drowned in its infinity.

I am sometimes asked, "What's so special about Trinitarian theology—don't most orthodox churches believe in the Trinity?" Yes, they do. Belief in the Trinity is considered the hallmark of authentic Christian doctrine. It was our acceptance of the Trinity that brought our denomination "in out of the cold," allowing us to break free from being considered a cult.

As I studied what various churches believe about the Trinity, I observed that while most consent to the doctrine, it does not have a central role in their faith. Many consider the Trinity to be an abstract idea, of interest to theologians but not of much use to the rest of us. This is sad because when the Trinity is not at the center, shaping all other doctrines, strange ideas and distortions arise. For example, those who proclaim a health/wealth/prosperity gospel tend to view God as a divine "vending machine." Others tend to view God as a mechanistic version of fate who has determined everything from before creation—including who will be saved and who will be damned. I find it hard to accept a God who creates billions of people just for the purpose of condemning and damning them for eternity!

Trinitarian theology puts the Trinity at the center of all doctrinal understanding, influencing everything we believe and understand about God. As theologian Catherine LaCugna wrote in her book *God for Us:*

> The doctrine of the Trinity is, ultimately…a teaching not about the abstract nature of God, nor about God in isolation from everything

other than God, but a teaching about God's life with us and our life with each other. Trinitarian theology could be described as par excellence a theology of relationship, which explores the mysteries of love, relationship, personhood and communion within the framework of God's self-revelation in the person of Christ and the activity of the Spirit. [Note: While I appreciate much of what is in this book, I don't agree with all of it.]

We know of this triune life of God from Jesus, who is God's self-revelation in person. It should be our rule that anything we say about the Trinity must come from Jesus' life, teaching, death, resurrection, ascension and promised return.

I have seen many diagrams that attempt to explain the Trinity. The best of them fall short and some are confusing. It is impossible to explain the nature of God in a diagram. However, a good one can help us grasp some aspects of the doctrine. You may find helpful the diagram shown below. It summarizes early church teaching, pointing out that correct biblical understanding concerning the nature of God upholds three essential beliefs about God. It also indicates that we end up denying that God is Triune when even one of these beliefs is rejected.

The three sides of the triangle in the diagram represent these three essential beliefs, and the point of the triangle across from each side represents the corresponding error when that particular belief is denied:

- Denial of the Three Persons results in Modalism (sometimes referred to as the Oneness teaching), the erroneous belief that God appears to us in three ways or modes, wears three hats, acts in three different roles or just has three different names.

- Denial of the Equality of Persons results in Subordinationism, the erroneous belief that one of the divine Persons is less than fully and truly God.

- Denial of Monotheism (the idea of the Unity of God) results in Polytheism, the erroneous belief in two or more separate gods (including the error of tri-

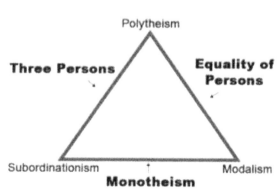

THE GOD REVEALED IN JESUS CHRIST

theism—a belief in three gods).

When we are careful to uphold all three of these essential beliefs about God, we avoid the corresponding false teachings and thus bear faithful witness to the glorious mystery of the Trinity.

I thank God daily for answering our many prayers to reveal to us greater truth. His revealing himself to each of us as the Triune God was a miraculous moment for each one of us.

Joseph Tkach

BEWARE THEOLOGICAL LABELS

As our understanding of who God is (our theology) developed, we began using the term "Incarnational Trinitarian theology" to identify and summarize our understanding. However, use of that term (and others like it) might cause some problems. First, it might confuse some who are not trained in theology. Second, it might be used by some who do not understand it well. Third, it might be overused and thus become cliché. Last, it might become a denominational label that could lead some to misunderstand what we actually believe and teach.

It is helpful to think of Incarnational Trinitarian theology as describing *how* we believe rather than merely what we believe. All orthodox Christians accept the doctrines of the Trinity and the Incarnation. But for us, they are more than two doctrines on a list of many—they are the heart of our faith and worship.

Why is that not so for all Christians? Partly because these truths are deep mysteries beyond our fallen human imaginations. Also, these doctrines are sometimes poorly taught or not taught at all. Thus it is easy to drift away from this defining core and begin to emphasize secondary (even tertiary) issues. When that happens, everything becomes distorted.

This was seen clearly in the way Jewish religious leaders resisted Jesus. Those leaders looked to Scripture as a source of truth, but disagreed about its details. Nevertheless, they were united against Jesus. So Jesus told them,

> You have your heads in your Bibles constantly because you think you'll find eternal life there. But you miss the forest for the trees. These Scriptures are all about me! And here I am, standing right before you, and you aren't willing to receive from me the life you say you want. (John 5:39-40, *The Message*)

Note how Jesus placed himself at the center as the living key to interpreting Scripture. He himself was the source of their life. If they would accept and understand that, they would put their petty disagreements in perspective and come together in acknowledging him as Messiah. Instead, they saw him as a heretic and plotted to kill him.

As Christians today, we can make the same mistake. Even if we accept Jesus as Lord and Savior, we can sideline the fundamental truths that define who he is. The result is the fragmenting of Christianity into competing "schools" of thought with their own doctrinal distinctives. This leads to a "my Christianity is better than yours" mentality. Though the distinctives may be accurate, they emphasize peripheral matters. The result is that the reality of who God is and what he has done for us in his Son is diminished, if not lost. Division within the Body of Christ results.

That is why we need to avoid using labels in ways that imply that we are setting ourselves apart as having a Christianity that is superior in comparison to others. The reason we use a label is to remind ourselves (and others, if they are interested) of the focus of our renewal—the reality of what is revealed in Jesus Christ according to Scripture.

Also, in using a label, we must avoid implying that we are slavishly beholden to some systematic theology or to certain theologians—even those identified as Incarnational or Trinitarian. There are approximately 50 systematic theologies in existence today. However, there is no single concrete, uniform, particular school of thought called "Trinitarian theology."

For example, Barth, the Torrance brothers and Thomas Oden drew on many other theologians throughout the ages and on the writings of the early church councils. Rather than seeking to establish a new theology, they were seeking to serve Jesus Christ and to build up his church through their teaching and research. They might be described as "Incarnational Trinitarian theologians" because they saw that these elements of Christian faith were being neglected or even forgotten. They discerned that the church needed to get back on the central path of Christian faith.

When we use the term "Incarnational Trinitarian theology," we are referring to the fact that Jesus is the lens through which we read and interpret the Bible and how we have come to know God. Consequently, any other doctrinal points should flow from and fit with the Trinitarian nature of God. Our role in the administration of our denomination is to pass on the best formulations of Christian theology that we can find—especially on the major issues. We are blessed to incorporate the ideas of the great theologians of Christian history, and we can learn from those alive today. But we do not do so slavishly, and biblical revelation always has the controlling authority.

So, when we say that we believe and teach Incarnational Trinitarian theology, we are describing how we understand and believe Scripture based on Jesus as the centerpiece of God's plan for humanity. It is perhaps more like your computer's operating system rather than one of the many programs you load into it. Individual doctrines are like the software applications, which must be able to interface with the operating system if they are to work properly. But it's the operating system that orders, organizes, prioritizes and produces all other useful results.

The focus of our renewal as a denomination has been the very theological issues that have been central to historical, orthodox Christianity. We are not the only branch of the church that neglected or even misunderstood the doctrines of the Trinity and the Incarnation. We hope that we might benefit other parts of the Body of Christ with what we have learned. It is in this spirit that we offer our *Speaking of Life* and *You're Included* videos. If you have not viewed them, I urge you to do so. They will help us all keep the Center in the center, feed our continuing renewal in the Spirit, and enable us to join with all Christians down through the ages in giving witness to the glory of our triune God: Father, Son and Holy Spirit.

Joseph Tkach

ANSWERING QUESTIONS
ABOUT OUR THEOLOGY

The label, "Incarnational Trinitarian theology" is descriptive rather than prescriptive for our doctrinal statements. Our critics sometimes want to label our theological perspective as Barthian or Torrancian or whatever. But at best, such labels are only partially descriptive. Any similarities are definitely not prescriptive.

Prescriptive for us is the reality of who God has revealed himself to be in Jesus Christ according to Scripture. Our theological formulations are derived from and meant to point faithfully to that reality, which exceeds what can be contained in our theological understandings.

When we quote any theologians positively, or even when the historic Christian creeds are referenced, they are being used as illustrative of our theological position, not as a source or final norm of it. They show that other members of the Body of Christ at other times and places grasped the biblical revelation in a way similar to how we have come to understand it. It demonstrates that we are concerned not to be esoteric or eccentric in our teaching and that we believe that other members of the Body of Christ can be helpful to us, saying at least as well, if not better than ourselves, how we understand God's Word.

Given what is noted above, the label "Incarnational Trinitarian theology" is not meant to indicate that we hold to a special (or superior) form of Christianity. It indicates that the center and heart of our faith and worship corresponds to the center and heart of the revelation of the gospel itself – just as the historic, orthodox church has done down to this day. This label reminds us of the core reality of who God is and has revealed himself to be in and through Jesus Christ, according to Scripture. It also represents the nature of our renewal and restoration to true Christian faith, which we have come to share with the Christian church. If others have been pushed or pulled off-center, we hold out to them these foundational truths, from which flow all other Christian doctrines, that they might also be renewed and restored in their faith and worship.

Some critics say we don't make distinctions between believers and non-believers because of the way we speak of God having a oneness of mind, heart and purpose towards all. Though it is not true, they say we teach universalism. Why do they come to this wrong conclusion? Because they make inferences from our statements about God to our views about his creatures. "If God regards all the same way, then all must regard God the same way." But we do not come to our understanding through logical inferences made from a single affirmation about God. That would be bad theology and bad logic. No simple logical inference is ever *necessarily* true, most especially when moving from God to talking about creatures.

It seems that their critique of our theology is a mirror-image of how their own theology works. Seeing a difference between believers and non-believers, they then imagine a corresponding difference in God. They make a simple logical inference, but this time in the reverse direction: from a description of the differences among humans to what God then must prescribe for that difference among humans. We do not reason in that way. Doing so would, in our view, constitute mythological projection, which is idolatry. Doing so would mean concluding something about what God prescribes from a description of individual creatures or a class of them. John Calvin made this mistake in reasoning in his polemical writings about predestination. Thankfully, he did not succumb to that faulty reasoning in most of his writings on theology (in his *Institutes* and elsewhere).

Typically, the difference between our viewpoint and that of those who criticize it, is that we start with God's self-revelation as the criterion for our statements about God ("only God reveals God"). We do not start with our own, or even the Bible's descriptions of how humans respond differently to God and then logically infer something about who God is and what God wants for his human creatures. Descriptions of human creatures and of their potential eternal situations, either by means of our own observations or by reference to isolated biblical passages interpreted out of context, do not prescribe for us a definitive revelation of who God is and what he wants. Jesus Christ alone, according to divine revelation (Scripture) alone, prescribes for us our trust in and understanding of God's heart, mind, purposes and character. On that basis, we conclude that God is a redeemer who has a redemptive nature and heart, does not want any to perish, but wants all to repent and receive eternal life. That is, God is identical in character to Jesus Christ, our Lord and Savior.

Some condemn or dismiss our theological stance by labeling it universalism, Aminianism or Calvinism. However, we have no need to be aligned with a particular school of theology. Though each school has understandings deserving our consideration, each also has significant weaknesses that obscure important, even crucial elements of the biblical revelation. Those weaknesses have not only been identified by us but have been brought to light in the ongoing discussions and debates down through the history of the church. While we share faith in the same realities as do all Christians, our theological understanding and articulation does not fall neatly along the lines drawn in the typical universalist-Arminian-Calvinist debates.

Those who are satisfied with one of these primary theological traditions and insist that these are the only options, will probably not be able to properly hear our theological testimony or grasp its source and norm the way we do. Their critiques likely will assume that we have bought into the one or two theological options they have rejected – ones that might include being "incarnational" or "Trinitarian."

While we can offer our reasons for why and how we understand the Christian faith the way we do, we don't have to accept any labels nor defend the one we use. We are simply trying to be as faithful as we can in understanding and explaining the biblical revelation. We hold out our convictions to our members for their benefit and to others in hope that they might be renewed and blessed as we have been as the Lord has corrected and restored us.

It was not a particular theology or theologian who transformed Grace Communion International. Rather, it was Jesus Christ, speaking through his Holy Word, who revealed to us the true nature and character of God. Grace Communion International was grasped by the gospel of Jesus Christ, as our Lord placed himself at the center of our worship and faith. If the label "Incarnational Trinitarian theology" properly *describes* that transformation, then we accept it. However, we have no need to defend a label, for it *prescribes* nothing.

Gary Deddo

WHY BOTHER WITH THEOLOGY?

Many people find theology to be complicated, confusing and even irrelevant. They wonder why they should bother with it at all. "Surely," they exclaim, "the Bible isn't that difficult! Why read the works of head-in-the-clouds theologians with their long sentences and fancy terms?"

Sadly, it is common to ridicule things we don't understand. But doing so is a formula for continuing in ignorance and possibly falling into heresy.

I acknowledge that some academic theologians are hard to understand. In fact, it is unusual to find a genuine scholar who is also a gifted communicator. People in academic circles often deal in lofty ideas, and speak and write mainly with their peer group in mind. They leave it to others to bring those ideas down to earth. The situation is not unlike the difference between the practices of a science like physics and technology. The experimental scientist in his laboratory discovers a new process or material, and leaves it mostly to others to harness the idea into something practical for the ordinary person.

Theology has been called "faith seeking understanding," and we should not despise it. As Christians we trust God, but God has made us to want to understand the one we trust, and why we trust him. Our God apparently wants us to grow in our knowledge and trust in him, having our minds more and more transformed. But knowledge about God is not something that we humans can just come up with on our own by thinking about it. The only way we can know anything true about God is to listen to what he tells us about himself.

God has chosen to preserve the revelation of himself to us in the Bible, a collection of inspired writings compiled over many centuries under the supervision of the Holy Spirit. However, even the most diligent study of the Bible does not automatically convey to us a right or full understanding of who God is.

Most heresies come from wrong understandings of who God is, often promoted by one or a few individuals who fail to grasp how God has revealed himself in the Bible and ultimately in Jesus Christ, and who have given little or no attention to the biblically based teaching of the church down through the ages.

What then do we need? First, we need the Holy Spirit to enable us to understand what God reveals in the Bible about himself and give us the humility to receive it. The Bible and the work of the Spirit together are enough to bring the humble reader (or hearer) with a mustard seed's worth of faith to an initial trust that repents of unbelief and acknowledges that Jesus is Lord and that he alone brings us God's gracious salvation.

Second, growth in our knowledge of who God is calls for a comprehensive grasp of the whole of Scripture with Jesus Christ at the center of it all. No one can do that for themselves, even in a lifetime. We need the wisdom of others.

Third, we may misunderstand some or much of what we read in the Bible due to assumptions we bring with us into our study of the Bible. We need help to remove these obstacles to spiritual growth.

Fourth, we will not instantly know how best to communicate our understanding to those around us. Some people are called to help sort all these things out. This is where theology comes in.

The word *theology* comes from a combination of two Greek words, *theos*, meaning God, and *logia*, meaning knowledge or study – *study of God*. Theologians are members of the body of Christ who are called to synthesize and sum up the biblical witness to the nature, character, mind, purposes and will of God. In doing this they survey the results of others in the history of the church who attempted to do the same. They also analyze our contemporary context to discern the best words, concepts, stories, analogies or illustrations that most faithfully convey the truth and reality of who God is. The result is theology. While not all theologies are equally faithful, the church is wise to make use of those results that do help it keep its proclamation of the gospel resting on the firm foundation of God's own revelation of himself in Jesus Christ according to Scripture.

The church as a whole has an ongoing responsibility to examine its beliefs and practices critically, in the light of God's revelation. Theology, therefore, represents the Christian community's continuous quest for faithful doctrine as it humbly seeks God's wisdom and follows the Holy Spirit's lead into all truth. The church ought to make use of those members of the Body who are specially called to help it do that. Until Christ returns in glory, the church cannot assume that it has reached its goal. That is why theology should be a never-ending process of critical self-examination. Theology can thus serve the church by combating heresies, or false teachings, and helping us find the most faithful ways we can speak the truth in love today in our current context.

My point is that theology – good theology based in a profound respect for the biblical revelation and a sound understanding of its intent, background, context and comprehensive meaning for today – is a vital ingredient to a growing Christian faith. The 21st-century is posing unprecedented challenges that are not addressed directly in the inspired Scriptures. Times change, but "Jesus Christ is the same yesterday and today and forever" (Hebrews 13:8). At the Last Supper, Jesus told his disciples,

> I have much more to say to you, more than you can now bear. But when he, the Spirit of truth, comes, he will guide you into all the truth. He will not speak on his own; he will speak only what he hears, and he will tell you what is yet to come. He will glorify me because it is from me that he will receive what he will make known to you. All that belongs to the Father is mine. That is why I said the Spirit will receive from me what he will make known to you. (John 16:12-15)

So let's not despise the understanding that comes from good theology, even though it sometimes comes wrapped in difficult language. As the "resident theologian" to the people you serve, strive to understand it and then serve it up to your people in a way they can understand.

Joseph Tkach

THEOLOGY:
WHAT DIFFERENCE DOES IT MAKE?

"Don't talk to me about theology. Just teach me the Bible."

To the average Christian, theology might sound like something hopelessly complicated, frustratingly confusing and thoroughly irrelevant. Anybody can read the Bible (although people often come to very different conclusions). So why do we need head-in-the-clouds theologians with their long sentences and fancy terms?

Faith seeking understanding

Theology has been called "faith seeking understanding." We have faith in God, but God has made us to want to understand who we are trusting and why we trust him. That's where theology comes in. The word *theology* comes from a combination of two Greek words, *theos,* meaning God, and *logia,* meaning knowledge or study – study of God.

When properly used, theology can serve the church by combating heresies, or false teachings. Most heresies come from wrong understandings of who God is, understandings that don't square with the way God has revealed himself in the Bible. The church's gospel needs to rest on the firm foundation of God's revelation of himself.

Revelation

Knowledge about God is not something that we humans can just come up with on our own by thinking it out. The only way we can know anything true about God is to listen to what God tells us about himself. The main way God has chosen to reveal himself to us is through the Bible, a collection of inspired writings compiled over many centuries under the supervision of the Holy Spirit. But even diligent study of the Bible, in itself, cannot convey to us right understanding of who God is.

We need more than mere study – we need the Holy Spirit to enable our minds to understand what God reveals in the Bible about himself. The bottom line is that true knowledge of God comes only from God, not merely by human study, reasoning or experience.

The church has an ongoing responsibility to critically examine its beliefs and practices in the light of God's revelation. Theology is the Christian community's continuous quest for truth as it humbly seeks God's wisdom and follows the Holy Spirit's lead into all truth. Until Christ returns in glory, the church cannot assume that it has reached its goal.

That is why theology should never become a mere restatement of the church's creeds and doctrines, but should rather be a never-ending process of critical self-examination. It is only as we stand in the divine Light of God's mystery that we find true knowledge of God.

Paul called that divine mystery "Christ in you, the hope of glory" (Colossians 1:27), the mystery that through Christ it pleased God "to reconcile to himself all things, whether things on earth or things in heaven, by making peace through his blood, shed on the cross" (verse 20).

The Christian church's proclamation and practice are always in need of examination and fine-tuning, sometimes even major reform, as it continues to grow in the grace and knowledge of the Lord Jesus Christ.

Dynamic theology

The word *dynamic* is a good word to describe this constant effort of the Christian church to look at itself and the world in the light of God's self-revelation and then to let the Holy Spirit conform it accordingly to be a people who reflect and proclaim God as God truly is. We see this *dynamic* quality in theology throughout church history. The apostles reinterpreted the Scriptures when they proclaimed Jesus as the Messiah.

God's new act of self-revelation in Jesus Christ brought new light to the Bible, light that the Holy Spirit opened the eyes of the apostles to see. In the fourth century, Athanasius, bishop of Alexandria, used descriptive words in the creeds that were not in the Bible in order to help Gentiles understand the meaning of the biblical revelation of God. In the 16th century, John Calvin and Martin Luther contended for the renewal of the church in light of the demand of the biblical truth that salvation comes only by grace through faith in Jesus Christ.

In the 1800s, John McLeod Campbell attempted to broaden the Church of Scotland's narrow view on the nature of Jesus' atonement for humanity, and was thrown out for his efforts.

In modern times, no one has been more effective in calling the church to a dynamic theology rooted in active faith than Karl Barth, who "gave the Bible back to Europe" after liberal Protestant theology had nearly swallowed up the church by embracing Enlightenment humanism and the "natural theology" of the German church, and ended up supporting Hitler.

Listening to God

Whenever the church fails to hear the voice of God and instead gives in to its own assumptions and presuppositions, it becomes weak and ineffective.

It loses relevance in the eyes of those it is trying to reach with the gospel message. The same is true of any part of the Body of Christ when it wraps itself up in its own preconceived ideas and traditions. It becomes bogged down, stuck or *static,* the opposite of *dynamic,* and loses its effectiveness in spreading the gospel.

When that happens, the church begins to fragment or break up, Christians become alienated from one another, and Jesus' command that we love one another fades into the background. Then, gospel proclamation becomes merely a set of words, a proposition that people unthinkingly agree with. The power behind it to offer healing to sinful minds loses its force. Relationships become external, only surface contacts that miss the deep union and communion with Jesus and one another where genuine healing, peace and joy become real possibilities. Static religion is a barrier that can prevent believers from becoming the real people God intends them to be in Jesus Christ.

'Double predestination'

The doctrine of election or double predestination has long been a distinctive doctrine in the Reformed theological tradition (the tradition that stands in the shadow of John Calvin). Calvin himself struggled with this issue, and his teaching on it has been interpreted by many as saying, "From eternity God has decreed some to salvation and others to damnation."

This interpretation of the doctrine of election fosters a fatalistic view of God as an arbitrary tyrant and an enemy of human freedom. Such an approach to the doctrine makes it anything but good news as proclaimed in God's self-revelation in Jesus Christ. The biblical witness describes the electing grace of God as astonishing, but not dreadful! God, who loves in freedom, offers his grace freely to all who will receive it.

Karl Barth

In correcting this view, Karl Barth recast the Reformed doctrine of election by centering rejection and election in Jesus Christ. He laid out the full biblical doctrine of election in Volume II of his *Church Dogmatics* in a way that is consistent with the whole of God's revelation.

Barth forcefully demonstrated that within a Trinitarian context, the doctrine of election has one central purpose: it declares that God's works in creation, reconciliation and redemption are fully realized in the free grace of God made known in Jesus Christ.

It affirms that the triune God who lives eternally in loving communion graciously wills to include others in that communion. The Creator Redeemer deeply desires a relationship with his creation. Relationships by nature are dynamic, not static. Relationships penetrate the abyss of our existence and turn it into real life.

In the *Dogmatics*, where Barth rethought the doctrine of election in a Trinitarian, Creator Redeemer context, he called it "the sum of the gospel." In Christ God elected *all* of humanity in covenant partnership to share in his life of communion by freely and graciously choosing to be God for humanity.

Jesus Christ is both the Elected and the Rejected for our sakes, and individual election and rejection can be understood as real only in him. The Son of God is the Elect on our behalf. As the universal elected human, his vicarious, or substitutionary, election is at the same time both to the condemnation of death (the cross) in our place and to eternal life (the resurrection) in our place. This atoning and reconciling work of Jesus Christ in the incarnation was complete in the redeeming of fallen humanity.

We must therefore say yes to God's yes for us in Christ Jesus and embrace and begin to live in the joy and light of what he has already secured for us — union, communion and participation with him in a new creation.

New creation

In his important contribution to the doctrine of election, Barth writes:

> For in God's union with this one man, Jesus Christ, he has shown his love to all and his solidarity with all. In this One he has taken upon himself the sin and guilt of all, and therefore rescued them all by higher right from the judgment which they had rightly incurred, so that he is really the true consolation of all.

Everything changed at the cross. The entire creation, whether it knows it or not, has been, is being and will be redeemed, transformed and made new in Jesus Christ. We are becoming a new creation in him.

Thomas F. Torrance, premier student and interpreter of Karl Barth, served as editor when Barth's *Church Dogmatics* was translated into English. Torrance believed that Volume II was some of the finest theology ever written. He agreed with Barth that all of humanity has been redeemed and elected in Christ. Professor Torrance, in his book *The Mediation of Christ,* lays out the biblical revelation that Jesus is not only our atoning reconciler through his vicarious life, death and resurrection, but serves as our perfect response to God's grace.

Jesus took our fallenness and judgment on himself, assuming sin, death and evil in order to redeem the creation at all levels and transform everything that stood against us into a new creation. We have been freed from our depraved and rebellious natures for an internal relationship with the One who both justifies and sanctifies us.

Torrance goes on to explain that "the unassumed is the unhealed." What Christ has not taken upon himself has not been saved. Jesus took our alienated mind on himself, becoming what we are in order to reconcile us to God. He thereby cleansed, healed and sanctified sinful humanity in the depths of its being in his vicarious loving act of incarnation for us.

Instead of sinning like all other human beings, he condemned sin in our flesh by living a life of perfect holiness within our flesh, and through his obedient Sonship he transformed our hostile and disobedient humanity into a true, loving relationship with the Father.

In the Son, the triune God took up our human nature into his Being, and he thereby transformed our nature. He redeemed us and reconciled us. By making our sinful nature his own and healing it, Jesus Christ became the Mediator between God and a fallen humanity.

Our election in the one man Jesus Christ fulfills God's purpose for the creation and defines God as the God who loves in freedom. Torrance explains that "all of grace" does not mean "nothing of humanity," but *all of grace means all of humanity.* That is, we cannot hold onto even one percent of ourselves.

By grace through faith, we participate in God's love for the creation in a relational way that was not possible before. That means that we love others as God loves us because by grace Jesus Christ is in us and we are in him. This can happen only within the miracle of a new creation. God's revelation to humanity comes from the Father through the Son in the Spirit, and a redeemed humanity now responds by faith in the Spirit through the Son to the Father.

We have been called to holiness in Christ. We enjoy freedom in him from the sin, death, evil, misery and judgment that stood against us. We return God's love for us through thanksgiving, worship and service in the community of faith. In all his healing and saving relations with us, Jesus Christ is engaged in personalizing and humanizing us – making us real people in him. In all our relations with him, he makes us more truly and fully human in our response of faith. This takes place in us through the creative power of the Holy Spirit as he unites us to the perfect humanity of the Lord Jesus Christ.

All of grace means all of humanity. The grace of Jesus Christ who was crucified and resurrected for us does not eliminate the humanity he came to save. God's unconditional grace brings into the light all that we are and do.

Even in our repenting and believing we cannot rely on our own response, but in faith we rely only on the response that Christ has offered to the Father in our place and on our behalf! In his humanity, Jesus, the new Adam, became our vicarious response to God in all things, including faith, conversion, worship, celebration of the sacraments and evangelism.

Ignored

Unfortunately, Karl Barth has been ignored or misinterpreted by many American evangelicals, and Thomas Torrance is often presented as too hard to understand. But to fail to appreciate the dynamic nature of theology displayed in Barth's reworking of the doctrine of election causes many Christians to remain caught in the behavioralism trap, struggling to understand where God draws the line between human behavior and salvation.

The great Reformation principle of ongoing reformation should free us from old worldviews and behavior-based theologies that inhibit growth, promote stagnation and prevent ecumenical cooperation within the Body of Christ. Yet today doesn't the church often find itself robbed of the joy of grace as it shadowboxes with various forms of legalism? For this reason the church is not uncommonly characterized as a bastion of judgmentalism and exclusivism rather than as a testament to grace.

We all have a theology – a way that we think about and understand God – whether we know it or not. And our theology affects how we think about and understand God's grace and salvation.

If our theology is dynamic and relational, we will be open to hear God's ever-present word of salvation, which he freely gives us by his grace though Jesus Christ alone. On the other hand, if our theology is static, we will shrivel into a religion of legalism, judgmentalism and spiritual stagnation. Instead of knowing Jesus as he is, in a way that seasons all our relationships with mercy, patience, kindness and peace, we will know judgment, exclusivity and condemnation of those who fail to meet our carefully defined standards of godliness.

New creation in freedom

Theology does make a difference. How we understand God affects the way we understand salvation and how we live the Christian life. God is not the prisoner of some static, humanly reasoned idea about what he must and should be.

Humans are not capable of reasoning out who God is and what he must be like. God tells us who he is and what he is like, and he is free to be exactly how he chooses to be, and he has revealed himself in Jesus Christ as being the God who loves us, is for us and who chooses to make humanity's cause – including your cause and my cause – his own.

In Jesus Christ, we are freed from our sinful minds, from our boasting and despair, and graciously renewed to experience God's *shalom* peace in his loving faith community.

Recommended reading

Michael Jinkins, *Invitation to Theology*
Thomas Torrance, *The Mediation of Christ*
Karl Barth, *Dogmatics in Outline*
James Torrance, *Worship, Community and the Triune God of Grace*
Thomas Torrance, *The Christian Doctrine of God: One Being Three Persons*
Thomas Torrance, *The Trinitarian Faith*
Ray Anderson, *Theology, Death and Dying*
C. Baxter Kruger, *The Great Dance*
Donald Bloesch, The Christian Foundations series (seven books)

Terry Akers and J. Michael Feazell

THEOLOGY AFFECTS THE WAY WE LIVE

Ideas have consequences. The way we think about God affects the way we respond to him. In other words, our *theology* affects the way we live. Some people think theology is dull and irrelevant, but perhaps that is because they think God is dull and irrelevant; they would rather get on with their life without dragging God into the discussion.

Everyone has a theology, whether they know it or not. They have some concepts of what God is like. They may think he is distant and unconcerned, or harsh and angry, or even that he doesn't exist. All these ideas affect the way we live. If we believe God is distant and unconcerned, we may be angry because we are suffering from the sins of other people, and God doesn't seem to care. We may need help, but God doesn't seem to answer our cries for help. Or we may indulge our baser desires or take advantage of others, thinking God doesn't care one way or the other.

Living by faith

My point is that the way we *think* about God affects the way we live. This is implied throughout the Bible, which repeatedly connects doctrine and behavior.

God cares about us, Jesus said, so we should not worry. Worry comes from a lack of faith that God is good, powerful, merciful and will not cease to love us and do what is good and right for us. If we don't trust God, we may think that he doesn't care, or that he doesn't have the power to take care of us, or that he is harsh, unforgiving or unpredictable toward us.

But when we trust in God, we do not worry even when bad things happen to us. We are confident that God is faithful to us, suffering with us, holding us, and that he will use even our pain to make us stronger and bless us. He works all things, even bad things, for good. He brings light out of our darkness. Our belief about God's power and love affects the way we react to the situations we face.

Paul uses a similar kind of logic in his letters. He explains that we are saved by grace through the work of Jesus our Savior, and then he writes, Therefore we should be living sacrifices, set apart to do God's will, putting off the old self and putting on the new, acting like the new people that God has declared us to be. In other words, our theology should affect the way we live.

The book of Hebrews uses similar logic at several points. After explaining a concept, the author says, Therefore let us hold fast to our confession, therefore let us approach the throne with confidence, therefore let us encourage one another. He sees a close connection between ideas and consequences, between doctrine and practice.

Need for an accurate view

Since the way we think about God affects the way we live, we want to have the best understanding of God we can. If we think of God as a powerful physical being, then we will tend to focus on physical life, on external behavior, on a future based on physical things. We will tend to neglect spiritual qualities such as grace and love, and give little attention to concepts such as the heavenly and the eternal.

On the other hand, when we think of God as eternal and triune, then we see a God for whom relationships are essential to his very being, for whom love is essential, a God who gives himself when he gives his Son, a God who lives within us when his Spirit is in us.

The triune God is a God who has fellowship with us directly, not through intermediaries. In contrast, a God who is only Father, but not Father, Son and Holy Spirit, unity in Trinity, is more likely to be seen as aloof, distant, legalistic, stressing law rather than mercy. This is how many people view God. If such a God sent his Son to die on the cross, he would be sending another being to appease his angry judgment, rather than (as actually happened) taking humanity into his own being and redeeming it through union with his own sinless Son, with whom he, with the Spirit, is one God.

It is not my intention here to discuss the nature of God in detail. We have already published quite a bit of material on that, and it is on our website. We have an article summarizing it and listing a number of books for further study ("An Introduction to God"). It highlights two qualities of God – his greatness and his goodness. God always uses his enormous power to further his covenant of love and grace toward his people. He is gentle, loving, slow to anger and full of mercy.

Trust

Here, I want to focus on the "so what" question. How is this relevant to us? What difference does it make in our lives? How do we respond to a God who is simultaneously powerful and gentle? When we realize that God has all power to do anything he wants, and that he always uses it for the good of humanity, then we can have absolute confidence that we are in good hands.

He has both the ability and the covenanted purpose to work all things, including all our rebellion, hatred and betrayal against him and one another, toward our redemption and glorification in Jesus Christ. He is completely trustworthy – worthy of our trust.

When we are in the midst of trials, sickness, suffering and even dying, we can be confident that God is still with us, that he cares for us, that he has everything under control. It may not look like it, and we certainly do not feel in control, but we can be confident that God isn't caught off guard. He can and does redeem any situation, any misfortune, for our good.

We need never doubt God's love for us. "God demonstrates his own love for us in this: While we were still sinners, Christ died for us" (Romans 5:8). "This is how we know what love is: Jesus Christ laid down his life for us" (1 John 3:16). The God who did not spare his own Son can be counted on to give us through his Son everything we need for eternal happiness.

God did not send somebody else: The Son of God, essential to the Godhead, became human so that he could die for us and rise again for us (Hebrews 2:14). We were redeemed not by the blood of animals, not by the blood of a very good man, but by the blood of the God who became human.

We can be confident that he loves us. Every time we take communion, we are reminded of the extent of his love for us – both of his death wherein we are forgiven, and his resurrection wherein we are given union with him and presented holy and blameless to God. He has earned our trust.

"God is faithful," Paul tells us. "He will not let you be tempted beyond what you can bear" (1 Corinthians 10:13). "The Lord is faithful, and he will strengthen and protect you from the evil one" (2 Thessalonians 3:3). Even "if we are faithless, he will remain faithful" (2 Timothy 2:13). He is not going to change his mind about wanting us, about calling us, about being merciful to us. "Let us hold unswervingly to the hope we profess, for he who promised is faithful" (Hebrews 10:23).

He has made a commitment to us, a covenant with us, to redeem us, to give us eternal life, to love us forever. He will not be without us. He is trustworthy, but how do we respond to him? Do we worry? Do we struggle to be worthy of his love? Or do we trust him?

We need never doubt God's power, either. This is shown in the resurrection of Jesus from death. This is the God who has power over death itself, power over all the beings he created, power over all other powers (Colossians 2:15). He triumphed over all things through the cross, and this is demonstrated through his resurrection. Death could not hold him, for he is the author of life (Acts 3:15).

The same power that raised Jesus from death will also give immortal life to us (Romans 8:11). We can trust that he has the power, and the desire, to fulfill all his promises toward us. We can trust him with everything – and that's a good thing, since it is foolish to trust in anything else.

Of ourselves, we will fail. Left to itself, even the sun will fail. Our only hope is in a God who has power greater than the sun, greater than the universe, more faithful than time and space, full of love and faithfulness toward us. We have that sure hope in Jesus our Savior.

Joseph Tkach

THEOLOGY IN PERSPECTIVE

Good theology is important, for bad theology distorts our understanding of God and our relationship with him. However, it's important to note that we are not saved by theology. We need to keep it in perspective.

Christianity has never been theologically or doctrinally perfect. We often hear preachers urging people to "get back to the faith once delivered." By this, they usually mean the early apostolic church, which they assume had a complete and uncorrupted understanding of the faith. However, those apostolic churches were not perfect. They too had to grow in their understanding of what was "sound doctrine."

Much of the New Testament is polemic – it was written to correct various wrong ideas. In Corinth, for example, some Christians were tolerating incest, suing one another in court, offending each other by their understanding of what they were permitted to eat, and becoming drunk at the Lord's Supper. Some thought they should be celibate even if married and others thought they should divorce their non-Christian spouses. Paul had to correct these ideas, and history tells us that he had only limited success. But the people were Christian despite their lack of complete doctrinal understanding.

There are many examples of the disciples failing to understand Jesus, even when he was with them. For example, after Jesus miraculously fed thousands of people, he and the disciples got into a boat and Jesus warned them, "Watch out for the yeast of the Pharisees and that of Herod" (Mark 8:14). The disciples concluded that Jesus meant that, since they hadn't brought any bread they would have to buy some on the other shore; moreover, they shouldn't buy any bread from a Pharisee or Herodian because something was incorrect about the yeast they used.

Why didn't they just ask Jesus what he meant? Perhaps because they were afraid of looking foolish (that happens today, too!). Jesus chided them for not understanding something that they should have been able to grasp. The disciples didn't need to worry about bread or yeast. Jesus had just shown them that he could make bread miraculously. They could remember facts (verses 19-20), but they didn't always draw right conclusions from those facts. The miracle of the loaves was not just a way to save money – it also had a much deeper meaning that the disciples had failed to understand (Mark 6:52). It figuratively symbolized the fact that Jesus is our source of life.

I am encouraged to know that Jesus' own disciples frequently didn't fully comprehend what he was doing. Nevertheless, Jesus still co-ministered with them, as he does with us. It demonstrates that any "success" we have is the result of God's guidance, not our human ability to figure things out exactly.

Those first disciples were thrown into confusion by Jesus' death even though he explained it to them more than once. But, like us, they could absorb only so much at a time. If you follow the flow of the conversation at the Last Supper, you can see by their questions and frequent attempts to change the subject that the disciples did not understand what was going on. So Jesus told them, "I have much more to say to you, more than you can now bear. But when he, the Spirit of truth, comes, he will guide you into all the truth" (John 16:12-13).

After his resurrection, Jesus appeared to his disciples and instructed them for 40 days, after which he ascended to heaven. While with them, he said, "Do not leave Jerusalem, but wait for the gift my Father promised, which you have heard me speak about. For John baptized with water, but in a few days you will be baptized with the Holy Spirit" (Acts 1:4-5).

Jesus' words were fulfilled on the day of Pentecost. As we read in Acts 2:4, the disciples were filled with the Holy Spirit, and through his guidance, what had been isolated facts and an unsound theology came together in a new and exciting way. The apostle Peter preached his first public sermon, urging his audience to repent, to believe in Jesus as their Messiah and to receive the gift of the Holy Spirit (verse 38). On that day, some 3,000 people were baptized and became the part of the people of God (verse 41). The church had been born.

From that day on, the Holy Spirit has continued to guide the church into "all the truth," helping the church to "prove the world to be in the wrong about sin and righteousness and judgment" (John 16:9). The New Testament writers, led by the Holy Spirit, showed those first Christians how to live godly lives in the turbulent environment of the first century. He is doing the same with us today, as we struggle to "get it right" while facing the complex and controversial challenges of our time.

We need to remember that the ultimate object of our faith and the only object of our worship is our Triune God, not our theological statements. We want to tune our theological understandings as best we can, to do nothing less and nothing more than serve our faith in and worship of the Father, Son and Spirit. By the Spirit and the Word, our theological understandings can be continually sanctified. Each year on Pentecost Sunday we celebrate the descent of the Spirit and the birth of the church. While we are not yet perfect, the children of God have been given the good and perfect gift of the Spirit, who will in the end enable all of us to share in Jesus' own perfection!

Joseph Tkach

STRONG THEOLOGY
VS. WEAK THEOLOGY

One of the best definitions of theology is the one ascribed to Anselm of Canterbury (1033-1109), who called it "faith seeking understanding." The converse of this – "understanding seeking faith" is known as apologetics. Pursued properly, both disciplines can lead us to dig deeper and deeper, coming to appreciate more and more the simple, yet profound statement that "God is love."

But just digging deeper does not guarantee that our conclusions will be good. We need to dig in the right direction. As we see in 2 Timothy 3:7, it is possible to be "always learning but never able to come to a knowledge of the truth."

Theology has been described as being weak or strong based upon its arrangement and understanding of various doctrines and/or a specific understanding of the attributes of God. When I first heard this, I thought of it in terms of correct and incorrect doctrine. However, it is more than that. Doctrine is only one ingredient of authentic Christianity. It is important – it is essential that the church teach right doctrines. However, doctrine is not all that we must include in our worship of our Creator, Savior and Sanctifier. Doctrine does not save us. No matter how much we know, it doesn't do us any good if we don't have love (1 Corinthians 13:2).

I first realized a distinction when, with Dr. Mike Feazell, I attended a large conference several years ago. In one session it was noted that there was a tremendous evangelistic opportunity to be had in the wake of the attacks we now refer to as *9/11*. The presenter suggested that we celebrate the firefighters, police officers and other heroes who saved the lives of others, sometimes losing their own in the process – a powerful analogy of what Jesus has done for humanity.

During a later talk, a serious contradiction became apparent, although most seemed oblivious to it. Another presenter, in order to motivate us to evangelism, emphasized that unless someone had made a conscious decision for Christ, God would send them to hell forever. Mike, putting the two presentations together, elbowed me and said, "So, how do you celebrate a hero who gave his life to save others but who had been sent to hell forever because he had not accepted Jesus as his Savior? What is there to celebrate about a hero who is now burning in hell?"

"That's the problem with a weak theology," I replied.

Our theology defines how we understand God's nature, character, heart, mind and purpose. It fills out for us how God views us and others and what kind of relationship he wants with us.

Strong theology has a clear and coherent grasp of who God is and what God wants for us: God is exactly like Jesus all the way down. He is the fullness of deity, bearing the stamp of the character of God. He is the visible image of the Father and the Spirit. In Jesus, what you see is what you get.

Weak theology, however, presents God in bits and pieces, often leaving us with a view of a God who is of two minds, or who has two different wills, or even two different sides to his character. Sometimes Jesus is presented as one "side" of God who wants to save us by grace and the Father as the other "side" who wants to condemn us under the Law. This God has two wills, two purposes, two attitudes towards his creation and therefore has two kinds of relationship with us. This God is *for* some of us, but *against* others.

Weak theology leaves us with two minds toward others. We're supposed to love others, even our enemies, and present the gospel to them and encourage them to surrender their lives to Christ who died for them. But if we believe God only loves some and will only call some to himself but is against others and just as happy to send them to hell, it's hard, if not impossible, to have the same attitude and hope for all. We are left with the sense that we're not being totally truthful when we present the gospel as if it's for everyone.

While some people may somehow reject the gospel of grace no matter what we or even God does for them, perhaps for all eternity, God's revelation to us of his single mind, will and purpose for all is made clear by Paul:

> For God was pleased to have all his fullness dwell in him, and through him to reconcile to himself all things, whether things on earth or things in heaven, by making peace through his blood, shed on the cross. (Colossians 1:19-20)

Weak theology undermines this vital truth, leaving us with the impression that Jesus only shows us one side of God, not the fullness of God, and that God is interested in reconciling only some things, not everything. Weak theology can lead to an "us vs. them" elitist mentality where, after the evangelistic meeting is over, we minister to those on the "inside" far differently from those on the "outside."

While weak theology leads us down this dark and conflicted path of exclusivism, strong theology affirms that God loves everyone profoundly and places love above all other gifts from God:

> If I have the gift of prophecy and can fathom all mysteries and all knowledge, and if I have a faith that can move mountains, but do not

have love, I am nothing. (1 Corinthians 13:2)

While weak theology leads us to erect barriers between people, strong theology understands that God, who is no respecter of persons, "wants all people to be saved and to come to a knowledge of the truth" (1 Timothy 2:3-4). Led by this truth, we are encouraged to join with Paul in tearing down barriers that divide people from God and one another:

> Though I am free and belong to no one, I have made myself a slave to everyone, to win as many as possible. To the Jews I became like a Jew, to win the Jews. To those under the law I became like one under the law (though I myself am not under the law), so as to win those under the law. To those not having the law I became like one not having the law (though I am not free from God's law but am under Christ's law), so as to win those not having the law. To the weak I became weak, to win the weak. I have become all things to all people so that by all possible means I might save some. I do all this for the sake of the gospel, that I may share in its blessings. (1 Corinthians 9:19-23)

While weak theology includes or excludes people from coming under God's reconciling work, strong theology recognizes that Jesus' atonement has pre-qualified everyone for salvation. Note Paul's words to the Christians in Colossae:

> Giving thanks to the Father, who has qualified us to share in the inheritance of the saints in light. For He rescued us from the domain of darkness, and transferred us to the kingdom of his beloved Son, in whom we have redemption, the forgiveness of sins. (Colossians 1:12-14, NAS)

To sum it up, whereas weak theology begins with bad news, hoping to convince (or frighten) people into hoping there is good news, strong theology starts and ends with the good news for all:

> God so loved the world that he gave his one and only Son, that whoever believes in him shall not perish but have eternal life. For God did not send his Son into the world to condemn the world, but to save the world through him. (John 3:16-17)

Strong theology is profoundly and consistently evangelical, while weak theology is a pretender. As we dig deep into theology, it is important that we dig in the proper direction.

Joseph Tkach

FOUNDATIONS OF THEOLOGY FOR GCI

By Joseph Tkach, Mike Feazell, Dan Rogers, and Michael Morrison
Transcript of a video presentation

Joseph Tkach: Acts 17:11 tells us that the Bereans "examined the Scriptures every day" to see if what Paul said about Jesus was true. The Bereans were engaged in theology — studying to know God. The English word "theology" comes from two Greek words, *theos* and *logia* — meaning "God" and "knowledge." Theology is what we as Christian believers do — we involve ourselves in "God knowledge" or "God study" seeking to know God as fully as we can. Theology is simply the study of God. What we believe, and what a Christological, or Trinitarian, theology is all about, is that theology itself needs to emerge from God's witness to himself in Scripture.

Michael Morrison: The idea of studying theology, or even thinking about theology, can be frightening to many people. But everyone has a theology, whether they know it or not. Even atheists have a theology. A college student once admitted to the college chaplain that she did not believe in God. The chaplain was curious, so he asked: "What sort of god is it that you don't believe in?" She described an old man in the sky, someone who is just looking for people to do something wrong so he can zap them. The chaplain replied, "If that's what you mean by the word *god,* then I'd be an atheist, too. I don't believe in that kind of god, either."

JT: A person's theology is just their beliefs about God. Some people think that God is an angry judge; others believe that he is like a grandfather who means well but can't do much. Others see him as a cosmic concierge who exists to grant us our every desire. Some people think of God as far off and unknowable; others think of him as near and accessible. Some people think God never changes his mind; others think that he is always changing in response to the prayers of his people. How people view God affects how they read and interpret the Bible.

MM: When Paul tells us that Adam brought condemnation on everyone, and that Jesus brought justification for everyone, then we have to think about what that means about humanity and about Jesus and about salvation. When Paul says that we were baptized into Christ's death, or when Jesus says, "If you have seen me you have seen the Father," we need to think about what that means — and that's theology.

A study of theology helps us learn to put all our various doctrines or beliefs or teachings together, to see if they are consistent with one another, or if they seem to contradict one another. But we don't do theology just according to what sounds good to us. We are not the authority — God is. If he didn't reveal himself to us, then we wouldn't know anything for sure about him. But he has revealed himself to us, and in two ways — in Scripture, and in Jesus — and we know Jesus through Scripture as well. So Scripture should provide our foundation for theological thought.

J. Michael Feazell: At the heart of all our doctrines and beliefs in our denomination is the Bible. Yet, as is clear from our own history (not to mention the history of the Christian church in general), people do not agree on how the Bible should be interpreted. A person's theology, or their perspective on who God is and how he relates to humanity and how humanity relates to him, is like a lens though which people interpret what they read in the Bible. What we believe, and what a Christological, or Trinitarian, theology is all about, is that theology needs to emerge from God's own witness to himself in Scripture. God's own witness to himself in Scripture is Jesus Christ. "If you have seen me," Jesus said, "You have seen the Father."

Dan Rogers: In Jesus, God fully revealed himself to humanity. Karl Barth once said you really can't do theology. If theology is the study of God, the knowledge of God, how can the human mind ever study God? Well, there is a way — as he then pointed out. God fully revealed himself in Jesus Christ.

JT: In our denomination, our theology is what gives cohesion and structure to our beliefs and establishes priority for our doctrines. It has developed over the years as we have worked through various doctrinal issues, all the while being careful to maintain a Bible-based understanding of who God is and how he relates to humanity.

JMF: God is known by faith, and by that we mean that we know God not merely as we hear about him through the Scriptures, but as we actually put our trust in him. In that obedient life, the Spirit engages us to think about and reflect on what God reveals about himself. That is why a Christological, or Christ-centered, theology is important, so that we have the right starting place for our journey of growing in the grace and knowledge of God.

JT: As our theology developed, we found the writings of Thomas and James Torrance and Karl Barth to be especially helpful because of their intense focus on the biblical revelation of God through Jesus Christ.

MM: We have a Christ-centered, or Trinitarian, theology. That means not only that we accept the doctrine of the Trinity, but that this doctrine lies at the heart of all other doctrines. The central Bible truth that Jesus Christ is God in the flesh, that he and the Father with the Spirit are one God, forms the basis for how we understand everything we read in Scripture.

In John 14, the apostle Philip asked Jesus, "Lord, show us the Father." Jesus replied, "If you have seen me, you have seen the Father. I am in the Father, and the Father is in me." In other words, Jesus reveals to us what the Father is like. Jesus shows us a God who is love, is compassion, patience, kindness, faithfulness, and goodness. God is like that all the time.

Some people imagine that the Father is angry at humanity and really wants to punish everyone, but that the Son intervened for us and paid the price to save us from his Father's wrath. That's quite confused, because the Bible says that the Father is just like Jesus. The Father loved the world so much that he sent his Son to save the world. It's not like Jesus was working behind his Father's back — no, it's just the opposite: the Father was working in and through Jesus. The Father is just as eager to save humanity as Jesus is.

When Jesus was born, he was Immanuel, which means "God with us." When the Word became a human being, he showed us that God is present with humanity, and he is working for humanity. We are his creations, and he doesn't want to let us go to ruin. When God came in human flesh, he, as a representative of humanity, was able to do what other humans had not been able to do. As the perfect human, Jesus offered God perfect worship, and a perfect sacrifice, and God accepted this worship that was offered on behalf of the human race. Just as in Adam we are all condemned, so also in Christ we are all acquitted, and accepted, and welcomed into the love and fellowship of the Trinity.

DR: As we study Jesus, we begin to see God and his relationship with us as his creation — with humanity. So we began to view the Scriptures through that lens, and we noticed that many others had done likewise; men such as Athanasius and in our modern times theologians like Karl Barth had looked through this same lens, and we began to interact, to participate in a dialectical discussion with the writings and the thoughts of these great Christians from ages past. As we did, we began to focus more and more on a certain theology, the theology of adoption, the theology of God's love for humanity. How God wanted to take us into himself and share his life with us because he is a God of love — a God who gives, and a God who shares.

JT: Thomas Torrance is widely considered to be one of the premier Christian theologians of the 20th century. He was awarded the Templeton Foundation Prize for Progress in Religion in 1978, and his book, *Theological Science,* received the first "Collins Award" in Britain for the best work in theology, ethics, and sociology relevant to Christianity for 1967-69. Torrance founded the *Scottish Journal of Theology* and served as moderator of the General

Assembly of the Church of Scotland in 1976-77. He served for more than 25 years as chair of Christian Dogmatics at the University of Edinburgh, and is author of more than 30 books and hundreds of articles.

Torrance, following in the theological tradition of Athanasius and Gregory of Nazianzus, is a leading proponent of what is called Trinitarian theology: theology rooted in God's own revelation of himself through the Scriptures in the person of Jesus Christ. In the Scriptures, human life and human death find their meaning only in the life and death and resurrection of Jesus Christ, the Son of God, who in becoming human for our sakes has brought humanity into the eternal joyous fellowship of the Father, Son and Spirit. Because Christ has done in our place and on our behalf everything needed for our salvation, all that remains for us is to repent and believe in him as our Lord and Savior.

JMF: When we take seriously passages about the width and breadth of God's gracious and powerful reconciling work in Jesus Christ, such as Colossian 1:19-20, some people respond with "You're just teaching universalism." Colossians 1:19-20 says: "God was pleased to have all his fullness dwell in him, and through him to reconcile to himself all things, whether things on earth or things in heaven, by making peace through his blood, shed on the cross." Paul wrote the passage, not us, not Karl Barth, not Thomas Torrance.

Barth, responding to accusations that he was teaching universalism, said, "There is no theological justification for setting any limits on our side to the friendliness of God towards humanity which appeared in Jesus Christ." We have no reason to make apologies for the wideness of God's grace. Paul also wrote, in 1 Timothy 2:4, that God "wants all men to be saved and to come to a knowledge of the truth." Still, as Barth pointed out, God declares an eternal "No" to sin, and God's "No" is the power of God by which evil is overthrown and negated, and its power and future denied. God rejects and opposes all opposition to himself, and yet in Jesus Christ, God's elect, all humanity is indeed elect and reconciled, as Colossians says.

But kingdom life is none other than a life of faith in Jesus, not a life of unbelief. That means that even though all humanity is elect in Christ, unbelieving elect aren't living a kingdom life; they aren't living in the joy of fellowship with the Father and the Son and the Spirit. So if it were to be that everyone would ultimately enter into the life of the kingdom (and that is not something we are given to know), but if it were to be, it would only be after repentance, which is turning to God, and faith in Jesus Christ. "Now this is eternal life," Jesus said in a prayer to the Father, "that they may know you, the only true God, and Jesus Christ whom you have sent." There is no salvation outside of a life of faith in Jesus Christ.

That's what hell is all about—life outside the fellowship of the Father, Son and Spirit—life, if you can call it that, in the dark, outside the king's banquet, being left to the miserable fruit of one's own self-centeredness. Call it fiery, call it outer darkness, call it weeping and gnashing of teeth — the Bible uses all those metaphors in describing the existence of those who refuse to embrace his grace and love, that amazing grace and love God has even for his enemies.

JT: The Bible confronts us with a wonderful, amazing, reconciliation in Christ that is so broad as to encompass not only all things on earth, but even all things in heaven, Colossians tells us in no uncertain terms. Yet God calls on humanity to receive, to accept, that grace he so powerfully bestows on all humanity in Jesus Christ. But for those who refuse it, who persist in their rebellion, and in their rejection of God's grace for them, hell is what remains for them. As Robert Capon puts it, God will not allow them to spoil the party for everyone else.

MM: Ancient Greek philosophers reasoned that since God is perfect, that must mean that he never changes, and that he never has any feelings, because if he would ever change, then that would mean that he wasn't perfect before the change. So they thought of God as static, the so-called "unmoved mover" who made everything happen, but who could not ever change course, because to do so would call his perfection and his power into question. This kind of God would never dirty himself by getting involved with people and their problems. He was far off, watching, but not directly and personally involved. This concept of God has often affected even how Christians think about God.

But the Bible reveals a different sort of God — one who is not constrained by the limits of a philosopher's logic. God is completely sovereign — he can do whatever he wants to do — and he is not limited by any external rules or ideas or human logic. If he wants the eternal Word to become a human being, then he does it, even though it constitutes a change. The God of the Bible is free to be whoever he wants to be — free to become what he was not before: the Creator; and free to create human beings who would be free, who could go astray, and God is even free to become one of those human beings in order to rescue humanity from its rebellion and alienation.

In this theological thinking, it is not our logic that is in charge — God is the one in charge, and our task, our desire, is to try to understand God not the way that we might reason him out to be by our finite forms of logic, but rather to seek to understand God the way that he has revealed himself through the Bible in the person of Jesus Christ.

Throughout church history, people have defined theology as "faith seeking understanding." We believe, and now we want to understand as much as we can about what we believe. It's like we've fallen in love with someone, and we want to find out as much as we can about that person. Theology is faith, trying to understand more about the God who loves us. We must seek that understanding in the context of God's own revelation of himself as Father, Son and Spirit revealed to us perfectly in Jesus, the Son of God made flesh for our sakes.

JT: When it comes to theologies, it is not so much a matter of a particular theological perspective being totally "right" or totally "wrong." It is more a case of how adequate a particular theology is in fully addressing believers' biblical understanding of God and how God relates to humanity. We have found that of all approaches to Christian theology, Christo-centric, or Trinitarian, theology reflects and adheres most faithfully and carefully to what God reveals about himself and humanity in the Bible.

We should keep in mind that theology is a journey, not a destination. We will always be seeking as clear and adequate a theological vision as we can, in order to soundly convey the biblical vision and understanding God has given us over 15-plus years of doctrinal reformation. Theology includes the task of seeking adequate thought-forms to convey doctrinal truths in a rapidly changing world.

JMF: Many people today, even believers, are afraid: They're afraid of their standing with God, worried that they're not measuring up, that they're not doing enough, worried that their sins and failures have cut them off from God's love. That's what theologies that start from ideas of, say, holiness, or of judgment, cause. Instead of taking confidence in Jesus, and knowing that Jesus has already done for them everything God requires of them, instead of knowing that Jesus is their perfection, their obedience, their faithfulness, they suffer under a burden of guilt and anxiety.

When we know that it isn't our righteousness but Jesus' righteousness that has already put us in good standing with God, then we are freed from ourselves and our sinfulness to trust in Jesus and to take up our cross and follow Jesus as we could never be free to do when we're afraid that God is mad at us. A sound, biblically rooted theology will always start with and be centered in Christology, because in Scripture we are confronted with a God who chooses to be God in Jesus, with Jesus and for Jesus. If we let the Bible forge our theology, we cannot look outside of Jesus to understand who God is, or to define God.

MM: In Jesus we meet God as God really is, the way God has revealed himself to be, as the God who is for us, because he is for Jesus. We find that the Father loves us unconditionally, that he sent Jesus not out of anger and a need to punish someone, but out of his immeasurable love and his unbending commitment to our redemption. The love we see in Jesus is none other than the love of the Father, because the Father is in the Son and the Son in the Father and they are one. That means that when we know Jesus Christ, we know God the Father.

JMF: In Jesus, God reveals himself as our Creator and our Judge, and also as our Reconciler and Redeemer. In other words, the God who made us and whom we stand under as our Judge is also the one who reconciles and redeems us. That means we can believe him and trust him instead of being afraid of him and hiding from him. In Jesus, we are free for obedience and faith because we aren't relying on our own obedience and faith, but on his. That takes our minds off ourselves and rests them in Jesus.

JT: In Trinitarian theology, which is centered on Jesus as God's perfect revelation of himself, we see that 1) God is free in the fullness of his divine love and power to be with us and for us and 2) that humanity, secure in God's grace manifest in Jesus, is free to be with God and for God. That is because Jesus is both the fullness of God and the fullness of humanity, exactly as God reveals himself in the Bible.

MM: The Christian life is a response to God's grace. It is letting God's grace work in us, change us, and shine through us. Paul said, "It is not I who live, but Christ lives in me." His grace works in us, and as we are united to Christ, we have a new life, and we walk in newness of life, in a new way — a way that is being transformed by Christ in us.

We are not working our way into salvation, or trying to obey Jesus in order to be a child of God. No, by grace God has already said that we are his children. That is who we are, and that does not change. God says to us, "You belong to me. Now, I invite you to live a new way, a better way, a way that gives meaning and purpose to life. I invite you — I urge you — to join and enjoy the life of love — the way that has worked for all eternity. I invite you to the banquet, to the party, to the never-ending fellowship of the Father, Son, and Holy Spirit."

DR: As we began to look at certain doctrines, every doctrine was viewed through the lens of Jesus Christ. As time has gone by, we have seen that our statement of beliefs has held up very well and we are coming more and more into a fuller and fuller understanding of the implications of this theology of adoption, of God as Trinity and as God fully revealed in the person of Jesus Christ.

JT: The articles and Statement of Beliefs posted on our website express the official doctrines of our fellowship and discuss our theological vision. We are adding high-quality biblical studies, Christian living and theological material to our website continually. It is important that our preaching and teaching reflect sound theology, and that it remain rooted in the good news, the biblical revelation of Jesus Christ as the incarnate Son of God in whom we live and move and have our being.

Christo-centric, or Trinitarian, theology originates as far back as the early Church Fathers with Irenaeus, Athanasius and the Cappadocian Fathers. Some of the greatest theologians in modern history have devoted their life's work to explaining the relationship between God's triune nature and his redemptive work on behalf of humanity. Theologians whose work has been of special help to us in understanding and articulating a sound, Bible-based theology include Karl Barth, Thomas and James Torrance, Michael Jinkins [now president of Louisville Seminary], Ray Anderson, [recently deceased] professor of theology and ministry at Fuller Theological Seminary, Colin Gunton, Robert Capon, Gary Deddo, C. Baxter Kruger, Donald Bloesch, Michael Green and others. We have also found the writings of C.S. Lewis of particular value, although Lewis was not a theologian, per se.

Although it is not likely that you or I would necessarily agree with every single statement in any particular book, we are able to recommend a number of books on theology that we believe provide a sound and faithful reflection of biblical doctrine. These would include such books as:

Invitation to Theology, by Michael Jinkins

The Mediation of Christ, by Thomas Torrance

Dogmatics in Outline, by Karl Barth

Worship, Community & The Triune God of Grace, by James Torrance

The Christian Doctrine of God: One Being Three Persons, by T.F. Torrance

The Trinitarian Faith, by Thomas Torrance

Theology, Death and Dying, by Ray Anderson

Judas and Jesus: Amazing Grace for the Wounded Soul, by Ray Anderson

On the Incarnation, by St. Athanasius

The Christian Foundations Series by Donald Bloesch

The Parables of Judgment, The Parables of Grace, and The Parables of the Kingdom, by Robert Capon

The One, the Three, and the Many, by Colin Gunton

Across All Worlds, by Baxter Kruger
The Great Dance, by Baxter Kruger
The Promise of Trinitarian Theology, by Elmer Colyer
How to Read Thomas F. Torrance, by Elmer Colyer
The Humanity of God, by Karl Barth
Mere Christianity, by C.S. Lewis
The Great Divorce, by C.S. Lewis

This is by no means a complete list, but it's a good start. Most pastors will find Michael Jinkins' *Invitation to Theology* especially helpful as a one-volume, easy-to-read, basic theology text.

I want to take this and every possible occasion to thank all of you who labor in the gospel for your faithful work and to let you know how much all of us here in Glendora appreciate your service in Christ to his people. May God bless and keep you always in his faithful embrace.

WHO'S AFRAID
OF THE JUDGMENT OF GOD?

Imagine a courtroom scene. You are accused of a crime and now on trial. Problem is, you know you are guilty. But as you walk in, you notice the judge gives you a reassuring nod of recognition, as if he had known you all your life. He summons you to the bench. "Don't worry about a thing," he tells you with a warm fatherly smile. "I know all about this case. In fact, I'm going to be your defense attorney."

The late theologian Shirley C. Guthrie would explain that this is the way we should picture what the Bible calls the Judgment. "Must we talk about the wrath of God?" Guthrie asked. "Yes," he answers. "But God's wrath is not like that of the gods. It is the wrath of the God who was in Christ reconciling the world to God's self" (*Christian Doctrine*, pages 261-262).

Theological strait-jackets

Unfortunately, instead of allowing Jesus' love, compassion and kindness to shape their understanding of God, many Christians gravitate toward what we might call a "forensic" model of salvation. "Forensic" is a penal or legal term. This model sees God the Father as stern and vengeful, a frightening God from whom we need Jesus to save us. It assumes that the starting place for understanding God is not Jesus Christ, but "the law," or the commands of the Bible. This model sees the law as so important that even God is subject to it. Since God is concerned first about the demands of his law and only secondly about the well-being of humans, he will punish them for lawbreaking in the same way that the State and human courts and legal systems do — through a straightforward proving of guilt, a guilty verdict, followed by an appropriate punishment.

Front and center in the forensic model is God's anger against sinning humanity. God is offended, and someone must pay. Jesus steps forward and takes the full force of God's wrath against human sin. That means we have had our penalty paid for us, but this model does nothing for a restored relationship of love and trust. This "offended deity" picture forgets that first and foremost, God is love (1 John 4:16), that God is joyously working to bring "many children to glory," and that our salvation was in his mind "from the creation of the world" (Revelation 13:8).

This forensic model also forgets something even more basic — that Jesus Christ and the Father along with the Holy Spirit are the three Persons of the one God, and that the Son or Word made Incarnate in Jesus was the perfect revelation of the Father in human form. The Father is not some angry, vengeful deity that we need protection from; he is just like Jesus. Jesus, remember, is "the exact representation" of the being of God (Hebrews 1:3). The Father is full of compassion and mercy, a God who "desires mercy and not sacrifice," just like Jesus. Jesus is the starting place for understanding God; the law is not.

God is not schizophrenic. He does not have a split personality. There is not one "good God," Jesus, and one "bad God," the Father. There is one God — Father, Son and Spirit — who loves us unconditionally and has in Jesus made full provision not only for our sins to be forgiven and removed, but also for us to be fully included in the love relationship that the Son has shared with the Father from eternity.

Adoption

God is not in the business of training obedient servants, but in building a family. The apostle Paul used the word "adoption" in describing the kind of relationship that God has created for humanity in Jesus Christ (Ephesians 1:4-5). Through the Incarnation of the Son — by Jesus becoming one of us and taking up our cause as his own — God has drawn us into and made us part of the intimate relationship that Jesus has with the Father.

We see the power of this intimate love that God has for humanity in the parable of the Prodigal Son. The repentant son is welcomed home by the Father and restored to full rights of being part of the family (Luke 15:11-24). This depicts the God who was in Christ reconciling the world to himself (2 Corinthians 5:19). The death of Christ was not an act of divine child abuse, as some critics of Christianity have said. It was a divine rescue springing from God's love for us (John 3:16), an intervention designed to restore a purpose of which we were unaware in our ignorance and darkness (verses 19-20).

Set against this majestic purpose, God's wrath can be seen for what it is —anger not at the humanity he sent Jesus to save, but at sin, which destroys the relationship he has always intended for us in Christ. God is not some resentful, selfish parent in an emotional stew because we have not played by his rules. God is Father, Son and Spirit, loving, faithful and unconditionally committed to bringing humanity into the joy of knowing him for who he really is.

Mercy vs. judgment

God, however, will never be at peace with sin. The great human tragedy is that we have been unaware of the pardon and reconciliation the Father has brought about through Jesus Christ. We have loved darkness rather than light and have chosen to ignore what the Father offers us through the Son.

Through Christ, the disconnect between the world and God has been removed once and for all. The great majority of unbelievers are people who through weakness or ignorance are resisting the influence of the life-giving Holy Spirit of Christ, the Person of the Godhead who beckons to us to abandon our addiction to darkness and sin — who testifies in our hearts to God's saving, atoning and reconciling work in Jesus on our behalf (John 14:25-27; 15:26).

Jesus did not just *bring* good news, he *was* good news. The overwhelming emphasis of his teaching was mercy, not vengeance. His hallmark sayings reflect the God who is love, in whose mind mercy rejoices against judgment (James 2:13). Thus, what was hinted at in parts of the Old Testament becomes the major theme in the Gospels — "I will have mercy and not sacrifice." Jesus' word pictures show us a forgiving father, a Good Samaritan, seeking shepherds and splendidly generous employers, healings, exorcisms, a Great Physician who pleaded "Come to me, all you who are weary and burdened, and I will give you rest" (Matthew 11:28).

Neil Earle

WE WERE ALWAYS ON HIS MIND

The doctrine of the Trinity has been with us for more than 1,600 years. Most Christians consider it to be one of the "givens" of their faith, and don't give it much thought. Theologian J.I. Packer noted that the Trinity is usually considered a little-thought-about piece of "theological lumber" that no one pays much attention to.[1]

But whatever your level of understanding of the doctrine of the Trinity, one thing you can know for sure: The Triune God is unchangeably committed to including you in the wonderful fellowship of the life of the Father, the Son and Holy Spirit.

Communion

The doctrine of the Trinity teaches that there are not three Gods, only one, and that God, the only true God, the God of the Bible, is Father, Son and Holy Spirit. This has always been a concept that is difficult to put into words. But let's try. The Father, Son and Spirit, we might say, mutually indwell one another, that is, the life they share is perfectly interpenetrating. In other words, there is no such thing as the Father apart from the Son and the Spirit. There is no such thing as the Son apart from the Father and the Spirit. And there is no Holy Spirit apart from the Father and the Son.

That means that when you are in Christ, you are included in the fellowship and joy of the life of the Triune God. It means the Father receives you and has fellowship with you as he does with Jesus. It means that the love that God once and for all demonstrated in the Incarnation of Jesus Christ is no less than the love the Father has always had for you even before you were a believer, and he always will have that love for you.

It means that God has declared in Christ that you belong to him, that you are included, that you matter. That's why the Christian life is all about love: God's love for you and God's love in you.

God did not make us to be alone. To be created in God's image, as the Bible says humanity is (Genesis 1:27), is to be created for loving relationships, for communion with God and with one another. The systematic theologian Colin Gunton put it this way: "God is already 'in advance' of creation, a communion of persons existing in loving relations."[2]

Mutual indwelling

This union/communion of Father, Son and Spirit was referred to as *perichoresis* by the early Greek fathers of the church. They used the word in the sense of *mutual indwelling*.[3]

Why does this matter? Because that inner life of love in the Triune God is what God shares with *us* in Jesus Christ. Theologian Michael Jinkins describes it this way:

> Through the self-giving of Jesus Christ, through God's self-emptying assumption of our humanity, God shares God's own inner life and being in communion with us, uniting us to himself by the Word through the power of the Holy Spirit. Thus the God who is Love brings us into a real participation in the eternal life of God.[4]

Too "theological" sounding? Let's make it simpler. Paul told the pagans at Athens that we all "live and move and have our being" in God (Acts 17:28). The God in whom we live and have our being is the Father, the Son and the Holy Spirit, each existing in the other in perfect communion and love. The Son became human so that we humans can join him in that perfect communion of love that he shares with the Father and the Spirit. We learn this from God's perfect revelation of himself in Jesus Christ in the Scriptures:

- "I am the way and the truth and the life. No one comes to the Father except through me. If you really knew me, you would know my Father as well" (John 14:6-7).
- "Don't you believe that I am in the Father, and that the Father is in me?… Believe me when I say that I am in the Father and the Father is in me" (John 14:10-11).
- "On that day you will realize that I am in my Father, and you are in me, and I am in you" (John 14:20).
- "I pray also for those who will believe in me through their message, that all of them may be one, Father, just as you are in me and I am in you" (John 17:20-21).
- "God was pleased to have all his fullness dwell in him [Jesus Christ], and through him to reconcile to himself all things, whether things on earth or things in heaven, by making peace through his blood, shed on the cross" (Colossians 1:19-20).

Salvation flows from God's absolute love for and faithfulness to humanity, not from a desperate attempt to repair the damages of sin. God's gracious purpose for humanity existed *before* sin ever entered the picture (Ephesians 1:4). God has assured our future – he has, as Jesus said, "been pleased to give you the kingdom" (Luke 12:32). Jesus has taken us with him where he is (Ephesians 2:6).

God has purposed to never be without us. "God was pleased to have all his fullness dwell in him, and through him to reconcile to himself all things, whether things on earth or things in heaven, by making peace through his blood, shed on the cross" (Colossians 1:19-20). We often forget that, but God never does.

In his embrace

In Jesus Christ through the Holy Spirit by the will of the Father, we mortal, sinning human beings, in spite of ourselves, are graciously and lovingly held in the divine embrace of the triune God. That is exactly what the Father intended for us from the beginning. "In love he predestined us to be adopted as his sons through Jesus Christ, in accordance with his pleasure and will – to the praise of his glorious grace, which he has freely given us in the One he loves" (Ephesians 1:5-6).

Redemption starts with God's nature, his absolute and unquenchable love for humanity, not with human sin. Through the incarnation of the Son, his becoming one of us and making us one with him, God includes us humans in the all-embracing love of the Father for the Son and the Son for the Father. God made us for this very reason – so that in Christ we can be his beloved children. This has been God's will for us from before creation:

> For he chose us in him before the creation of the world to be holy and blameless in his sight. In love he predestined us to be adopted as his sons through Jesus Christ, in accordance with his pleasure and will – to the praise of his glorious grace, which he has freely given us in the One he loves…. He made known to us the mystery of his will according to his good pleasure, which he purposed in Christ…to bring all things in heaven and earth together under one head, even Christ. (Ephesians 1:4-6, 9-10)

Through the atoning incarnation of the Son, humans are already forgiven, reconciled and saved in him. Divine amnesty has been proclaimed for all humanity in Christ. The sin that entered the human experience through Adam cannot hold a candle to the overwhelming flood of God's grace through Jesus Christ. "Consequently," the apostle Paul wrote, "just as one trespass resulted in condemnation for all people, so also one righteous act resulted in justification and life for all people" (Romans 5:18).

Universal salvation?

So will everyone automatically – perhaps even against their will – enter into the joy of knowing and loving God? Such a thing is an oxymoron, a self-contradiction, because it is impossible for you to love someone against your will. God draws all humanity to himself (John 12:32), but he does not force anyone to come. God wants everyone to come to faith (1 Timothy 2:4), but he does not force anyone. God loves every person (John 3:16), but he doesn't force anyone to love him – love has to be voluntary, freely given, or it is not love.

Contrary to the idea of universal salvation, only those who trust Jesus are able to love him and experience the joy of his salvation. Those who don't trust him, who refuse his forgiveness or the salvation he has already won for them, whether because they don't want it or simply because they don't care, can't love him and enjoy fellowship with him. For those who consider God their enemy, God's constant love for them is grossly annoying. The more they are confronted with his love, the more they hate him. For those who hate God, life in God's world is hell.

As C.S. Lewis put it, "The damned are, in one sense, successful, rebels to the end; that the doors of hell are locked on the inside."[5] Or as Robert Capon explained: "There is no sin you can commit that God in Jesus hasn't forgiven already. The only way you can get yourself into permanent [trouble] is to refuse forgiveness. *That's* hell."[6]

Always on his mind

The doctrine of the Trinity is far more than a creed to be recited or words printed on a statement of faith. The central biblical truth that God is Father, Son and Holy Spirit actually shapes our faith and our lives as Christians. The wonderful and beautiful fellowship shared by the Father, Son, and Spirit is the fellowship of love into which our Savior Jesus places us through his life, death, resurrection and ascension as God in the flesh (John 16:27; 1 John 1:2-3).

From before all time, the Triune God determined to bring humanity into the indescribable life and fellowship and joy that Father, Son and Holy Spirit share together as the one true God (Ephesians 1:4-10). In Jesus Christ, the Son of God incarnate, we have been made acceptable to the Father, and in Jesus we are included in the fellowship and joy of the shared life of the Trinity (Ephesians 2:4-6). The church is made up of those who have already come to faith in Christ. But redemption applies to all (1 John 2:1-2). The gap has been bridged. The price has been paid. The way is open for the human race – like the prodigal son in the parable - to come home.

Jesus' life, death, resurrection and ascension are proof of the total and unwavering devotion of the Father to his loving purpose of including humanity in the joy and fellowship of the life of the Trinity. Jesus is the proof that the Father will never abandon us. In Jesus, the Father has adopted us and made us his beloved children, and he will never forsake his plans for us.

When we trust Jesus to be our all in all, it is not an empty trust. He *is* our all in all. In him, our sins are forgiven, our hearts are made new, and we are included in the life he shares with the Father and the Spirit.

Salvation is the result of the Father's ever-faithful love and power, proven through Jesus Christ and ministered to us by the Holy Spirit. It's not our faith that saves us. It's God alone – Father, Son and Spirit – who saves us. God gives us faith as a gift to open our eyes to the truth of who he is – and who we are, as his beloved children.

God's eternal and almighty word of love and inclusion for you will never be silenced (Romans 8:32, 38-39). You belong to him, and nothing in heaven or earth can ever change that.

Endnotes

[1] James Packer, *God's Words* (Baker, 1998), 44.

[2] Colin Gunton, *The Triune Creator: A Historical and Systematic Study* (Eerdmans, 1998), 9.

[3] Other theological terms that describe this inner communion of the Father, Son and Spirit are *coinherence,* each existing within the other) and *circumincessio* (the Latin equivalent of *perichoresis).*

[4] Michael Jinkins, *Invitation to Theology* (InterVarsity, 2001), 92.

[5] C.S. Lewis, *The Problem of Pain* (Collier, 1962), chapter 8, page 127).

[6] Robert Farrar Capon, *The Mystery of Christ* (Eerdmans, 1993), 10.

Joseph Tkach

WHO IS GOD?

Charles Haddon Spurgeon was England's best-known preacher for most of the second half of the 19th century. In a sermon he gave when he was only 20, Spurgeon declared that the proper study for a Christian is the Godhead. Here is a quote from that sermon—it's one of my favorites:

> The highest science, the loftiest speculation, the mightiest philosophy, which can ever engage the attention of a child of God, is the name, the nature, the person, the work, the doings, and the existence of the great God whom he calls his Father. There is something exceedingly improving to the mind in a contemplation of the Divinity. It is a subject so vast, that all our thoughts are lost in its immensity; so deep, that our pride is drowned in its infinity. Other subjects we can compass and grapple with; in them we feel a kind of self-content, and go our way with the thought, "Behold I am wise." But when we come to this master-science, finding that our plumb-line cannot sound its depth, and that our eagle eye cannot see its height, we turn away with the thought, that vain man would be wise, but he is like a wild ass's colt; and with the solemn exclamation, "I am but of yesterday, and know nothing." No subject of contemplation will tend more to humble the mind, than thoughts of God.

As have many other preachers and teachers, Spurgeon reminds us that the great and central question of Christianity is this: "Who is God?"

God's own answer is not a proposition, but a person: the incarnate Son of God, Jesus Christ. As the self-revelation of God, Jesus is the focal point of our knowledge of God's nature. Jesus, who takes us to the Father and sends us the Spirit, teaches us to ask, "Who is God?," then bids us look to him for the definitive answer.

Throughout history, many great thinkers pondered the question, "Who is God?" Unfortunately, they often did not, or in certain cases (before the Incarnation) could not, make Jesus the living center of their investigations. Working from the central revelation of God in Jesus Christ, the doctrine of the Trinity was developed to answer the false reasoning and heretical ideas about God that had infiltrated the church in the first three centuries of its existence. Though the Trinity doctrine doesn't answer all questions about God's nature, it helps us focus on who God is without wandering away from sound doctrine.

The early Christians were not unique in developing errors of reasoning as they pondered the nature of God. Theologians and philosophers of every age got it wrong and our time is no exception. Old ideas have a way or repackaging themselves and worming their way into contemporary thinking. It is important that we are aware of two errors that are prevalent in our day. Both lead to wrong conclusions and a distorted picture of who God is.

The first error is a modern version of pantheism—the idea that God is a part of his creation instead of being distinct from it and Lord over it. Though Scripture tells us that creation tells us about God (Romans 1:20), there is an important difference between believing that God is *present to everything* and believing that *everything is God*.

Unfortunately, a belief in the divine spirituality of everything (often referred to as "the Universe") is common today. Hungry for spirituality and put off by traditional religion, many people are seeking "enlightenment" in obscure and fringe ideas. Go into any large bookstore and you'll find whole sections devoted to fantasy fiction and the occult. Video gamers are obsessed with ever more bizarre themes and fantastic creatures wielding supernatural powers. Technology is blurring the line between fantasy and reality, and the spiritual landscape is becoming cluttered with offbeat ideas.

The same thing happened in the early years of the church. People had an appetite for magic and mystery. As a result, many non-apostolic epistles and gospels were in circulation—offering a mix of truth and bizarre ideas about God, reflecting the popular culture of that day. Paul reminds us what happens when people lose their spiritual moorings:

> For although they knew God, they neither glorified him as God nor gave thanks to him, but their thinking became futile and their foolish hearts were darkened. Although they claimed to be wise, they became fools and exchanged the glory of the immortal God for images made to look like a mortal human being and birds and animals and reptiles (Romans 1:21-23).

A second prevalent error in our day concerning the nature of God is conceiving of God as a spirit force that dwells in everyone individually. From this perspective, God is viewed as a genie that we carry with us, making use of him as the need arises. It's as though God is a cosmic smartphone with all kinds of useful apps.

Following this line of faulty reasoning, we wrongly conclude that when we travel, we are taking God somewhere that he is not already present. God becomes dependent upon us and is limited by our limitations. As a result, God can't be more faithful than we are. Though this false idea may boost our sense of self-importance, it is a false sense of importance that negates the grace of God.

The truth of God's nature, revealed in Jesus, is the opposite of this error. As the authors of the New Testament remind us, God remains faithful even when we are faithless. Our true importance is related to our identify as children of the God who not only dwells within us by his Spirit, but far beyond us. Our calling is to join God in what he is doing. We do so with great anticipation knowing that he has been at work long before we arrive on the scene. We are greatly privileged to share in what the Holy Spirit is doing to turn people around and to draw them into a reconciled relationship with the Father and the Son.

The more clearly we understand who God is, the better will be our understanding of who we are and of our calling to live in communion with Christ by the Holy Spirit.

Joseph Tkach

THE GOD REVEALED IN JESUS CHRIST

AN INTRODUCTION TO GOD

As Christians, our most basic religious belief is that God exists. By the capitalized word "God," we mean the God described in the Bible: a good and powerful spirit being who created all things, who cares about us, who cares about what we do, who is involved in our lives, and who offers us an eternity with his goodness.

Humans cannot understand God in totality, but we can have a solid beginning point for understanding who God is and what God is doing in our lives. Let's focus on the qualities of God that a new believer, for example, might find most helpful.

His existence

Many people, even long-time believers, want proof of God's existence. But there is no way to "prove" God's existence so that everyone is convinced. It is probably better to talk in terms of evidence, rather than proof. The evidence gives us confidence that God exists and is the sort of being the Bible describes.

God "has not left himself without testimony," Paul told the pagans in Lystra (Acts 14:17). Well then, what is the evidence?

Creation. Psalm 19:1 tells us, "The heavens declare the glory of God." Romans 1:20 tells us, "Since the creation of the world God's invisible qualities—his eternal power and divine nature—have been clearly seen, being understood from what has been made." Creation itself tells us something about God.

It is reasonable for us to believe that something caused the earth, sun and stars to be the way they are. Scientists say the universe began with a big bang, and it is reasonable for us to believe that something caused the bang. That something, we believe, was God.

Design. Creation shows signs of order, of laws of physics. If various properties of matter were different, then earth would not exist, or humans could not exist. If the size or orbit of earth were different, then conditions on this planet would not permit human life. Some people believe that this is a cosmic accident; others believe that the more reasonable explanation is that the solar system was designed by an intelligent Creator.

Life. Life is based on incredibly complex chemicals and reactions. Some people believe that life had an intelligent cause; others believe that it happened by chance. Some have faith that scientists will eventually demonstrate a non-god origin for life. But for many people, the existence of life is evidence of a Creator God.

Humans. Humans are self-conscious creatures who explore the universe, who ponder the meaning of life, who seek significance. Physical hunger suggests the existence of food; thirst suggests that there is something that can quench our thirst. Does our intellectual yearning for purpose suggest that there is in fact a meaning to be found? Many people claim to have found meaning in relationship with God.

Morality. Is right and wrong a matter of opinion, of majority rule, or is there some supra-human authority that defines good and evil? If there is no God, then humans have no basis for proclaiming anything evil, no reason to condemn racism, genocide, torture or any atrocity. The existence of evil is therefore evidence that God exists. If there is no God, then there is no basis for authority except power. It is reasonable to believe in God.

Greatness

What sort of being is God? Bigger than we can imagine! If he created the universe, then he is bigger than the universe—and not limited by time, space or energy, for he existed before time, space, matter and energy did.

2 Timothy 1:9 mentions something God did "before the beginning of time." Time had a beginning, and God existed before that. He has a timeless existence that cannot be measured by years. He is eternal, of infinite age— and infinity plus several billion is still infinity. Mathematics is too limited to describe God's existence.

Since God created matter, he existed before matter, and he is not made of matter. He is spirit—but he is not "made of spirit." God is not made at all; he simply *is*, and he exists as spirit. He defines existence—he defines spirit and he defines matter.

God existed before matter did, and the dimensions and properties of matter do not apply to him. He cannot be measured in miles or kilowatts. Solomon acknowledged that even the highest heavens could not contain God (1 Kings 8:27). He fills heaven and earth (Jeremiah 23:23); he is everywhere, or omnipresent. There is no place in the universe where he does not exist.

How powerful is God? If God can cause a big bang, design solar systems, create the codes in DNA and manage all these levels of power, then he must be unlimited in power, or omnipotent. "With God all things are possible," Luke 1:37 tells us. God can do whatever he wants to do.

God's creativity demonstrates an intelligence greater than we can understand. He controls the universe, constantly causing its continued existence (Hebrews 1:3). That means he must know what is happening throughout the universe; he is unlimited in intelligence—he is omniscient. He knows whatever he wants to know.

God defines right and wrong, and is by definition right, and he has the power to always do right. "God cannot be tempted with evil" (James 1:13). He is consistently and perfectly righteous (Psalm 11:7). His standards are right, his decisions are right, and he judges the world in righteousness, for he is, in his very nature, good and right.

In all these ways, God is so different from us that we have special words that we use only for God. Only God is omniscient, omnipresent, omnipotent, eternal. We are matter; he is spirit. We are mortal; he is eternal. This great difference between us and God, this otherness, is called his *transcendence*. It means that he transcends us, is beyond us, is not like us.

Other ancient cultures believed in gods and goddesses who fought with one another, who acted selfishly, who could not be trusted. But the Bible reveals a God who is in complete control, who needs nothing from anyone, who therefore acts only to help others. He is perfectly consistent, his behavior is perfectly righteous and completely trustworthy. This is what the Bible means when it says that God is holy: morally perfect.

This makes life much simpler. People do not have to try to please 10 or 20 different gods; there is only one. The Creator of all is still the Ruler of all, and he will be the Judge of all. Our past, our present and our future are all determined by the one God, the All-knowing, All-powerful, Eternal One.

Goodness

If all we knew about God is that he had incredible power over us, we might obey him out of fear, with bent knee and resentful heart. But God has revealed to us another aspect of his nature: The incredibly great God is also incredibly gentle and good.

One of Jesus' disciples asked him, "Show us the Father" (John 14:8). He wanted to know what God was like. He knew the stories of the burning bush, the pillar of cloud and fire at Mt. Sinai, the science-fiction throne that Ezekiel saw, and the whisper that Elijah heard (Exodus 3:4; 13:21; 1 Kings 19:12; Ezekiel 1). God can appear in all these ways, but what is he really like? Where should we look?

Jesus said, "Anyone who has seen me has seen the Father" (John 14:9). If we want to know what God is like, we need to look at Jesus. We can learn a bit about God from nature; we can learn more from the way he revealed himself in the Old Testament, but we learn the most from the way that God has revealed himself in Jesus.

Jesus shows us what God is like. Jesus is called Immanuel, which means God with us (Matthew 1:23). He lived without sin, without selfishness. He is a person of compassion. He has feelings of love and joy, disappointment and anger. He cares about individuals. He calls for righteousness, and he forgives sin. He served others, even in his suffering and death.

God is like that. He described himself to Moses in this way: "The Lord, the compassionate and gracious God, slow to anger, abounding in love and faithfulness, maintaining love to thousands, and forgiving wickedness, rebellion and sin. Yet he does not leave the guilty unpunished" (Exodus 34:6-7).

The God who is above all creation is also free to work within creation. This is his *immanence,* his being with us. Although God is larger than the universe and everywhere within the universe, he is with believers in a way that he is not with unbelievers. The enormous God is always close to us. He is near and far at the same time (Jeremiah 23:23).

In Jesus, he entered human history, space and time. He worked in human flesh, showing us what life ought to be like in the flesh, and showing us that God wants more for our lives than merely flesh. We are offered eternal life, life beyond the physical limits we know now. We are offered spirit life, as the Spirit of God himself comes into us to live in us and make us children of God (Romans 8:11; 1 John 3:2). God continues to be with us, working in space and time to help us.

The great and powerful God is also the gentle and gracious God; the perfectly righteous Judge is also the merciful and patient Savior. The God who is angry at sin also provides salvation from sin. He is mighty in mercy, great in gentleness. This is what we should expect from a Being who can create the codes in DNA, the colors in a rainbow and the delicate wisps on dandelion seeds. We would not exist at all, except for the fact that God is kind and gentle.

God describes his relationship to us in several ways. In one analogy, he is a father and we are his children. In another, he is the husband and all believers together are his wife. Or he is a king and we are his subjects. He is a shepherd and we are the sheep. In all these analogies, God puts himself in a situation of responsibility to protect and provide for the needs of his people.

God knows how tiny we are. He knows he could obliterate us in the snap of a finger, in the slightest miscalculation of cosmic forces. But in Jesus, God shows us how much he loves us, how much he cares for us. Jesus was humble, willing even to suffer, if it would help us. He knows the kind of pain we go through, because he has felt it. He knows the pain that evil causes, and he accepted it, showing us that we can trust God.

God has plans for us, for he has made us to be like himself (Genesis 1:27). He invites us to become more like himself—in goodness, not in power. In Jesus, God gives us an example to follow: an example of humility, selfless service, love and compassion, faith and hope.

"God is love," John wrote (1 John 4:8). God demonstrated his love by sending Jesus to die for our sins, so barriers between us and God might be removed, so we might live with him in eternal joy. God's love is not wishful thinking—it is action that helps us in our deepest need.

We learn more about God from the crucifixion of Jesus than from his resurrection. Jesus shows us that God is willing to suffer pain, even pain caused by the people who are being helped. His love invites us, encourages us. He does not force us to do his will.

God's love for us, shown most clearly in Jesus Christ, is our example: "This is love: not that we loved God, but that he loved us and sent his Son as an atoning sacrifice for our sins. Dear friends, since God so loved us, we also ought to love one another" (1 John 4:10-11). If we live in love, then eternal life will be a joy not only for us but also for those who live with us.

If we follow Jesus in life, we will also follow him in death, and then in resurrection. The same God who raised Jesus from the dead will also raise us and give us life eternal (Romans 8:11). But if we do not learn to love, then we will not enjoy everlasting life. So God is teaching us to love, at a pace we can follow, giving us a perfect example, changing our hearts by the Holy Spirit working in us. The Power who controls the nuclear furnaces of the sun is working gently in our hearts, wooing us, winning our affection, winning our allegiance.

God gives us meaning in life, direction for life, hope for life eternal. We can trust him, even when we suffer for doing good. God's goodness is backed up by his power; his love is guided by his wisdom. He has all the forces of the universe at his control, and he is using them for our benefit. "In all things God works for the good of those who love him" (Romans 8:28).

Response

How do we respond to a God so great and gentle, so terrible and tender? We respond with worship: awe at his glory, praise for his works, reverence for his holiness, respect for his power, repentance in the presence of his perfection, obedience in the authority found in his truth and wisdom.

To his mercy, we respond with thankfulness; to his grace, with our allegiance; to his goodness, with our love. We admire him, we adore him, we give ourselves to him even as we wish we had more to give. Just as he has shown his love for us, we let him change us so that we love the people around us. We use all that we have, all that we are, all that he gives us, to serve others, just as Jesus did.

This is the God we pray to, knowing that he hears every word, that he knows every thought, that he knows what we need, that he cares about our feelings, that he wants to live with us forever, that he has the power to fulfill every request, and that he has the wisdom not to.

God has proven himself faithful in Jesus Christ. God exists to serve, not to be selfish. His power is always used in love. Our God is supreme in power, and supreme in love. We can trust him in absolutely everything.

Five facts to know about God

- God is omnipotent—able to do whatever he wants. He is the Almighty.
- God is immortal, constant in character, always reliable. He is the Eternal.
- God is omnipresent—unlimited by space and time. He is always near.
- God is omniscient—knowing all truth and all wisdom. Father knows best.
- God is consistently good, never selfish. God is love.

For further reading

Now that you've had an introduction to God, wouldn't you like to know him better? We get to know God in several ways: through nature, through our experience with the Holy Spirit, through the Scriptures, through spiritual disciplines and through the words of other believers.

To learn more about God, read the Bible, especially the New Testament. Try a modern translation such as *The Message,* by Eugene Peterson, or *The New Living Translation,* published by Tyndale. For evidence of God's existence, we recommend the following (easiest listed first):

Paul Little, *Know Why You Believe*
C.S. Lewis, *Mere Christianity*
Lee Strobel, *The Case for a Creator*
Peter Kreeft and Ronald Tacelli, *Handbook of Christian Apologetics*
C. Stephen Evans, *Why Believe?*
James Sire, *Why Should Anyone Believe Anything at All?*

William Lane Craig, *Reasonable Faith*
C.S. Lewis, *Miracles*
Alister McGrath, *Intellectuals Don't Need God and Other Modern Myths*
For discussions of the attributes of God:
Max Anders, *God: Knowing Our Creator*
Paul Little, *Know What You Believe,* chapter 2
Gilbert Bilezekian, *Christianity 101,* chapter 2
J.I. Packer, *Knowing God*
Millard Erickson, *Introducing Christian Doctrine,* chapters 8-15
Donald G. Bloesch, *God the Almighty*

Things to think about

1. Do the evils in this world weaken our faith in God, or strengthen it?
2. If God is good, why did he make humans fallible, able to choose wrong?
3. What does God say about the way we use his creation?
4. How can God be distant to one person, but near to another?
5. Can we trust a God who has all power but isn't always good? Can we trust one who is always good but is limited in power?
6. In what way is God like Jesus, and in what way is he different?
7. Does God's mercy cause you to admire him, or to ignore him?

Michael Morrison

KNOWING GOD

In Psalm 113:5-6, the psalmist asks: "Who is like the Lord our God, the One who sits enthroned on high, who stoops down to look on the heavens and the earth?"

We still are asking that question.

The self-help sections of bookstores and online catalogs offer seemingly countless books addressing ways to know God from Christian, quasi-Christian and other religious perspectives. Some of these books teach universalism; others teach pantheism or panentheism. Those with a New Age perspective promise keys to finding secret knowledge concerning God.

It seems that many people are seeking to know God or at least to connect with some sort of "higher power." That should not surprise us since God created humans in his image, giving us a "spiritual appetite." Theologian and philosopher Blaise Pascal is credited with saying that within each person there is a "God-shaped hole looking to be filled" [see endnote 1 for what he actually said]. That being so, one would hope that a person sincerely seeking to know God would receive clear direction from all Christian churches. Sadly, that is not always the case.

Given our limited minds, we humans are unable to fully comprehend all there is to know about God. Paul put it this way: "Oh, the depth of the riches of the wisdom and knowledge of God! How unsearchable his judgments, and his paths beyond tracing out!" (Romans 11:33). Though God lives in "unapproachable light" (1 Timothy 6:16), he has not left us completely in the dark. Note Jesus' remarkable statement in Matthew 11:27: "All things have been committed to me by my Father. No one knows the Son except the Father, and no one knows the Father except the Son and those to whom the Son chooses to reveal him." I love how the second-century Christian teacher Irenaeus explained this verse in *Against Heresies*:

> No one can know the Father apart from God's Word, that is, unless the Son reveals him, and no one can know the Son unless the Father so wills. Now the Son fulfills the Father's good pleasure: the Father sends, the Son is sent, and he comes. The Father is beyond our sight and comprehension; but he is known by his Word, who tells us of him who surpasses all telling. In turn, the Father alone has knowledge of his Word. And the Lord has revealed both truths. Therefore, the Son reveals the knowledge of the Father by his revelation of himself. Knowledge of the Father consists in the self-revelation of the Son, for all is revealed through the Word.

This means that no one can know God unless and until God reveals himself. And he has chosen to reveal himself through Jesus. The word *reveal* comes from the Greek word *apokalupto* meaning to take off the cover—to disclose or reveal. It is the opposite of *kalupto*, which means to cover up; hide. The Old Testament speaks of the Shekinah glory of God, present within the innermost part of the Tabernacle behind the veil. No one was allowed beyond that veil except the high priest, and then only once a year. For most of the time, God remained hidden behind the veil. So when Jesus said he had come to reveal the Father, his followers were understandably intrigued.

When Philip asked Jesus to show the disciples the Father, Jesus replied: "Don't you know me, Philip, even after I have been among you such a long time? Anyone who has seen me has seen the Father" (John 14:9). God sent his Son to "pull back the covers" and reveal who he is through his Son. We must be careful not to let preconceptions of what God is like determine our thinking and behavior toward God. Only Jesus has perfect and complete knowledge of God. And he shares that knowledge with us.

Through the life and ministry of Jesus, we get the best look at what God is like this side of our resurrection in glory. Jesus alone is one with the Father and the Holy Spirit. He alone brings "insider knowledge" of the whole of God as the eternal Son of God. He alone is God's self-revelation in time and space, flesh and blood. In Jesus, God has come to us in person, meeting us face-to-face so that we may know him truly and personally.

Jesus shared himself and what he knew with his disciples, whom he called his friends. And he commissioned them, and those who follow them, to go into the world and make that knowledge known—not through books and programs offering esoteric, "hidden knowledge" or esoteric, private experiences. And certainly not through a complex web of philosophical arguments and counter-arguments. Jesus told his followers that they could come to know God through relationships, including relationships with each other and with those outside the Christian community. He said that the clearest sign that would point others to him would be the love that his followers have for each other—a love reflecting God's own love for all people.

---

1 Pascal said: "What else does this craving, and this helplessness, proclaim but that there was once in man a true happiness, of which all that now remains is the empty print and trace? This he tries in vain to fill with everything around him, seeking in things that are not there the help he cannot find in those that are, though none can help, since this infinite abyss can be filled only with an infinite and immutable object; in other words by God himself" (148/428).

Joseph Tkach

GRACE COMMUNION INTERNATIONAL

LET GOD BE GOD

May I ask you a couple of personal questions?

You don't have to respond out loud; silent answers will do. The answers are for you, not for me.

Here's the first question: Has your child ever gotten a bit rebellious, uncooperative or disrespectful?

And here's the second: Did you punish him or her? Remember, just a silent answer. No need to raise your hand.

Now let me ask you this: How long did the punishment last? More to the point, Did you decree that the punishment would last forever?

The very idea of it sounds crazy, doesn't it?

We, as weak and imperfect parents, forgive our kids for their "sins" against us. We might even punish them, but I wonder how many of us would think it fitting, or even sane, to punish them for the rest of their, or our, lives.

Yet some Christians would have us believe that God, our heavenly Father, who is not weak and imperfect, punishes forever and ever people who have never even heard the gospel. And fascinatingly, these same people call God the God of grace and mercy.

Let's think about it for a moment. Jesus tells us to love our enemies, and yet some Christians think God not only hates his enemies, but burns them mercilessly and relentlessly for eternity.

Jesus prayed for his killers, saying, "Father, forgive them, because they don't know what they're doing." But some Christians teach that God only forgives certain people, the ones he predestined to forgive before he even created the Earth. Which, if true, means that Jesus' prayer didn't make a whole lot of difference.

On our heads?

How often have you heard someone giving their "witness" speak about how miserable and guilty they felt over failing to present the gospel to someone who died? One Christian youth leader recently told a group of college kids a morbid story about how he met a person and talked to him, and felt an urge to present the gospel, but then didn't actually do it during their conversation. Then he learned that the man died, hit by a car, later that same day.

"That man is in hell right now," he told the young, wide-eyed, Christian students, "suffering indescribable agony." Then with a dramatic pause, he added, "and all that's on my head." He told them how he suffers nightmares

96

about what he has done, and how he lies in bed sobbing over the horrible truth that because of him, this poor wretch will suffer the torments of fiery hell forever.

I marvel at the way some people can so expertly juggle their faith on the one hand that God so loved the world that he sent Jesus, with their faith (yes, it takes faith) on the other hand that God is so shockingly inept at saving people that he sends them to hell based on our incompetence. Standing steadfastly in faith in God's power and love with one part of their minds, they believe at the same time that God's hands are tied to save people if we fail to get to them in time.

"You are saved by grace and not by works," they say (rightly so), and yet they somehow have taken a most baffling detour to come up with the patently anti-gospel idea that people's eternal destiny is determined by *our* success or failure in the work of evangelizing.

Nobody slips through Jesus' fingers

As much as we humans love our kids, how much more does God love them? It's a rhetorical question— God loves them infinitely more than we are even able to love them.

Jesus said, "Which of you fathers, if your son asks for a fish, will give him a snake instead?... If you then, though you are evil, know how to give good gifts to your children, how much more will your Father in heaven give the Holy Spirit to those who ask him!" (Luke 11:11-12).

God really does love the world. And the salvation of what God loves depends on God, not how good we are at telling the gospel story. And God is really good at what he does.

So if you're carrying a burden of guilt about someone you didn't get the gospel to before he or she died, why not hand that burden over to Jesus? Nobody slips through his fingers, and nobody goes to hell because of you. (Who do you think you are, anyway?)

Our God is good and merciful and strong. And you can trust him to be that way for everybody, not just for you.

J. Michael Feazell

GRACE COMMUNION INTERNATIONAL

PREDESTINATION:
DOES GOD CHOOSE YOUR FATE?

"I am wondering about predestination. Are some people predestined to be saved and the rest predestined not to be saved?"

Thank you for asking! The doctrine of predestination is sometimes referred to as "election," in the sense that God *chooses* people for his own purposes. For example, Abraham was chosen, or elected, by God, as were his son and grandson, Isaac and Jacob. Other chosen ones included Moses, Joshua, David, the prophets, and of course, the Israelites were the "chosen people."

The apostle Paul wrote about predestination, or election, in several passages. In Romans 8:28-30 and Ephesians 1:3-6, he emphasized that election is "in Christ," and that it is a matter of God's own choice for God's own purposes. In Romans 9-11, Paul takes the topic of election further by exploring Israel's rejection of her Messiah.

In the course of his argument in Romans 9-11, Paul asks the question,

> What if God, desiring to show his wrath and to make known his power, has endured with much patience the objects of wrath that are made for destruction; and what if he has done so in order to make known the riches of his glory for the objects of mercy, which he has prepared beforehand for glory—including us whom he has called, not from the Jews only but also from the Gentiles? (Romans 9:22-24)

As you might expect, this passage has been much debated over the centuries. Taken out of its context, it might sound as though some people are predestined to be saved and the rest are predestined for destruction. But that is not what the passage says, nor is it the argument Paul is making.

Paul argues in Romans 9 and 10 that Israel has failed to be found righteous before God because they sought after righteousness their own way instead of putting their trust in Christ (9:31-32; 10:3). This does not mean that God's covenant promises have failed, however, because God is free to have mercy on whomever he chooses (9:15) and is using Israel's unfaithfulness to draw the Gentiles to himself though faith (9:16, 22-26, 30; 10:11-13).

Next, Paul asks, "Have they stumbled so as to fall? By no means! But through their stumbling salvation has come to the Gentiles, so as to make Israel jealous. Now if their stumbling means riches for the world, and if their defeat means riches for Gentiles, how much more will their full inclusion mean!" (11:11-12).

Yes, Paul argues, Israel has rejected Christ and therefore, except for a believing remnant, falls under the covenant judgments. But that is not the end of the story, even for those who rejected Christ. Paul declares in verse 23, "And even those of Israel, if they do not persist in unbelief, will be grafted in, for God has the power to graft them in again."

These people rejected Christ, yet God does not abandon them. The God who is forever faithful to his covenant love is so powerful that he can and does provide opportunity for unbelievers to become believers, even dead unbelievers (many of the unbelieving Israelites were dead, but God's work of mercy involves all of them, see 11:32). We aren't told how or when God does it, only that it is so.

Paul continues: "So that you may not claim to be wiser than you are, brothers and sisters, I want you to understand this mystery: a hardening has come upon part of Israel, until the full number of the Gentiles has come in. And so all Israel will be saved; as it is written, 'Out of Zion will come the Deliverer; he will banish ungodliness from Jacob. And this is my covenant with them, when I take away their sins'" (verses 25-27).

God works in his own ways and in his own times, but his work is aimed toward one final outcome, his desire for all people to be saved: "For God has imprisoned all in disobedience so that he may be merciful to all. O the depth of the riches and wisdom and knowledge of God! How unsearchable are his judgments and how inscrutable his ways!" (verses 32-33).

Even if God were to predestine some to destruction and some to salvation, it would be his right; pots don't tell the potter how to make them. But the good news, the gospel truth, is that even though God has every right to destroy us all, he instead takes our sins on himself in Christ and forgives us and saves us.

The "objects of God's wrath" who were "prepared for destruction" in Romans 9:22 are unbelieving Israel, the same unbelieving Israel who will be "grafted back in" if they don't persist in unbelief (11:23). In other words, Romans 9:22 is not a proof that some people are predestined by God for damnation. We need to read the context to see Paul's full teaching on it.

Common ideas

Probably the best-known view on predestination is the one called "Calvinism." This view of predestination is named after the Reformation theologian, John Calvin. It was constructed in this form by some of his followers at the Synod of Dort in 1618, and is the general position of what are called Reformed churches, which includes many Presbyterians, Congregationalists and Dutch and German Reformed Churches. (However, many of the members of these churches are unaware of the doctrines that were so crucial in the formation of these denominations.)

The Calvinist view, though there are variations, is usually defined using the acronym TULIP. It looks like this:

Total depravity
Unconditional election
Limited atonement
Irresistible grace
Perseverance of the saints

Because TULIP has five points, its adherents are often called "five-point Calvinists." Let's look at each point of the TULIP.

1. "Total depravity" refers to the sinful condition of human beings. It means that there is no part of the human condition that has not been touched and tainted by sin. Therefore, all humans are unfit for the kingdom of God apart from Christ.

2. "Unconditional election" means that through his free sovereignty God chose some before the world was made to be saved by grace without any conditions being required or met for that choice.

3. "Limited atonement" means that Jesus' sacrifice is not effective for all humans. It is effective only for those who were predestined to be saved, not for those who are predestined to be damned.

4. "Irresistible grace" means that the grace God gives to those predestined to be saved cannot be resisted. God's grace has saved them no matter how hard they might resist it. The idea is that if a human could ultimately refuse God's grace, then it would mean that God's will can be thwarted by humans, which would undermine the Calvinist view of God's sovereignty.

5. "Perseverance of the saints" means that those predestined to be saved will not only become believers, but they will remain under the grace of God and will not ever permanently fall away.

Practical terms

Let's now look at how the TULIP plays out in practical terms: First, it is based on a certain concept of the sovereignty, or ruling power, of God. In this concept, nothing can ever happen that God did not, before all time and Creation, decide and design to happen. Therefore, God not only knew all along who would be saved and who would be damned, he is the one who decided it. This view is sometimes called "double predestination."

A number of theologians who teach predestination of the saved, however, do not take a stance on predestination of the damned. They explain it along these lines: Since all humans are sinners and lost without God's grace, those who are not elected to be saved simply receive the just reward of their rebellion. It is not that God specifically predestined, or elected, them to be damned, it is just that since God didn't elect them to receive grace and be saved, they simply wind up getting what they deserve.

This view is sometimes called "single predestination." Whether single or double, it boils down to this: God made lots of people; they are all sinners and can do nothing about that themselves; God extends grace and mercy to a select few and all the others are condemned.

In practical terms, it works like this: If you're saved, you're saved, but if you're damned, you're damned, and there is nothing you can do about it either way. Further, there is no way of knowing for sure whether you are saved or damned.

However, you can have some evidence that you might be saved—good works. So, it is a good idea to do lots of good works. The more you do, the more likely you might be saved. If you don't have any good works, it is good evidence that you are probably damned (but even that is not certain). So what this doctrine gives with one hand (assurance of salvation for the elect), it takes away with the other (the only evidence you have that you are saved is your changed life in terms of good works, and you can't even be sure that proves anything).

This doctrine is bad news for most of humanity (the damned, the non-elect), and it is hard to call it good news even for the elect (they never know for certain in this life whether they are elect or damned). The real gospel, on the other hand, is good news.

Aristotelian influence

The TULIP viewpoint on predestination is based on a Ptolemaic/Aristotelian concept of the way in which God is sovereign. That is, the idea of predestination that is commonly called "Calvinist" and consists of the TULIP formulation explained above, rests on a marriage of Christianity with the earth-centered concept of the cosmos formulated by the Greek astronomer, Ptolemy, and on a concept of God that was formulated by the Greek philosopher, Aristotle. It does not rest on the concept of God we can read about in the Hebrew Bible. To put it another way, it is rooted in

Greek philosophy and not in God's own revelation of himself in the Bible.

Aristotle taught that God is "the unmoved mover." God is not only the original source or fount of all things, he is static, unmoved and unmovable, because, Aristotle reasoned, in order to be the original source and fount of all things, God cannot be capable of being acted upon, or moved by anything else. Further, God cannot change, since any change on his part would render him not God, because, after all, God is that which causes change, not that which changes. (In Aristotle's view, as you might have guessed, God was an impersonal force.)

With this "unmoved mover" idea of God lying behind our reasoning, how are we to understand the way in which the Christian God is sovereign, that is, the way in which God is in complete control of the universe? Well, to review, the TULIP idea is that if God is truly sovereign, truly in complete control, then everything that happens must ultimately be caused by God. In other words, if something ever happened that was not ultimately caused by God, then God would not be in complete control. And since God is in complete control, then everything must ultimately be caused by God.

Further, God is not only omnipotent, or all-powerful (sovereign), he is also omniscient, that is, all-knowing. In other words, TULIP reasons, there is nothing that can ever happen that God has not always known would happen.

So what do we have so far? First, since God is sovereign, that is, completely in control of everything, nothing happens that God is not ultimately the cause of. Second, since God knows everything that is going to happen, nothing can ever happen that 1) God doesn't already know about, and 2) that God hasn't caused to happen.

Logically, this means that God is "immutable," that is, that God cannot change. In this view, if God could change, it would mean he was not already perfect to begin with.

Dilemma

TULIP posits a God who is omnipotent, omniscient and immutable. It appears to have safeguarded God's sovereignty with an airtight formulation of what it means for God to be completely in charge of the universe. But a huge dilemma has appeared: God is good, but there is evil in the world.

How did that happen? In this world in which God 1) is the cause of everything that happens, 2) knows everything that will happen from the beginning because he is the cause of it, and 3) cannot change because any change would mean he is not perfect, how did sin get in?

Did God want evil in his universe? If he did, then he would have to be the ultimate cause of the evil. On the other hand, if God did not want evil in his universe, but it is there anyway, then God must not be in complete control. And the dilemma mushrooms. If nothing happens that God has not caused to happen (including catastrophes of nature, birth defects and acts of terror), then somehow God is also the cause of human sin. And even more disturbing, if people are sinners because God made them that way, then on what basis can we say that God is just in his damning of them? And, of course, the whole idea of free will among humans becomes merely an exercise in semantical gymnastics.

TULIP plays out in some startlingly non-biblical ways. The Bible says God hates sin, yet this construct says he made some folks damned sinners on purpose. The Bible says "for God so loved the world" (John 3:16) and that God wants "all to come to repentance" (2 Peter 3:9)and Christ says "I will draw all men to myself" (John 12:32), yet the TULIP construct posits a God who "loves" some (most, as it turns out) by damning them before they ever drew breath.

The Bible, in striking contrast, presents God as interacting with humans in meaningful ways and even records some fascinating conversations with people in which God learns something or changes his mind.

So where does five-point Calvinism leave us? It leaves most of us predestined human wretches in hell, where God supposedly created us to go, and, according to this construct, he enjoys our eternal torment as a tribute to his supreme justice and righteousness.

The Bible draws the picture rather differently, thank God. And it might be a good idea for us to draw our picture from the Bible too, instead of reading the Bible with our assumptions about God being colored by philosophies alien to the biblical world. Let's see what we can learn about how the Bible unpacks God's sovereignty.

Sovereign

Three questions arise immediately. Can God be sovereign and perfect and also be able to change? Can God be in control of the universe and also give humans true freedom? Can God create a universe in which he is an active partner with humanity without determining every choice humans must make?

The answer to all three questions, from a biblical perspective, is Yes, God can.

After all, God is God; he can do what he, of his own free will, decides to do in accord with who he is. Consider the fact that the Holy Spirit inspired biblical writers to record occasions in which God did, in fact, change.

The Bible shows us that God created a world for himself in which he can and does abide, work, enjoy himself and rest. The universe depends on God for every moment of its existence, the Bible tells us, yet God takes pleasure in what he has made and is quite actively involved in its life and journey.

Consider the biblical picture of God. He loves a cool breeze (Genesis 3:8). He walks and talks with people (Exodus 33:11). He finds out things about them (Genesis 22:12). He makes friends (James 2:23) and gets betrayed by them (2 Samuel 12:7-9).

This God, the God of the Bible, is indeed sovereign, yet not so "otherly" that he cannot enjoy the world he made. When he finished making it, he proceeded to rest in it. And he even calls on us to join him in his rest. He is a God who freely makes things and then sets out to use and enjoy what he has made.

Is such a God, who doesn't seem to mind "getting his hands dirty," truly in control? It seems to me, and you may disagree, that such a God is in far more control, and has far more power, in fact, than the sort of God described by the TULIP.

As we saw above, TULIP, which describes a Calvinist view of predestination, is an acronym that stands for total depravity, unconditional election, limited atonement, irresistible grace and perseverance of the saints. The "God of the TULIP" has to create what amounts to a grand DVD recording of entirely predetermined outcomes and characters who can't wrestle with him, talk back to him, challenge him, or, conversely, can't truly love him, except as he has written it all into the prearranged script. He is in control, to be sure, but of what? Of what amounts to a magnificent cosmic screenplay.

But the God of the Bible, who, in his own divine freedom, has created a real universe—a universe that is truly free, with truly free people—exercises his awesome creativity and genius continually, because, in spite of sinning and rebellious humans, he does bring about his purpose for them.

God is neither threatened by, nor overcome by, human free will and the time and chance he built into his universe, but works within them to bring about a human redemption that is purified in the midst of authentic relationships. He is constantly bringing good out of evil and light out of darkness through his indescribable grace freely demonstrated most supremely in Jesus Christ.

The God of the Bible does not force anyone to trust him. He doesn't remove anyone's freedom to refuse him. Yet, he is infinitely creative in his means of knocking on the doors of our human castles, inviting, even urging, us to invite him in. This is the God who became one of us in Jesus Christ. This is the God who is united with us and in communion with us through Christ. This is the God who loves us and who calls on us to love one another as he loves us.

Divine freedom

God is free to be who he is. "I Am Who I Am," or "I Will Be Who I Will Be," is who this God says he is (Exodus 3:14). He is free to create the universe and humanity and interact with them in whatever way pleases him, and what pleases him is to be faithful to and with his Creation.

The fact that God is *able* to create a windup, predetermined universe does not mean that he had to. The Ptolemaic-Aristotelian concept of God, reflected in TULIP, demands that God had to. It demands that a proper, logical, totally sovereign God could have done things no other way. That concept, in its effort to safeguard God's sovereignty, winds up tying God's hands by limiting him to one particular and nonbiblical way of being sovereign with his Creation.

If, on the other hand, we are to take the biblical record of God's self-disclosure seriously, we must conclude that God is free both to create and to interact with his Creation in any way he pleases, because he is free to be and do as he pleases in accord with who he is (and he is "I Am Who I Am").

Our freedom to be who we are in Christ is not a freedom that we have simply by virtue of existing. It is a freedom given to us by God, entrusted to us, and dependent on God's own freedom to give it to us.

In other words, we are free to accept or reject God's grace only because God holds us in the palm of his hand, not because we have personal sovereignty in and of ourselves. People can reject God, but in rejecting God they are also rejecting themselves, because their freedom is upheld only by the God they are rejecting.

Immutable and impassible

In our efforts to discuss and describe God, we have no choice but to use analogies and comparisons to created things we know about. But we must keep in mind that in all our analogies and comparisons, God is not even on the same plane as any of the created things—whether objects, roles or passions—we might use in describing him. Even the pronoun "he" is only an analogy; we should not get the idea that God is actually male or female. (The term "Father" refers to the relationship between the Father and the Son

[John 1:14, 18, 34] and the Father and creation [Ephesians 3:14-15]; the Father is infinitely greater than any human concept of "father.")

God—Father, Son and Spirit—is the source and cause of all being and existence. He brings everything into being without anything bringing him into being. He is pure Being, that "Is-ness" from which all other being flows. All things depend on him for their existence, and he depends on nothing for his existence.

When we say God is "immutable" or "unchangeable," we do not mean that God cannot change as he, in his uncreated freedom, chooses to change. We mean that God cannot be changed by anything outside himself, as though he were a created being.

But what about Malachi 3:6: "For I the Lord do not change"? This and other passages about God's unchangeableness are declarations of God's faithfulness to his covenant promise. ("Therefore you, O children of Jacob, have not perished," he continues.) And within that unchanging faithfulness to his beloved people there are many ups and downs, twists in the tale, disappointments and surprises. In other words, God declares that despite all your trials of faith and doubt, he will not change his mind about loving you and saving you.

God's covenant faithfulness is the theme throughout the Bible. God made promises to Abraham, and those promises included the salvation of the whole world through the seed of Abraham (Galatians 3:16, 29). The Bible is the record of God's faithfulness to those promises.

So, when we say that God is "immutable" (unchangeable) and "impassible" (incapable of feeling), we do not mean that God cannot change or feel. We mean, rather, that God cannot be changed or moved or hurt against his will by anything outside himself.

But in his divine freedom, God can, and does, of himself, change and feel. In other words, God cannot be acted on against his will, but he certainly, in his divine freedom, acts. When God created the universe, he freely in grace and love became something new—Creator—and he did so in the freedom of his grace and love. Likewise, when the Son became flesh in the Incarnation, God became something new—human like us and for our sakes. God did not have to create, nor did he have to become flesh, but he did so in his divine freedom out of the abundance of his grace and love.

In control

In his eternal serenity and tranquility, God is not depressed, confused, worried, or bowled over by human sin, tragedy and disaster. After all, he knows his power and purpose and what he is bringing out of it all. As Michael Jinkins put it, "God the Creator is intimately, passionately involved in creation continuously from beginning to end and at every nanosecond in between…. All things spring continuously from the God who loves them into existence, loves them redemptively throughout their existence and loves them toward God's final and full purpose" (*Invitation to Theology*, InterVarsity Press, 2001, p. 90).

The universe is not "on its own." While there is indeed "cause and effect," "cause and effect" is not all there is. The universe functions according to general rules laid out by its Creator, but it is not detached from its Creator's free and gracious will and creatively sustaining presence.

God made things in such a way that they bump and collide their way through what we might call a "randomly ordered" existence. We are subject to "time and chance," yet we believe, as Christians, that our loving God uses these very real, and often painful vicissitudes of "time and chance" to mysteriously and graciously bring us out of darkness into his marvelous light.

Always faithful

The "God" of Plato and Aristotle could not change, because for "God" to change would mean that "God" was not already perfect. So "God" was called the "unmoved mover." But the God of the Bible has no problem with changing whenever he decides to, and he remains perfect and perfectly God all the while. He haggled with Abraham over the fate of Sodom, agreeing to change his plan under certain conditions (Genesis 18:16-33).

God changed his mind about saving the Israelites when they started worshiping the calf at Mount Sinai, then allowed Moses to talk him out of killing them all and starting the whole plan over with Moses' children (Exodus 32:7-14). He accommodated himself to Israel's desire for a king even though they were making a mistake and still will ultimately deliver them from their rebellion (1 Samuel 8; Hosea 11:9; 14:4). He changed his plan regarding wicked King Ahab's punishment (1 Kings 21:27-29).

God is sovereign, but God, who is none other than Father, Son and Spirit, is sovereign the way he chooses to be, not the way the greatest human thinkers conclude the ultimate cause of all things must logically be. God will be who God will be. And he has revealed himself to be, for us and with us, the Father of Jesus Christ, the Sender of the Holy Spirit, the Forgiver of sins, the Lover of souls, our Savior, our Deliverer, our Comforter, our Advocate, our Helper, our Strengthener, our Righteousness, our Peace, our Hope, our Life, our Light, our Friend and many other good and wonderful things.

God doesn't behave the way we would expect. We cannot package him to make him more appealing. We cannot mold him into our imagined idea of what a proper and respectable, board-certified God ought to be like.

God is not an unmoved mover who created a windup world of preprogrammed automatons. Nor is God "way out there," merely looking down and watching and judging us as some detached Super-being.

He is the immanent one, that is, God with us. He is here, has been all along, and always will be. All because he wants to be. Because he loves us. Because he made us real, to be real with him and in him and through him.

Far from some platonic impersonal "other," this God is ever active and involved in his creation. He gets his hands dirty. He takes this reeking and sin-infested hovel we have turned the world into, and by the power of the bloody and unjust crucifixion of his own incarnate self, cleans, redeems, transforms and ushers both us and it into the joy of his eternal kingdom.

In Christ Jesus, God brings humanity into union and communion with the very essence of who he is. We are one with him by his action on our behalf, not for our own sakes, but for the sake of Christ, who became for us the perfect human.

If we are in him, we are in union with God, not as Gods, but as humans in union with the God/man, Jesus, who is human and divine for our sakes. Our continual communion, or fellowship, with him is a continual confirmation of and participation in that grand truth—we are God's children in Christ.

Free in God's faithfulness

We must not get the idea that God *has* to create, or that Creation necessarily (that is, automatically, like a fire must produce heat) flows from him. God creates entirely in his divine freedom, not because he is a creation machine.

Nor must we get the idea that God creates because he is lonely, or because there was something "missing" in God that compelled him to create. God is not lonely. The triune God is utterly complete in every way, including in love, joy and perfection, without the Creation.

God does not need the Creation. God does not depend on the Creation. The Creation does not add anything to God that God "lacked." The Creation happened because God freely made it happen in the abundance of his joy and love, not because he had to or needed to, but simply because he wanted to.

So when we talk about God's covenant faithfulness, we can begin to see how certain our trust in God can be. God brought the world into being for the sheer joy of it, redeemed humanity because he loved the people he made, and holds all things, all existence, including yours and mine, in the palm of his hand.

We can trust him because we know we exist only because he says so. If he has gone to all the trouble, while we were still his enemies, to redeem us through the cross (the hard part), how much more certain can we be that he will through his life, now that we are his friends, see our salvation through to the end (the easy part) (Romans 5:8-11)?

God creates and God redeems because he wants to, not because we asked him to, or got him to, or talked him into it, or convinced him to, or behaved really well. He did it because he is good, because he is love, because he is who he is. Your behavior is not going to change who God is, nor who God is toward you. If it could, he would not be God, because God cannot be changed by any incantations or spells or nice or naughty deeds you can throw at him.

You cannot manipulate God or coerce him. You can only trust him and receive the good things he has given you, or not trust him and refuse the good things he has given you. You have that freedom, a created freedom that reflects and derives from God's own uncreated divine freedom. It is freedom to trust him, to commune with him, to love him. You can turn it into freedom to reject him if you want, but you don't have to.

Assurance of salvation

Since the blood of Christ covers all sin, and he atoned for the whole world (1 John 2:1-2), then predestination, or election, in the sense of being chosen by God to be his people only by his grace and not by works, applies, through Christ, to everyone (Ephesians 1:9-10). It is received and enjoyed only by those who accept it in faith, but it applies to everyone.

Some people are called to faith in Christ and experience his redemption before others do (verse 12). Those called to faith early are a living testament to the grace God has poured out on the world, a grace that will come fully into view at the appearing of Christ (Titus 2:11-14).

And it is all done according to the foreknowledge of the God of grace who has been working out in Christ his gracious plan for humanity from the beginning (Matthew 25:34). When it comes to assurance of salvation, we trust in God who justifies the ungodly, which we are. We are saved by grace alone, not by our works, so our assurance rests in the sure word of the God of free grace.

Here is what we know, then, by the testimony of Jesus Christ, to be certain: God loves us, and we do not have to fear that we won't be saved. He saves us in spite of our sins because he is faithful and full of grace. The only people who will not enjoy his salvation are those who do not want it.

Now someone will say that in this treatment of predestination we have oversimplified a complex theological matter, and no doubt we have. But this we know: God calls on us to trust him. And if you and I are to trust him, we have to know that our relationship with him matters. We have to know that we are more than hapless cogs in a deterministic gristmill of human pain, sorrow and tragedy. We have to know that God loves us, that he loves us so much that he sent his own Son to bail us out of a lifetime of horrible decisions, fool's errands and sin by taking all of it on himself in our place, even though we didn't deserve such mercy.

Without a doubt, we can trust a God like that. We can throw in our lot with him and follow him to the ends of the earth, because we owe him our lives now and forever.

Please do not take anything I have written here to mean that I think people who hold the TULIP position are in any way "lesser" Christians than those who don't. That would be a great mistake. Christians are people who put their faith in Jesus Christ, pure and simple. We are not measured by our theologies, but by God's grace freely given to us in Jesus Christ. Our faith is in him, not in theology books. Theology is important, but it is not the root of our salvation. Jesus is.

Devoted and faithful Christian theologians have struggled throughout the centuries to find adequate words and concepts to inform our faith about how God exercises his sovereignty in the world. They do not always agree. Even so, the Christian struggle to understand and talk about God theologically is a worthy pursuit. It reflect our desire as Christians to use the reasoning power God has given us to seek greater understanding of our biblically grounded and personally experienced faith.

Though we may disagree with one another on certain points (none of us has perfect understanding), as believers we are all God's children, washed in the blood of our Savior, and he calls on us to love one another.

In Christ, we can respect one another's views, hear the issues that we each raise, in humility form our own conclusions, and still love one another as fellow partakers of the mercies of God.

J. Michael Feazell

110

THE GOSPEL *REALLY* IS GOOD NEWS

When Americans gathered in churches around the nation on September 14, 2001, a day of mourning, they came to hear words of comfort, encouragement and hope. Yet, try as they might to bring hope to a grieving nation, a number of conservative Christian leaders unwittingly proclaimed a message that amounted to despair, hopelessness and fear for people whose loved ones had died in the terrorist attack without having first professed faith in Jesus Christ.

Many Christians are convinced that everyone who did not profess Christ before death, even those who never so much as heard of Christ, are now in hell, being tortured in agony by God—the God the same Christians ironically proclaim as compassionate, merciful, loving and full of grace. "God loves you," some of us Christians seem to be saying, but then comes the fine print: "If you don't say the sinner's prayer before you die, then my merciful Lord and Savior will torture you forever."

Good news

The gospel of Jesus Christ is good news. It remains forever, good news, the best news imaginable, for absolutely everybody and everything. It is not merely good news for the few who came to know Christ before they died; it is good news for the whole of creation—even for all those who died before they ever heard of Christ.

Jesus Christ is the atoning sacrifice not merely for the sins of Christians but for the sins of the whole world (1 John 2:2). The Creator is also the Redeemer of his creation (Colossians 1:15-20). Whether people know that truth before they die is not the thing that determines whether it is true. It depends entirely on Jesus Christ, not on human action or human response of any kind.

Jesus said, "For God so loved the world that he gave his only Son, so that everyone who believes in him may not perish but may have eternal life" (John 3:16, New Revised Standard Version from here to the end). It is God who loved the world and God who gave his Son, and he gave him to save what he loved—the world. Whoever believes in the Son whom God sent will enter into eternal life (better translated "the life of the age to come").

The verse says nothing about that belief having to come prior to physical death. In fact, it says that believers will not perish, and since even believers die, it should be obvious that "perish" and "die" are not the same thing. Belief keeps people from perishing, but it does not keep them from dying. The kind of perishing that Jesus is talking about here, translated from the Greek word *apoletai,* is a spiritual death, not a physical one. It has to do with utter destruction, with being abolished, put an end to, or ruined. Those who believe in Jesus will not come to such a final end, but will, instead, enter into the life *(zoe)* of the age to come *(aeonion).*

Some enter into the life of the age to come, or kingdom life, while they still live and walk on the earth, but in the grand scheme of things, this happens to only a few of those who make up the "world" (or "*kosmos*") that God loves so much that he sent his Son to save it. What about the rest? This verse does not say that God cannot or won't bring to faith any of those who die physically before believing.

The idea that physical death is a barrier to God's ability to save, or to his ability to bring a person to faith in Christ, is a human interpretation; the Bible states no such thing. We are told that everyone dies, and then they are judged (Hebrews 9:27). But let us remember that their Judge, thank God, is none other than Jesus, the slaughtered Lamb of God who died for their sins—and that changes everything.

Creator and Redeemer

Where do we get this notion that God is only able to save live people and not dead ones? He conquered death, didn't he? He rose from the dead, didn't he? God doesn't hate the world; he loves it. He didn't create humanity for hell. Christ came to save the world, not to condemn it (John 3:17).

One Christian teacher told his Sunday School class on September 16, the first Sunday after the terrorist attacks, that God is perfect in hate as well as perfect in love, which accounts for why there is a hell as well as a heaven. He went on to explain how dualism (the idea that good and evil are equal and opposite forces in the universe) is a false doctrine. But doesn't he realize he posited a dualistic God with his explanation of God holding in tension perfect hate and perfect love?

God is absolutely just, and all sinners are judged and condemned, but the gospel, the good news, lets us in on the mystery that in Christ, God took that very sin and its judgment on himself for our sakes! Hell is indeed real and horrible. But it is precisely that hell, the hideous hell reserved for the ungodly, that Jesus bore in humanity's stead (2 Corinthians 5:21; Matthew 27:46; Galatians 3:13).

All humans are under condemnation because of sin (Romans 6:23), but the free gift of God is eternal life in Christ (same verse). That's why it is called grace. In Romans 5:15, Paul puts it like this: "But the free gift is not like the trespass. For if the many died through the one man's trespass [this "many" refers to everybody; there is no one who doesn't bear Adam's guilt], much more surely have the grace of God and the free gift in the grace of the one man, Jesus Christ, abounded for the many [the same "many"—absolutely everybody]" (Romans 5:15).

Paul is saying that as bad as our condemnation for sin is—and it is bad (it deserves hell)—it can't even hold a candle to the grace and the free gift in Christ. In other words, God's word of reconciliation in Christ is incredibly louder than his word of condemnation in Adam—the one completely eclipses the other ("much more surely"). That is why Paul can tell us in 2 Corinthians 5:19 that "in Christ God was reconciling the world [that's everybody, the "many" of Romans 5:15] to himself, not counting their trespasses against them…"

So, then, what about the family and friends of those who die without having professed faith in Christ? Does the gospel offer them any hope and encouragement about the fate of their dead loved ones? Indeed, the Gospel of John records Jesus declaring, "And I, when I am lifted up from the earth, will draw all people to myself" (John 12:32). That's good news, the gospel truth. Jesus didn't lay out a timetable, but he did declare that he would draw everybody to himself, not just a few who find out who he is before they die, but absolutely everybody.

Then it is no wonder that Paul wrote to the Christians in the city of Colosse that in Jesus Christ, God was pleased, *pleased,* mind you, to "reconcile to himself *all things,* whether on earth or in heaven, by making peace through the blood of his cross." (Colossians 1:20). That's good news. And it is, like Jesus said, good news for the whole world, not just for the limited few.

Paul wanted his readers to know that this Jesus, this Son of God raised from the dead, is not just some exciting leader of a new and improved religious concept. Paul is telling them that Jesus is none other than the Creator and Sustainer of all things (verses 16-17), and more than that, he is God's way of fixing absolutely everything that has gone wrong with the world from the beginning of history (verse 20)! In Christ, Paul was saying, God has moved once and for all to make good on all his promises that he made to Israel—promises that he would one day act in pure grace to forgive all sins everywhere and make everything new (see Acts 13:32-33; 3:20-21; Isaiah 43:19; Revelation 21:5; Romans 8:19-21).

Only for Christians

"But salvation is only for Christians," the fundamentalists howl. Yes, of course it is. But just who are "the Christians"? Are they only those who repeat the sinner's prayer? Are they only those who are baptized by immersion? Only those who belong to the "true" church? Only those who are absolved by a duly ordained priest? Only those who have ceased sinning? (Have you? I haven't.) Only those who come to know Jesus before they die?

Or does Jesus himself, the one into whose nail-pierced hands God has given all judgment, decide who is and is not ultimately to be included among those upon whom he will have mercy? And while he is at it, does he, the one who conquered death and grants eternal life to whomever he will, decide when he might bring a person to faith, or do we, the all-wise defenders of the true religion, make that determination for him?

Every Christian became a Christian at some point, that is, was brought to faith by the Holy Spirit. The fundamentalist assumption seems to suggest, however, that it is impossible for God to bring a person to faith after that person has died. But hold on, Jesus is the one who raises the dead. And he is the one who is the atoning sacrifice, not for our sins only, but for the sins of the whole world (1 John 2:2).

Great chasm

"But the parable of Lazarus," someone will argue. "Abraham says that there is a chasm fixed between his side and the rich man's side" (see Luke 16:19-31).

Jesus did not give this parable as a textbook on the afterlife. After all, how many Christians would want to describe heaven as "Abraham's bosom" with Jesus himself nowhere in sight? The parable was a message to the members of the first-century Jewish privileged class who rejected their Messiah, not a portrait of the resurrection life. And before we take even that further than Christ intended, remember what Paul wrote in Romans 11:32.

In the parable, the rich man was still unrepentant. He still saw himself as Lazarus' superior. He still saw Lazarus as existing only to serve his personal needs. Maybe it is not unreasonable to think that the rich man's persistent unbelief is what kept the gulf fixed, not some arbitrary cosmic necessity. Remember, Jesus himself bridges the otherwise impassable chasm from our sinful condition to reconciliation with God. Jesus underscores this point, the point of the parable—that salvation comes only through faith in him—when he says, "If they do not listen to Moses and the prophets, neither will they be convinced even if someone rises from the dead" (Luke 16:31).

God is in the business of saving people, not torturing them. Jesus is Redeemer, and whether we believe it or not, he is awfully good at what he does. He is the Savior of the world (John 3:17), not the Savior of a fraction of the world. "God so loved the world" (verse 16)—not merely one out of 1,000.

God has ways, and his ways are higher than our ways.

Jesus tells us, "Love your enemies" (Matthew 5:43). Surely we believe he loves his own enemies. Or do we believe that Jesus hates his enemies while he calls on us to love ours, and that his hatred accounts for why there is a hell? Give me a break. Jesus asks us to love our enemies precisely because *he* loves them. "Father, forgive them, for they don't know what they are doing," Jesus prayed of those who murdered him (Luke 23:34).

Certainly, those who continue to refuse Jesus' grace even after they understand it receive the fruit of their own stupidity. There is no place left for people who refuse to enter the Lamb's banquet, except outer darkness (another of the metaphors Jesus used to describe the state of alienation from God; see Matthew 22:13; 25:30).

Mercy to all

Paul makes the amazing assertion in Romans 11:32 that God "has imprisoned all in disobedience so that he may be merciful to all." And yes, the Greek words here do mean *all*, not some, but *all*. All are sinners, and in Christ all are shown mercy—whether they like it or not; whether they take it or not; whether they know it before they die or not.

And what can you say to such a thing, but what Paul says in the next verse:

O, the depth of the riches and wisdom and knowledge of God! How unsearchable are his judgments and how inscrutable his ways! For who has known the mind of the Lord? Or who has been his counselor? Or who has given a gift to him, to receive a gift in return? For from him and through him and to him are all things. To him be the glory forever. Amen. (verses 33-36)

In fact, it would seem that his ways are so unfathomable that many of us Christians simply cannot believe that the gospel can be that good. And some of us seem to know the mind of God so well that we just *know* that everybody goes straight to hell if they aren't Christians yet when they die. But Paul's point is precisely that the unbelievable extent of God's mercy is simply beyond our ken—a mystery revealed only in Christ: God has done something in Jesus Christ that nobody would ever have guessed in a million years.

In his letter to the Christians at Ephesus, Paul says that this is what God had in mind all along (Ephesians 1:9-10). It was the whole point of God's calling of Abraham, of his choosing of Israel and David, and of the covenants (Ephesians 3:5-6). God is saving even the aliens and strangers (2:12). He is even saving the ungodly (Romans 5:6). He really does draw all people to himself (John 12:32). The Son of God has been at work underneath all of history from the very beginning, bringing about the redemption, the reconciliation of all things to God (Colossians 1:15-20). God's grace has a logic all its own, a logic that often seems illogical to religious-minded people.

Only path to salvation

In short, Jesus Christ is the only path to salvation, and he draws absolutely everybody to himself—in his way, in his time. It might help if we could get our minds around the fact that there isn't anywhere to be in the universe except in Christ, since as Paul said, nothing exists that isn't created by him and upheld by him (Colossians 1:15-17). Those who finally reject him do so in spite of his love; it's not that he refuses them (he doesn't—he loves them, died for them and forgave them), but that they refuse him.

C.S. Lewis put it this way: "There are only two kinds of people in the end: those who say to God, 'Thy will be done' and those to whom God says, in the end, 'THY will be done.' All that are in Hell choose it. Without that self-choice, there could be no Hell. No soul that seriously and constantly desires joy will ever miss it. Those who seek, find. To those who knock, it is opened" (*The Great Divorce,* chapter 9).

Heroes in hell?

As I listened to Christians preach about the meaning of September 11, I thought of the heroic firefighters and police officers who sacrificed their lives trying to rescue victims of the attack on the World Trade Center. How is it that we Christians can call these people heroes and applaud their self-sacrifice on one hand, but declare that unless they confessed Christ before they expired they are being tortured in hell on the other? Their good works cannot save them, but Christ can.

The gospel declares that there is hope for those who died in the World Trade Center without yet having professed Christ. They will encounter the risen Lord on the other side of death, and he is the Judge—the one with nail holes in his hands—eternally ready to embrace and receive all his creatures who will come to him. He forgave them before they were born (Ephesians 1:4; Romans 5:6, 10). That part is done, just as it was done for us who believe now.

All that remains for them now is to throw down their crowns before him and receive his gift. Maybe some won't. Maybe some are so committed to loving themselves and hating others that they will see their risen Lord as their archenemy. That's a shame, no, more than that; it's a disaster of cosmic proportions, because he's not their archenemy. Because he loves them anyway. Because he would gather them into his arms like a hen gathers her chicks, if they would only let him.

But it is safe to say, if you believe passages like Romans 14:11 and Philippians 2:10, that by far most of the people who died in that attack will jump into Jesus' forgiving and merciful arms like a puppy runs to its mother at mealtime.

Jesus saves

"Jesus saves," Christians put on their posters and bumper stickers. It's true. He does. And he is the author and finisher of salvation, the beginning and goal of all creation, including all dead people. God did not send his Son into the world to condemn the world, Jesus said. Rather, he sent his Son into the world to save it (John 3:16-17).

Regardless of what some people say, God is out to save everybody (1 Timothy 2:4; 2 Pet. 3:9), not just a few. And guess what? He never gives up. He never stops loving. He never stops being who he is, was, and will always be for humanity—their Creator and their Redeemer. Nobody falls through the cracks.

Nobody was created for the purpose of sending to hell. If anybody winds up in hell—the tiny, meaningless, dark, nowhere corner of the eternal kingdom—then what causes them to stay there will be nothing but their own stubborn refusal to receive the grace God has for them. It will not be because God hates them, because he doesn't. It will not be because God is vindictive, because he isn't. It will be because 1) they hate the kingdom of God and refuse his grace, and 2) God won't let them spoil the fun for everybody else.

Positive message

The gospel is the message of hope for absolutely everybody. Christian preachers don't have to resort to threats of hell to coerce people to turn to Christ. They can proclaim the truth, the good news: "God loves you. He isn't mad at you. Jesus died for you because you're a sinner, and God loves you so much he has saved you from everything that is destroying you. So why should you keep on living as though this dangerous, cruel, unpredictable and unforgiving world is all you've got? Why don't you come and start experiencing God's love and enjoying the blessings of his kingdom? You already belong to him. He's already paid for your sins. What are you waiting for? He'll turn your sorrow into joy. He'll give you peace of heart like you've never known. He'll bring meaning and purpose to your life. He'll help you improve your relationships. He'll give you rest. Trust him. He's waiting for you."

This message is so good that it bubbles out of us. Paul wrote in Romans 5:10-11: "For if while we were enemies, we were reconciled to God through the death of his Son, much more surely, having been reconciled, will we be saved by his life. But more than that, we even boast in God through our Lord Jesus Christ, through whom we have now received reconciliation."

Talk about hope! Talk about grace! Through Christ's death, God reconciles his enemies, and through Christ's life, he saves them. No wonder we can boast in God through our Lord Jesus Christ—we are already experiencing in him what we are telling others about. They don't have to keep on living like they have no place at God's table; he's already reconciled them, they can come on home.

Christ saves sinners. It really is good news. It's the best news anybody can hear.

J. Michael Feazell

EMBRACING TRINITARIAN THEOLOGY

Almost ten years ago Jesus called me, and the two churches I serve, to a profound awakening in our understanding of the gospel. This article is a brief description of what we have learned in that journey.

After several years of reading the New Testament, praying, and being mentored by such Christian writers as Athanasius, T.F. and J.B. Torrance, Mike Feazell and C. Baxter Kruger, I had come to see that the Trinity is not just "a" doctrine. It is "the" doctrine of the gospel. The gospel is about nothing less than human participation in the eternal communion of the Father, Son and Spirit.

The triune God created humanity to participate through the Holy Spirit in the incarnate Son's communion with the Father. As Paul wrote to the church in Ephesus, "In love he predestined us for adoption to sonship through Jesus Christ, in accordance with his pleasure and will" (Ephesians 1:4-5).

James B. Torrance put it this way:

> He who was the eternal Son of God by nature, enjoying eternal communion with the Father, became the Son of Man that we 'sons and daughters of men' might become 'sons and daughters of God' by grace and be drawn into the Son's communion with the Father, that through the Spirit we too might call God "Father" (*Worship, Community and the Triune God of Grace,* p. 82, InterVarsity Press, 1996).

As I began to take seriously the statements in the Bible that speak of "all" being included in Christ, it became clear to me that the Father didn't create some people for adoption and some for destruction. In Christ he has adopted everyone and delivered everyone from sin and death. Paul wrote in Colossians 1:19-20, "God was pleased to have all his fullness dwell in him, and through him to reconcile to himself all things, whether things on earth or things in heaven, by making peace through his blood, shed on the cross." Jesus said in John 12:32, "I, when I am lifted up from the earth, will draw all people to myself."

A plan for all people

Beginning in September 2006, I began to make the Trinity foundational in my preaching to my congregations. I made it clear from the Bible that the Father's plan is humanity's adoption as his own beloved children in Jesus Christ through the power of the Holy Spirit. And I made it clear that in Jesus

God has delivered all of humanity from bondage to sin and death.

The reaction in my congregations ranged from cautious optimism to electric excitement. Jan Taylor remembers, "I felt uncertainty; I thought we were headed down a trail away from orthodoxy. Thankfully it didn't take long to recognize that just the opposite was true. It helped so much to see we were following the teachings of the early church as well as the teachings of renowned contemporary theologians."

Over the last five years our vision of the triune life of God and our understanding of grace has been broadened and deepened in ways we never expected.

Judy Pass says, "Five years ago I didn't understand the importance of the doctrine of the Trinity and how it is the framework by which we understand who Jesus is and what he's done for us." Bert Caruthers agrees: "The Father, the Son and the Holy Spirit finally make sense to me."

Maria Olson looks at it from the perspective of someone who didn't grow up in the church: "Five years ago I still had that mentality of 'I have to do good in order for God to love me.' Now I am one hundred percent convinced that God loves me no matter what I do, that I have been included and that there is nothing I or anyone can do that will ever change that."

For many of us, the change has been in how we view other people. Mary Jo Leaver says, "Now I understand everyone is included whether they know it or not. God's love in me overflows to everybody I meet: believer, nonbeliever, atheist, Buddhist, Muslim—everybody. I am free to love others without an agenda."

Suggestions for others

Based on what we have experienced, I would make three suggestions to any pastor or congregation embarking on this process:

1. Find a mentor in the gospel. Tim Brassell has been my mentor and he helps me, on a weekly basis, to shape my thinking, speaking, and doing in the light of the gospel.
2. Soak your mind in books, articles, and blogs that focus on the reality of who Jesus is for us and who we are in him, and you will find that the what of ministry begins to flow much more naturally.
3. Be bold. Those you are ministering to are the Father's adopted, forgiven children in Jesus whether they know it or not. In the Holy Spirit you can confidently, with wisdom and gentleness, proclaim this truth to them, and the Spirit will back you up.

Judy Pass says that "having a small group where you can discuss what you're learning, ask questions of others and listen to others helps a lot." Mike Gass recommends having an "openness to God." Bert Caruthers points out that it needs to be a journey we take together. She says, "Be willing to be a learner and empower your people to learn by giving them the tools and resources to discover the truth of the Trinity with you."

More than one person mentioned the helpfulness of such resources as *The Great Dance* by C. Baxter Kruger, *The Shack* by William P. Young, and the *You're Included* interview series at www.youreincluded.org.

This growth in our understanding of the gospel is changing the way we do ministry. Jan Taylor says, "Every ministry is done in a relational context, and we no longer view the world as separated into 'sacred' and 'secular.' There is freedom in knowing that we are in Jesus no matter what we are doing. We don't have to be doing something church related in order for it to be ministry."

And always remember, Lloyd Briggie says, "Keep an open mind—don't put limits on God's love!"

Jonathan Stepp

According to the New Testament, that life of communion with the Father did not begin at Bethlehem. He who was the eternal Son of God by nature, enjoying eternal communion with the Father, became the Son of Man that we "sons and daughters of men" might become "sons and daughter of God" by grace and be drawn into the Son's communion with the Father, that through the Spirit we too might call God "Father." The eternal Word who was with God and who was God, the only begotten Son of the Father, who created all things, took our humanity and "tabernacled" among us, that we might see the glory of the Father, and ourselves become sons and daughters of God (Jn 1:11-14). —James B. Torrance, p. 82.

GOD IS...

If you could ask God one question, what would it be? Maybe you would ask a big question: What is God's purpose for you? Or, what's going to happen to you after you die? Or perhaps, why does God let people suffer?

On the other hand, you might ask a question that seems minor but still perplexes you: Where did your puppy go after it ran away when you were 10? What would your life be like if you had married a lost sweetheart? Why did God make the sky blue?

But perhaps you might want to ask God about himself: Who are you? Or, what are you? Or, what do you want?

God's answer to such basic questions would go a long way toward answering other questions. Who and what God is, what God wants – these are aspects of God's nature. And the nature of God underlies everything else – why the universe is the way it is, who we are as humans, why our lives are the way they are, and what we should be doing with our time. Has anyone ever lived who didn't puzzle – at least a little – over such profound questions?

We humans can begin to grasp the answers. We can begin to understand the nature of God. Believe it or not, we can even come to share in that divine nature.

That is the subject of this series of six articles – what we can know about God, at least a little bit. Thinkers throughout history have viewed God in different ways. But God reveals himself to us – through his creation, through his Word, and most especially through his Son, Jesus Christ. God shows us who and what he is, what he does, and even a lot about why he does what he does. He also tells us how we should relate to him now – and how we will relate to him in eternity.

Philosophers discuss the nature of God, but this series of articles is not based on philosophy. It is based on the Bible, which God uses to reveal himself to us. We accept the Scriptures as an authoritative source of information about who and what God is. This is written for people who want to know what the Bible says about God. Those who want a more philosophical approach, or those who are more skeptical of biblical authority, will need to turn elsewhere, although they may find these articles of interest, as well.

The book of Isaiah tells us that God reveals himself to people who are humble and repentant, to those who respect God's Word (Isaiah 66:2).

Jesus said, "If anyone loves me, he will obey my teaching. My Father will love him, and we will come to him and make our home with him" (John 14:23). God wants to make his home with us. When God does, our questions will begin to be more fully answered.

IN SEARCH OF THE ETERNAL

Humans have always wrestled with questions like "How did we get here?" and "What should we be doing?" and "Where are we going?" Their pursuit of answers often led them back to fundamental issues such as whether God exists and what God is like. They framed in different ways the ideas they came up with.

Twisted paths back to Eden

Throughout history, people built their religious concepts on their desires to understand human origins and the purpose of life. In their own ways, they wanted to make contact with and relate to the Source of human life – and, presumably, the Authority over human destiny. Unfortunately, the human inability to understand spiritual reality perfectly gave rise to disagreement and more questions:

"Pantheism (Greek *pan*, 'all,' and *theos*, 'God') A term coined by John Toland (1670-1722), literally meaning 'everything God.' The view is that God is all and all is God. It differs from 'panentheism,' which views God as in all" (*Westminster Dictionary of Theological Terms*, 1996, p. 199). Pantheists saw God as being all that is, including all the forces and laws behind the universe. They depersonalized God and interpreted both good and evil as divine.

Polytheists believed in many gods. Each of these gods could help or hurt, but none held absolute power. Polytheism was the basis of many Middle Eastern and Greco-Roman forms of worship, and of the spirit and ancestor worship found in many tribal cultures.

"Theism (From Greek *theos*, 'God') Belief in a god. Also belief in one God (monotheism) in contrast to belief in many gods (polytheism)" (*Westminster Dictionary of Theological Terms*, p. 279).

Monotheists embraced a personal deity as the source, sustainer and goal of everything. Three of the world's most influential religions are monotheistic – Judaism, Christianity and Islam. All three claim their descent from Abraham.

Does God exist?

Historically, every culture has had a sense that God exists. Atheism does not provide satisfactory answers to humanity's questions about who we are and why we exist. Atheism cannot explain purpose, or distinguish between good and evil. Atheism has no authority, no proof of its philosophical assumptions. We see nature all around us, and science equips us to investigate the natural world. But science cannot explore the supernatural world. We cannot search for God with microscopes or deep space probes. If we are to know God, God must reveal himself to us. We want to know what the Creator is like, what his purpose is, and what must happen for us to come into harmony with him. So how does God reveal himself to us?

HOW GOD REVEALS HIMSELF

Imagine, for a moment, that you are God. You created all things – including human beings. You made humans in your own image (Genesis 1:26-27) and you want them to relate to you in a special way. Wouldn't you tell those humans about yourself? Wouldn't you tell them what you expect of them? Wouldn't you tell them how to come into the relationship you want to share with them?

People who believe that God is unknowable assume that God, for some reason, hides himself from his creation. But God does reveal himself, through his creation, in history, in the pages of the Bible, and through his Son, Jesus Christ. Let's look at what God shows us about himself.

Creation reveals God

Many people have looked at the cosmos and concluded from it that God exists, that God holds all power and that God works in order and harmony. Romans 1:20 tells us, "Since the creation of the world God's invisible qualities – his eternal power and divine nature – have been clearly seen, being understood from what has been made."

Looking at God's fabulous heavens made King David marvel that God even notices humans, who seem so insignificant next to God: "When I consider your heavens, the work of your fingers, the moon and the stars, which you have set in place, what is man that you are mindful of him, the son of man that you care for him?" (Psalm 8:3-4).

The patriarch Job questioned God. In reply, God described many of his marvels – and thus revealed his limitless authority and wisdom. Job was humbled by the exchange. You can read God's "speech" in chapters 38-41 of the book of Job. Job realized: "I know that you can do all things; no plan of yours can be thwarted.... Surely I spoke of things I did not understand, things too wonderful for me to know.... My ears had heard of you but now my eyes have seen you" (Job 42:2-3, 5).

God's purpose for humanity

What did God intend when he made all things and gave us life? Paul explained to the Athenians:

> From one man he made every nation of men, that they should inhabit the whole earth; and he determined the times set for them and the exact places where they should live. God did this so that men would seek him and perhaps reach out for him and find him, though

he is not far from each one of us. "For in him we live and move and have our being." As some of your own poets have said, "We are his offspring." (Acts 17:26-28)

Or, simply, as John wrote, "We love because he first loved us" (1 John 4:19).

History reveals God

Skeptics ask, "If God is real, why doesn't he show himself to the world?" This question assumes that God hasn't already shown himself to humanity. However, the Bible says that this assumption is not correct. From the time of the first family on, God has often communicated with human beings. But they, for the most part, have wanted nothing to do with God!

The story of Adam and Eve describes humanity's typical reaction. God created these people and spoke to them. But they disobeyed him, and then hid from him. "The man and his wife heard the sound of the Lord God as he was walking in the garden in the cool of the day, and they hid from the Lord God among the trees of the garden" (Genesis 3:8).

Disobedience separates us from God, makes us afraid of God, makes us want distance between us and God. The Bible is full of examples of how God reached out to sinning humans – but they rejected him. The book of Isaiah puts it this way: "Your iniquities have separated you from your God; your sins have hidden his face from you, so that he will not hear" (Isaiah 59:2). It is not that God is actually unable to hear, but that this is the person's perception.

Noah, "a preacher of righteousness" (2 Peter 2:5), warned his world about God's coming judgment. But they didn't listen – and they perished in the Flood. God destroyed sinful Sodom and Gomorrah in a fiery display (Genesis 19:28). But this supernatural rebuke did not convince anyone to change their ways.

Most of the Old Testament traces how God worked with the nation of Israel. But Israel often did not want to hear God. "Do not have God speak to us," they said (Exodus 20:19). God also intervened in the affairs of great powers such as Egypt, Nineveh, Babylon and Persia. But the effects were short-lived.

Many of God's servants met awful deaths at the hands of those to whom they brought God's message. People rejected the messengers of God because they did not like the message. They did not like what God was saying through his servants, because they did not like God.

Hebrews 1:1-2 tells us, "In the past God spoke to our forefathers through the prophets at many times and in various ways, but in these last days he has spoken to us by his Son." Jesus Christ came into the world to preach the gospel of salvation and the kingdom of God. The result? "He was in the world, and though the world was made through him, the world did not recognize him" (John 1:10). They killed him.

Jesus, as God in the flesh, was expressing God's loving concern for his people when he cried: "O Jerusalem, Jerusalem, you who kill the prophets and stone those sent to you, how often I have longed to gather your children together, as a hen gathers her chicks under her wings, but you were not willing" (Matthew 23:37).

God has revealed himself in many different ways, but most people have not wanted to see even the little part that they did.

The Bible record

The Bible reveals God in these ways:

- The Bible contains statements God makes about who and what he is.
- In Exodus 3:14, God revealed his name to Moses: "I am who I am." God's name reveals that God is self-existent, self-perpetuating life. The other names of God, found throughout the Bible, offer additional insight into who and what God is.
- "I am the Lord, and there is no other; apart from me there is no God.... There is no god apart from me, a righteous God and a Savior; there is none but me" (Isaiah 45:5, 21).
- In Isaiah 55:8, God tells us, "My thoughts are not your thoughts, neither are your ways my ways." God exists and acts on a higher plane than we humans do. We cannot understand all that he is, or all that he does.
- Jesus Christ described himself as the "I am" who lived before Abraham (verse 58). He was God in the flesh. He called himself "the light of the world" (John 8:12), "the gate" to eternal life (John 10:9), "the good shepherd" (verse 11), and "the way and the truth and the life" (John 14:6).

What a person does reveals much about what he or she is. In the same way, biblical statements about God's acts reveal him more fully to us.

"I am the Lord, who has made all things, who alone stretched out the heavens, who spread out the earth by myself," God says in Isaiah 44:24. God made all that is. And God rules what he made.

God also declares what he will do in the future: "I am God, and there is none like me. I make known the end from the beginning, from ancient times, what is still to come. I say: My purpose will stand, and I will do all that I please" (Isaiah 46:9-10).

God loves the world, and sent his Son for the salvation of the world. "God so loved the world that he gave his one and only Son, that whoever believes in him shall not perish but have eternal life" (John 3:16). Through Jesus, God is bringing children into his family. "He who overcomes will inherit all this, and I will be his God and he will be my son" (Revelation 21:7).

The Bible records the words of humans who describe what God is:

God has always interacted with people he chose to carry out his will. Many of those inspired servants left us, in the Bible, details about what God is like. "The Lord our God, the Lord is one," said Moses (Deuteronomy 6:4). God is one. The Bible proclaims monotheism, that there is only one God. (This concept will be taken up in more detail in chapter 3.)

Among the psalmist's many statements about God is this one: "For who is God besides the Lord? And who is the Rock except our God?" (Psalm 18:31). God alone deserves worship, and he strengthens those who worship him. The Psalms are full of insight about who and what God is.

Among the most comforting of Bible verses is 1 John 4:16, "God is love." A vital insight into God's love and his will for humanity is found in 2 Peter 3:9: "The Lord is...not wanting anyone to perish, but everyone to come to repentance." What is God's greatest desire for us, his creation, his children? That we be saved. And God's word does not return to him empty – it will accomplish what he sends it to do (Isaiah 55:11). Knowing that God intends to save us, and that he is perfectly able to do so, should give us great hope.

The Bible records the words of humans who describe what God has done and is doing:

God, as a loving Creator, formed humans in his own image and gave them dominion over the earth (Genesis 1:26).

Here's how God felt when he saw the earth corrupted by the evil that humans had chosen to do: "The Lord was grieved that he had made man on the earth, and his heart was filled with pain" (Genesis 6:6). God responded to the wickedness of the world by sending the Flood to start civilization over through Noah and his family (Genesis 7:23).

Centuries after the Flood, God called the patriarch Abraham and established with him a covenant through which "all peoples on earth will be blessed through you" (Genesis 12:1-3) – a reference to Jesus Christ, a descendant of Abraham.

When he formed the nation of Israel, God supernaturally brought them through the Red Sea and destroyed the Egyptian army: "The horse and its rider he has hurled into the sea" (Exodus 15:1).

The Israelites broke their agreement with God and gave themselves over to violence and injustice. Thus God allowed the nation to be attacked by foreign powers and, eventually, to be carried out of the Promised Land into slavery (Ezekiel 22:23-31; 36:15-21). Yet the merciful God promised to send into the world a Redeemer who would establish an everlasting covenant of righteousness with all those, Israelite or otherwise, who would turn to him in faith and repent of their sins (Isaiah 59:20-21).

In due time God sent into the world his Son, Jesus Christ. He proclaimed, "My Father's will is that everyone who looks to the Son and believes in him shall have eternal life, and I will raise him up at the last day" (John 6:40). God assured, "Everyone who calls on the name of the Lord will be saved" (Romans 10:13).

Today, God empowers his church to preach the gospel of the kingdom "in the whole world as a testimony to all nations" (Matthew 24:14). On the Day of Pentecost following the resurrection of Jesus Christ, God sent the Holy Spirit to unite the church as Christ's Body and to empower the preaching of the gospel, the good news of what God is doing (Acts 2:1-4).

The Bible is a book about God and humanity's relationship to him. Its rich message invites us to a lifetime of study to learn more about God, including what he is, what he has done, what he does, and what he plans to do.

But we know only in part. We are unable to know all there is of God, but we are able to understand what he has revealed to us. The Bible shows us that God is:

self-existing
not restricted by time
unbounded by place
unlimited in power
unlimited in knowledge
transcendent (having his existence beyond the physical universe)
immanent (involved with the universe).

What is God?

Suppose you are in a class in which a professor is trying to give the class a better understanding of God. She asks the students to close their eyes, relax and imagine God in their minds. "Think about what he must look like, what his throne would be like, how he would sound and what would be going on around him."

The students sit in their chairs, eyes shut, for a long time, each dreaming up a picture of God. "How are you doing?" the professor says. "Can you see God? Each of you by now must have some image. But do you know what?" – and then the professor shocks the class by exclaiming, "That's not God!"

"No!" the professor declares to the class. "That's not God! You cannot contain God in your mind! No human can have a full grasp of God, because God is God, and human beings are only physical, finite creatures! No image, no picture can do him justice."

Why is it hard to describe who and what God is? Because, as physical beings, our knowledge comes to us by way of our five senses – and human languages are designed in accordance with this knowledge. Our words, our grammar, our way of thinking, are all based on the physical world. But God is supernatural, eternal. He is infinite. He is invisible. We can still speak meaningfully about God, even though we are limited by our physical senses, but our words can never convey all that God is. We are limited in our languages.

What is "the image of God"?

Genesis 1:26 quotes God as saying, "Let us make man in our image, in our likeness, and let them rule over…all the creatures." Verse 27 tells us God followed through on his intent: "So God created man in his own image, in the image of God he created him; male and female he created them." Genesis 5:1 adds, "When God created man, he made him in the likeness of God."

How are we to understand what God means when he tells us we are made in his image and likeness? God's creation of humans in his image and likeness, recorded in Genesis 1:26-27, may be linked with the dominion God gave humans over the earth. In a sense, we act for God on earth when we exercise responsible lordship over the creation. "The context suggests that humanity is the image of God in the dominion it exercises over the rest of creation," notes *Harper's Bible Commentary* on Genesis 1:3-31 (Harper & Row, 1988, page 87).

The book *ABC's of the Bible* adds:

> Before undertaking his supreme creation, God announced his intention to make man in his image and likeness. The Hebrew word for "image" usually refers to a statue (often used in the Old Testament for pagan idols), while a different word for "likeness" suggests a physical resemblance. Later generations interpreted the terms more generally, however. They thought of themselves as resembling God

not in a physical sense, but in a spiritual sense by possessing ...intelligence, and the capacity to make moral distinctions" (Reader's Digest Association, 1991, page 16).

Insight into the image of God can also be gained from a consideration of the distinction between the material body and the immaterial spirit within humanity's own constitution. The *Baker Encyclopedia of the Bible* states:

> Recent discussions have focused on the unity and integrity of man. Thus it is man as a physical-spiritual unity who is in the image of God as Spirit. This explains why the same words can be used both of God and man. God sees and hears as men do, but men do so in a way appropriate to their constitution as physical-spiritual creatures (with ears and mouth) and God in a way appropriate to his nature as spiritual and uncreated. (article "Image of God," Baker Book House, 1988, page 1018)

The image to which humans ultimately must conform is that of Jesus Christ. Romans 8:29 tells us God desires that we "be conformed to the likeness of his Son"—Jesus Christ. *ABC's of the Bible* states, "The New Testament added to the notion that man was created in the image of God by proposing that Jesus was the sole embodiment of divine perfection" (page 16).

We are unique among earth's creatures in that God endowed us with rationality, free choice and moral responsibility. By creating us in his own image, God has given us the incomparable capacity to have a personal relationship with him.

Spiritual realities, human language

God shows us facets of himself throughout creation. He has intervened many times in history. The Bible tells us much about him. He even manifested himself in various ways to various people in the Bible. Still, since God is spirit, his fullness cannot be seen or heard or touched or smelled. The Bible gives us truths about God by using words that physical beings in their physical realm can grasp. But those words are not capable of completely defining God.

The Bible describes God as a rock and a fortress (Psalm 18:2), as a stronghold and a shield (Psalm 144:2) and as a consuming fire (Hebrews 12:29). We realize that God is not any of these physical things in a literal sense. But these metaphors, based on what we as humans can observe and understand, reveal important truths about God.

The Bible even attributes human form to God, revealing aspects of his character and his relationship with humans. This is called anthropomorphism "(From Greek *anthropos,* 'human,' *morphe,* 'form') the attribution of a human quality to God, such as 'eyes,' 'hands,' or 'arms'" (*Westminster Dictionary of Theological Terms,* p. 13).

Biblical passages describe God with:

> a body (Phil. 3:21),
> a head and hair (Rev. 1:14),
> a face (Gen. 32:30; Ex. 33:23; Rev. 1:16),
> eyes and ears (Deut. 11:12; Ps. 34:15; Rev. 1:14), a nose and nostrils (Gen. 8:21; Ex. 15:8),
> a mouth (Matt. 4:4; Rev. 1:16),
> lips (Job 11:5),
> a voice (Ps. 68:33; Rev. 1:15),
> a tongue and breath (Isa. 30:27-28),
> arms, hands and fingers (Ps. 44:2-3; 89:13; Heb. 1:3; 2 Chron. 18:18; Ex. 31:18; Deut. 9:10; Ps. 8:3; Rev. 1:16),
> shoulders (Isa. 9:6),
> a chest (Rev. 1:13),
> a back (Ex. 33:23),
> a waist (Ezek. 1:27)
> and feet (Ps. 18:9; Rev. 1:15).

The Bible also describes how God wants us to relate to him, often using familial language. Jesus taught us to pray to "Our Father in heaven" (Matthew 6:9). God will comfort his people as a mother comforts her child (Isaiah 66:13). In Revelation 21:7, God promises, "He who overcomes will inherit all this, and I will be his God and he will be my son."

Yes, God calls Christians to a family relationship – to be his children. The Bible paints the picture in words humans can get their minds around. But the picture, to use a term from the world of art, is impressionistic. It does not give us a complete grasp of the ultimate, glorious, spiritual reality. The joy and glory of our ultimate relationship with God as his children is far greater than our finite words can express.

> To all who received [Jesus Christ], to those who believed in his name, he gave the right to become children of God – children born not of natural descent, nor of human decision or a husband's will, but born of God. (John 1:12-13)

In the resurrection, when the fullness of salvation and the kingdom of God have come, we will be able to know God fully at last. As Paul wrote:

"Now we see but a poor reflection as in a mirror; then we shall see face to face. Now I know in part; then I shall know fully, even as I am fully known" (1 Corinthians 13:12).

"Anyone who has seen me has seen the Father"

God's self-revelation, as we have seen, encompasses creation, history and the Bible. But God also revealed himself by becoming a human. He became like us and walked and served and taught among us. God's greatest act of self-revelation was in Jesus Christ. "The Word became flesh," John 1:14 tell us, and this divine Word we know as Jesus Christ. The Son of God set aside the privileges of being God and came to earth as a man – fully human, who died for our sins, was resurrected from the dead, and started his church.

Christ's coming disturbed the people of his day. Why? Because their picture of God wasn't big enough, as we shall see in the next two chapters. Yet Jesus told his disciples, "Anyone who has seen me has seen the Father" (John 14:9). In short, God had revealed himself in Jesus Christ.

THE LORD OUR GOD, THE LORD IS ONE

Judaism. Christianity. Islam. These three great faiths all look to Abraham as their father. Abraham differed from others of his day in one vital respect: He worshiped only one God – the true God. Abraham worshiped the one true God. Monotheism, the belief that only one God exists, marks the starting point of true religion.

Abraham was not born in a monotheistic society. Centuries later, God reminded ancient Israel: "Long ago your forefathers, including Terah the father of Abraham and Nahor, lived beyond the River and worshiped other gods. But I took your father Abraham from the land beyond the River and led him throughout Canaan and gave him many descendants" (Joshua 24:2-3).

Before God called him, Abraham lived in Ur, though his relatives may have lived in Haran. The people of both places worshiped many gods. Ur, for instance, was the site of a great temple tower dedicated to the Sumerian moon-god, Nanna. Other temples at Ur honored An, Enlil, Enki and Nin-gal. God called Abraham out of this polytheistic setting: "Leave your country, your people and your father's household and go to the land I will show you. I will make you into a great nation" (Genesis 12:1-2).

Abraham obeyed God and moved (verse 4). In a sense, God's relationship with Israel began when he revealed himself to Abraham, their ancestor. God made a covenant with Abraham. God renewed that agreement with Abraham's son Isaac and, later, with Isaac's son Jacob. Abraham, Isaac and Jacob worshiped the one true God. This set them apart even from their close relatives. Laban, a grandson of Abraham's brother Nahor, embraced numerous household gods or idols (Genesis 31:30-35).

God rescues Israel from Egyptian idolatry

Decades later, Jacob (whose name God changed to Israel) and his children settled in Egypt. The children of Israel remained in Egypt for nearly three centuries. The Egyptians also worshiped many gods. *The International Standard Bible Encyclopedia* points out: "The first observation of a person coming to the study of Egyptian religion is the large number of deities, many of them in animal form, or human form with animal heads.... It is possible to list at least thirty-nine gods and goddesses" (vol. 4, page 101).

The children of Israel grew in number in Egypt but became enslaved by their Egyptian hosts. God revealed himself as the one true God through a series of miracles that led to Israel's liberation from Egypt. God then made a covenant between himself and the nation of Israel. God's revelation of himself to humanity, as these events show, has always centered on monotheism.

He revealed himself to Moses as the God of Abraham, Isaac and Jacob. The name God called himself, "I am" (Exodus 3:14), implies that other gods do not exist in the same way God does. God is. They are not!

Because Pharaoh refused to release Israel, God humbled Egypt with 10 miraculous plagues. Many of these plagues showed that Egypt's gods had no power. For example, one of the Egyptian gods had a head in the shape of a frog. God's plague of frogs upon Egypt ridiculed the worship of that god.

Even after witnessing the devastating effects the plagues had on his nation, Pharaoh still tried to prevent the Israelites from leaving. God finally swept the Egyptians "into the sea" (Exodus 14:27). This action demonstrated the impotence of Egypt's sea god. The children of Israel sang triumphantly (Exodus 15:1-21), exalting the omnipotent God of Israel.

The true God found – and lost

God led the Israelites out of Egypt and to the foot of Mt. Sinai, where they ratified a covenant. God stressed in the first of his Ten Commandments that he alone was to be worshiped: "You shall have no other gods before me" (Exodus 20:3). The Second Commandment forbade the making or worshiping of idols (verses 4-5).

Time and again, Moses pleaded with the Israelites not to worship idols (Deuteronomy 4:23-26; 7:5; 12:2-3; 29:14-18). He knew Israel would be tempted to follow the Canaanite gods when they arrived in the Promised Land.

A saying known as the *Shema'* (after the Hebrew word for "hear," which begins the saying) captured Israel's duty to God. The *Shema'* starts: "Hear, O Israel: The Lord our God, the Lord is one. Love the Lord your God with all your heart and with all your soul and with all your strength" (Deuteronomy 6:4-5).

However, Israel again and again lapsed into worshiping the Canaanite gods, among them El (a standard term for deity that is also applied to the true God), Baal, Dagon and Ashtoreth (also known as Astarte or Ishtar).

Baal worship particularly troubled the Israelites. As they colonized the land of Canaan, they became dependent on crop production. Baal, the storm god, was worshiped in fertility rites. *The International Standard Bible Encyclopedia* states, "The fertility cult, by virtue of its focus on the fertility of land and beasts, must always have had an attraction in a society such as ancient Israel where economy was based primarily on agriculture" (vol. 4, page 101).

God's prophets warned the Israelites to turn from their waywardness. Elijah asked the people: "How long will you waver between two opinions? If the Lord is God, follow him; but if Baal is God, follow him" (1 Kings 18:21). God answered Elijah's prayer to prove that he alone was God. The people acknowledged: "The Lord – he is God! The Lord – he is God!" (verse 39).

God revealed himself not merely as the greatest of all gods, but as the only true God: "I am the Lord, and there is no other; apart from me there is no God" (Isaiah 45:5). And: "Before me no god was formed, nor will there be one after me. I, even I, am the Lord, and apart from me there is no savior" (Isaiah 43:10-11).

Judaism – strictly monotheistic

The Jewish religion of Jesus' day was not merely henotheistic (holding that God is the greatest of many gods) nor monolatrous (permitting the worship of God alone but acknowledging that other gods might exist). It was strictly monotheistic, meaning there is only one God.

According to the *Theological Dictionary of the New Testament*, on no other point were the Jews more united than on the confession "God is one" (vol. 3, page 98). Reciting the *Shema'* remains part of Jewish worship today. Rabbi Akiba, who was killed in Palestine during the second century A.D., is said to have been brought to his execution at the time of the reading of the *Shema'* and to have repeated Deuteronomy 6:4 throughout his tortures, breathing his last on the word *one*.

What Jesus said about monotheism

When a scribe asked Jesus which command was greatest, Jesus replied by quoting the *Shema'*: "Hear, O Israel, the Lord our God, the Lord is one. Love the Lord your God with all your heart and with all your soul and with all your mind and with all your strength" (Mark 12:29-30). The scribe agreed: "Well said, teacher.... You are right in saying that God is one and there is no other but him" (verse 32).

In the next chapter, we will look at how Jesus' coming gave the New Testament church a deeper and broadened concept of God. (Jesus claimed to be the Son of God and to be one with the Father.)

Jesus reaffirmed monotheism. As the writers of the *Theological Dictionary of the New Testament* point out: "Early Christian monotheism is confirmed rather than shattered by the Christology of the [New Testament].... According to the Gospels Jesus himself sharpens the monotheistic confession" (vol. 3, page 102).

Mark 10:17-18 records one of Jesus' clearest affirmations of monotheism. When a man addressed him as "Good Teacher," Jesus answered: "Why do you call Me good? No one is good but One, that is, God" (New King James Version).

What the early church preached

Jesus commissioned his church to preach the gospel and to make disciples of all nations (Matthew 28:18-20). This soon involved preaching to Gentiles who were still immersed in polytheism.

When Paul and Barnabas preached and performed miracles at Lystra, the reaction of the people showed how steeped they were in polytheism: "When the crowd saw what Paul had done, they shouted in the Lycaonian language, 'The gods have come down to us in human form!' Barnabas they called Zeus, and Paul they called Hermes because he was the chief speaker" (Acts 14:11-12). Hermes and Zeus were two gods in the Greek pantheon. The Greek and Roman pantheons were well known in the New Testament world, and worship of the Greek and Roman gods was widespread.

Paul and Barnabas responded vigorously with the message of monotheism: "We too are only men, human like you. We are bringing you good news, telling you to turn from these worthless things to the living God, who made heaven and earth and sea and everything in them" (verse 15). Even then, Paul and Barnabas could scarcely restrain the people from sacrificing to them.

In Athens, Paul found many altars set up to honor different gods – even one with the inscription: "TO AN UNKNOWN GOD" (Acts 17:23). He used that altar as a starting point from which to explain monotheism to the Athenians.

At Ephesus, brisk sales of idols accompanied the worship of the Greek goddess Artemis. After Paul preached about the one true God, the idol trade slackened. The silversmith Demetrius was adversely affected economically. He told his fellow artisans, "Paul has convinced and led astray large numbers of people.... He says that man-made gods are no gods at all" (Acts 19:26).

Here is another case of one of God's servants preaching that gods made by hand are not gods at all. Just as the Old Testament does, the New Testament proclaims but one true God. The other gods aren't.

No other God

To the Christians at Corinth, Paul stated explicitly, "We know that an idol is nothing at all in the world and that there is no God but one" (1 Corinthians 8:4).

Monotheism underpins both the Old and New Testaments. God called Abraham, the father of the faithful, out from a polytheistic society. God revealed himself to Moses and Israel, and founded the old covenant on the worship of himself alone. God sent prophets to reiterate the message of monotheism. Finally, Jesus Christ himself reaffirmed monotheism. The New Testament church that Jesus founded fought against worship that fell short of true monotheism.

The church, from the days of the New Testament forward, has consistently preached what God long ago had revealed: "The Lord our God, the Lord is one."

JESUS REVEALS GOD

The Bible teaches that God is one. There are not two Gods, or three, or a thousand. Christianity is a monotheistic religion. That is why the coming of Jesus Christ aroused such strong controversy in the communities of his day.

"A stumbling block to Jews..."

God revealed himself to humanity through his Son, Jesus Christ, who is "the radiance of God's glory and the exact representation of his being" (Hebrews 1:3). Jesus called God his Father (Matthew 10:32-33; Luke 23:34; John 10:15) and said, "Anyone who has seen me has seen the Father" (John 14:9). He boldly claimed, "I and the Father are one" (John 10:30). After Jesus' resurrection, Thomas addressed him as "My Lord and my God!" (John 20:28). Jesus Christ was God.

Judaism could not accept this. "The Lord our God, the Lord is one," said the *Shema'* (Deuteronomy 6:4), which had long undergirded the Jewish faith. Yet here was a man with profound scriptural insight and miracle-working power who claimed to be the unique Son of God. Some Jewish leaders acknowledged that Jesus was a teacher come from God (John 3:2). But God's Son? How could God be one, and yet Jesus Christ also be God?

"For this reason the Jews tried all the harder to kill him," says John 5:18. "Not only was he breaking the Sabbath, but he was even calling God his own Father."

The Jews eventually condemned Christ to death because they thought he had, by his claims, blasphemed:

> The high priest asked him, "Are you the Christ, the Son of the Blessed One?" "I am," said Jesus. "And you will see the Son of Man sitting at the right hand of the Mighty One and coming on the clouds of heaven." The high priest tore his clothes. "Why do we need any more witnesses?" he asked. "You have heard the blasphemy. What do you think?" They all condemned him as worthy of death. (Mark 14:61-64)

"...Foolishness to Gentiles"

On the other hand, the Gentiles could not accept Jesus for who he said he was, either. The Greek philosophers thought that nothing could cross the gap from what was eternal and unchanging to what was temporal and material.

So the Greeks scoffed at John's statement: "In the beginning was the

Word, and the Word was with God, and the Word was God.... The Word became flesh and made his dwelling among us. We have seen his glory, the glory of the One and Only, who came from the Father, full of grace and truth" (John 1:1, 14).

For the unbelievers, this unbelievable story didn't end there. Not only did God become a human being and die, but he was raised from the dead and returned to his former glory (John 17:5). Paul wrote to the Ephesians that God had raised Christ "from the dead and seated him at his right hand in the heavenly realms" (Ephesians 1:20).

Elsewhere, Paul addressed the consternation with which the Jews and Greeks greeted the astounding story of Jesus Christ:

> Since in the wisdom of God the world through its wisdom did not know him, God was pleased through the foolishness of what was preached to save those who believe. Jews demand miraculous signs and Greeks look for wisdom, but we preach Christ crucified: a stumbling block to Jews and foolishness to Gentiles. (1 Corinthians 1:21-23)

Not everyone could understand and rejoice at the wonderful news of the gospel. Paul went on: "But to those whom God has called, both Jews and Greeks, Christ [is] the power of God and the wisdom of God. For the foolishness of God is wiser than man's wisdom, and the weakness of God is stronger than man's strength" (verses 24-25). And in Romans 1:16 Paul exclaimed, "I am not ashamed of the gospel, because it is the power of God for the salvation of everyone who believes: first for the Jew, then for the Gentile."

"I am the gate"

During his life on earth, Jesus, God in the flesh, smashed a lot of long-held and cherished – but false – beliefs about what God is, how God lives and what God wants. He illuminated truths that were only hints in Old Testament. He said that no one could be saved except through him: "I am the gate; whoever enters through me will be saved" (John 10:9).

"I am the way and the truth and the life," Jesus announced. "No one comes to the Father except through me" (John 14:6). And: "I am the vine; you are the branches. If a man remains in me and I in him, he will bear much fruit; apart from me you can do nothing. If anyone does not remain in me, he is like a branch that is thrown away and withers; such branches are picked up, thrown into the fire and burned" (John 15:5-6).

Jesus is God

Jesus did not do away with the monotheistic command in Deuteronomy 6:4. Rather, Jesus expanded beyond what anyone had imagined what it means for God to be one. The Gospel of John says that, while God is one and only one, the eternal Word existed with God and was God (John 1:1-2).

When the Word came in the flesh, though he was fully divine, he voluntarily set aside the prerogatives of divinity.

> [Jesus], being in very nature God, did not consider equality with God something to be grasped, but made himself nothing, taking the very nature of a servant, being made in human likeness. And being found in appearance as a man, he humbled himself and became obedient to death – even death on a cross! (Philippians 2:6-8)

Jesus was fully human and fully divine. He held all the power and authority of God, but he voluntarily, for our sakes, subjected himself to the limitations of human existence. During this period of incarnation, he, the Son, remained one with his Father in heaven.

"Anyone who has seen me has seen the Father," said Jesus (John 14:9). "By myself I can do nothing; I judge only as I hear, and my judgment is just, for I seek not to please myself but him who sent me," he said (John 5:30). And, "I do nothing on my own but speak just what the Father has taught me" (John 8:28).

Just before his crucifixion, Jesus told his disciples: "I came from the Father and entered the world; now I am leaving the world and going back to the Father" (John 16:28). Jesus came to earth to die for our sins. He came to found his church. He came to start the preaching of the gospel in all the world. Jesus also came to reveal God to humanity. In particular, he opened human understanding to the Father-Son relationship that exists within the Godhead.

The Gospel of John, for example, largely devotes itself to recording Jesus' work of revealing God the Father to humanity. Jesus' Passover discourse (John 13-17) is of special interest in this regard. What a startling truth about the nature of God! Even more startling is Jesus' further revelation about how God intends for humans to relate to him.

Humans share in the divine nature!

Jesus told his apostles: "Whoever has my commands and obeys them, he is the one who loves me. He who loves me will be loved by my Father, and I too will love him and show myself to him" (John 14:21). God wants to unite humans to him in a profound relationship of love – the love that the Father and Son share. God is revealed to those in whom that love works.

Jesus went on to explain: "If anyone loves me, he will obey my teaching. My Father will love him, and we will come to him and make our home with him. He who does not love me will not obey my teaching. These words you hear are not my own; they belong to the Father who sent me" (verses 23-24).

God lives in those who come to him through faith in Jesus Christ, committing themselves to live in allegiance to him. Peter preached: "Repent and be baptized, every one of you, in the name of Jesus Christ for the forgiveness of your sins. And you will receive the gift of the Holy Spirit" (Acts 2:38). The Holy Spirit also is God, as we shall see in the next chapter. The Holy Spirit lives in the believers.

Paul knew that God lived in him: "I have been crucified with Christ and I no longer live, but Christ lives in me. The life I live in the body, I live by faith in the Son of God, who loved me and gave himself for me" (Galatians 2:20). Because Christ lives in us and the Holy Spirit lives in us, God lives in us. But there is only one God.

God revealed himself fully in Jesus Christ. "For in Christ all the fullness of the Deity lives in bodily form" (Colossians 2:9). What can this revelation mean to us? By partaking of Christ, through faith in him, we can be partakers of God's own divine nature! Peter summed it up by saying,

> Divine power has given us everything we need for life and godliness through our knowledge of him who called us by his own glory and goodness. Through these he has given us his very great and precious promises, so that through them you may *participate in the divine nature* and escape the corruption in the world caused by evil desires. (2 Peter 1:3-4)

Christ – the perfect revelation of God

How did Jesus Christ reveal God?

Jesus revealed God's character in all he did and taught.

- Jesus died and was raised from death so that humans may be saved and reconciled to God, and that they may receive eternal life. Romans 5:10-11 says: "If, when we were God's enemies, we were reconciled to him through the death of his Son, how much more, having been reconciled, shall we be saved through his life! Not only is this so, but we also rejoice in God through our Lord Jesus Christ, through whom we have now received reconciliation."

- Jesus revealed God's plan to form a new spiritual community — the church — transcending racial and national barriers (Ephesians 2:14-22).
- Jesus revealed God as the Father of all who are reborn in Christ.
- Jesus revealed the glorious destiny God has promised to his people. The indwelling presence of the Spirit of God gives us a foretaste of that future glory here and now. The Spirit is "a deposit guaranteeing our inheritance" (Ephesians 1:14).
- Jesus also witnessed to the existence of the Father and the Son as one God. Our understanding of God's unity must allow for Father and Son, must allow for more than one Person within the Godhead. New Testament writers frequently applied the Old Testament names for God to Christ. By doing so, they showed not only what Christ is like, but what God is like, for Jesus is the revelation of the Father, and he and the Father are one. We learn about God as we study what Jesus Christ is like.

ONE IN THREE AND THREE IN ONE

The Bible never compromises the fact that God is one. Yet, Jesus' incarnation and work give us a greater depth of understanding of the way in which God is one. The New Testament testifies that Jesus Christ is God and that the Father is God. There is *more than one* Person in the *one* God.

The New Testament, as we shall see, also presents the Holy Spirit as divine and eternal. Whenever we say that the Holy Spirit does something, we mean that God does it. The Holy Spirit is God. That means the Bible reveals one God who exists eternally as Father, Son, and Holy Spirit. It is for this reason that Christians are to be baptized "in the name of the Father and of the Son and of the Holy Spirit" (Matthew 28:19).

Throughout the centuries, many ideas have been developed that might seem, at first glance, to make these biblical facts easier to understand. But we must be careful not to accept any idea that contradicts what the Bible says. Some ideas might make things seem simple, in the sense of making God easier to comprehend and easier to picture in our minds. But what is important is whether an idea is consistent with the Bible, not whether it is simple or easy.

The Bible tells us there is one and only one God, and then presents us with more than one Person called God. The Father is called God, the Son is called God, and the Holy Spirit is called God. All three are eternal, and all three do things that only God can do. So there is one God, and three in the One.

"One in three" – or "three in one" – is a concept that, at first glance, appears illogical. But neither is it logical for us to assume that God could not be more than what we would expect if we simply sat down, with no revelation, to figure it out for ourselves.

God reveals many things about himself, and we believe them, even though we cannot explain them all. For example, we cannot completely explain how God can be without beginning. This is beyond our ability to understand. We cannot explain what eternal existence is like, yet we know that God is without beginning. Likewise, the Bible reveals that God is one and only one, yet is also Father, Son, and Holy Spirit. We believe it even though it is not simple or easy to explain. We believe it because the Bible reveals it.

The Holy Spirit is God

Acts 5:3-4 calls the Holy Spirit God:

Peter said, "Ananias, how is it that Satan has so filled your heart that you have lied to the Holy Spirit and have kept for yourself some of the money you received for the land? Didn't it belong to you before it was sold? And after it was sold, wasn't the money at your disposal? What made you think of doing such a thing? You have not lied to men but to God."

When Ananias lied to the Holy Spirit, Peter says he was lying to God. He was not trying to deceive an impersonal force or an intermediate agency — he was trying to deceive God.

The New Testament ascribes to the Holy Spirit attributes that belong only to God. For instance, the Holy Spirit is omniscient, or unlimited in knowledge. "God has revealed it to us by his Spirit. The Spirit searches all things, even the deep things of God.... No one knows the thoughts of God except the Spirit of God" (1 Corinthians 2:10-11).

The Holy Spirit is omnipresent, or unlimited in place. "Do you not know that your body is a temple of the Holy Spirit, who is in you, whom you have received from God?" (1 Corinthians 6:19). The Holy Spirit is in believers everywhere, not limited to any one place (see also Psalm 139:7-8).

The Holy Spirit regenerates Christians, giving them new life. "No one can enter the kingdom of God unless he is born of water and the Spirit. Flesh gives birth to flesh, but the Spirit gives birth to spirit" (John 3:5-6).

The Holy Spirit speaks and foretells the future. "The Spirit clearly says that in later times some will abandon the faith and follow deceiving spirits and things taught by demons" (1 Timothy 4:1).

The Holy Spirit is equated with the Father and the Son in the baptismal ceremony. Christian converts are baptized "in the name of the Father and of the Son and of the Holy Spirit" (Matthew 28:19). There is one name, but three are included in the One.

The Spirit creates out of nothing (Psalm 104:30). Only God can create like that.

Hebrews 9:14 says the Holy Spirit is eternal. Only God is eternal.

Jesus told the apostles: "I will ask the Father, and he will give you another Counselor to be with you forever – the Spirit of truth. The world cannot accept him, because it neither sees him nor knows him. But you know him, for he lives with you and will be in you" (John 14:16-17).

Jesus identified the Counselor as the Holy Spirit: "The Counselor, the Holy Spirit, whom the Father will send in my name, will teach you all things and will remind you of everything I have said to you" (verse 26). The Counselor convicts the world of sin, an accomplishment that can rightly be ascribed only to God. He guides into all truth, something only God is capable of doing. As Paul affirmed, "We speak, not in words taught us by human wisdom but in words taught by the Spirit, expressing spiritual truths in spiritual words" (1 Corinthians 2:13).

Father, Son, and Holy Spirit: one God

When we understand that God is one, and that the Holy Spirit is God, just as the Father is God and the Son is God, we have no problem understanding a passage like Acts 13:2: "While they were worshiping the Lord and fasting, the Holy Spirit said, 'Set apart for me Barnabas and Saul for the work to which I have called them.'" Here Luke presents the Holy Spirit as speaking. The Holy Spirit is God at work in the church, speaking and calling people to do God's will.

The biblical revelation of the nature of God is beautiful. When the Holy Spirit speaks, or sends, or inspires, or leads, or sanctifies, or empowers, or gives gifts, it is God speaking, sending, inspiring, leading, sanctifying, empowering or giving gifts. But since God is one, and not three separate beings, the Holy Spirit is not a separate God.

God has one will, the will of the Father, which is also the will of the Son and of the Holy Spirit. It is not a matter of two or three separate God Beings deciding to be in perfect agreement with each other. This would contradict scriptures such as Isaiah 44:6-8. It is a matter of one God, one will. The Son is the very expression of the will of the Father. Similarly, the Holy Spirit constitutes the will of the Father at work in the world.

Paul says that "the Lord is the Spirit," and he speaks of "the Lord, who is the Spirit" (2 Corinthians 3:17-18). He says "the Spirit gives life" (verse 6), which is something only God can do. We know the Father, only because the Spirit enables us to believe that Jesus is the Son of God. Jesus dwells in us and the Father dwells in us, but that is only because the Spirit dwells in us (John 14:16-17, 23; Romans 8:9-11). Since God is one, if the Spirit is in us, then the Father and the Son are in us. The three can be distinguished, but not separated.

Paul equates the Spirit, the Lord, and God in 1 Corinthians 12:4-11. He says it is "the same God who inspires" in verse 6, and he says "these are the work of one and the same Spirit," and goes on to declare that the Spirit does all this as the Spirit wills (verse 11). How can the Spirit will? The Spirit wills because the Spirit is a person, and the Spirit is God, and God is one, and the will of the Father is the will of the Son and of the Holy Spirit.

To worship God is to worship the Father, the Son, and the Holy Spirit, the one and only one God. That does not mean we are to single out the Holy Spirit and worship the Holy Spirit as though the Holy Spirit is a separate Being. We do not direct our worship to the Holy Spirit specifically, but to God, who is Father, Son, and Holy Spirit. It is God in us (the Holy Spirit) who causes us to worship God. The Comforter (like the Son) will not speak on his own (John 16:13), but what the Father gives him he will speak. He does not direct us to himself, but to the Father through the Son. Likewise, we don't normally pray specifically to the Spirit – it is the Spirit in us who helps us in our prayers, and intercedes for us (Romans 8:26).

Unless God himself is in us, we would not be turned toward God at all. Unless God himself is in us, we would not know God, and we would not know his Son. That is why all the credit for our salvation goes to God and not to us. The fruit we bear is the fruit of the Spirit – that is, God's fruit, not ours. But God gives us the privilege, if we will accept it, of participating with him in his work.

The Father is the Creator and Source of all things. The Son is the Redeemer and Savior, and the one by whom God created all things. The Holy Spirit is the Comforter and Advocate. The Holy Spirit is God in us, the one who leads us to the Father through the Son. Through the Son, we are cleansed and saved so that we can have fellowship with him and the Father. The Spirit stirs our hearts and minds and inclines us toward belief in Jesus Christ, who is the way and the gate. The Spirit gives us gifts, the gifts of God, including faith, hope and love.

All this is the work of the one God, who reveals himself to us as Father, Son, and Holy Spirit. He is not a different God from the God of the Old Testament, but in the New Testament something more is revealed about him: He sent his Son as a human being to die for our sins and to be raised to glory, and he sent us his Spirit – the Comforter – to dwell in us, to lead us into all truth, to give us gifts, and to conform us to the image of Christ.

When we pray, reaching God is the goal of the prayer, yet it is also God who leads us toward that goal, and it is also God who is the Way along which we are led toward the goal. In other words, it is to God (the Father) we pray; it is God in us (the Holy Spirit) motivating us to pray; and God is also the Way (the Son) along which we are being led toward that goal.

The Father initiates the plan of salvation. The Son embodies and executes the atoning, redemptive plan for the salvation of humanity. The Holy Spirit applies the benefits, or gifts, of redemption to empower the actual salvation of the faithful believers. All this is the work of the one God, the God of the Bible.

Paul ended 2 Corinthians with the blessing: "May the grace of the Lord Jesus Christ, and the love of God, and the fellowship of the Holy Spirit be with you all" (2 Corinthians 13:14). In this verse, Paul highlights the love of God, which is shown to us through the grace he gives us in Jesus Christ and the unified fellowship with himself and one another he gives us through the Holy Spirit.

How many "Persons" is God?

Many people have only a hazy idea of what the Bible teaches about the oneness of God. Most do not really think about it. Some imagine three separate Beings. Some picture one Being with three heads. Others think of one Being who changes from Father to Son to Holy Spirit whenever he wills. It is easy to make such mistakes.

Many people use the word Trinity as a definition of the biblical teaching about God. However, if asked, most would not be able to explain what the Bible actually teaches about how God is one. In other words, what many people envision when they speak of the Trinity is not biblical. Some of the confusion lies in the use of the word Persons.

The word Persons, which is normally included in English-language definitions of the Trinity, causes people to think of three Beings. "One God who is three Persons – Father, Son, and Holy Spirit," is a common way the Trinity is explained. But the ordinary meaning of the word "person" is misleading when it is applied to God. It gives the impression that God has limits, and that his threeness lies in being three separate individuals – which is not the case.

The English word "person" is derived from the Latin word *persona*. The word *persona* was used by theologians to describe the Father, the Son, and the Holy Spirit in the Latin language, but it did not convey the same meaning as the English word "person" conveys today. It was a word originally used for a role that an actor portrayed in a play. It was also the word for "mask," because actors wore different masks for each character they portrayed.

Even this concept, though it does not allow the error of three Beings, is still weak and misleading when referring to God. It is misleading because the Father, the Son, and the Holy Spirit are not mere roles being played by God. An actor can play only one role at a time, quite unlike God, who is Father, Son, and Holy Spirit all the time.

Even though a Latin theologian may have understood what was meant by the word *persona*, the average person today would not. The English word "person" is easily misunderstood by the average individual when referring to

God, unless it is accompanied by an explanation that "Persons" in the Godhead should not be thought of in the same way as "persons" like humans.

When most English-speaking people think of one God who is three Persons, they cannot help but think in some way of three separate Beings. In other words, the terms *persons* and *beings* are usually thought of, in English, as meaning the same thing. But that is not how God is revealed in the Bible. There is only one God, not three. The Bible reveals that Father, Son, and Holy Spirit are the way the one true God of the Bible is, the way God exists always.

One God: three Hypostases

When we express the biblical truth that God is one and at the same time three, it is helpful to use words that do not imply three Gods. God's oneness cannot be compromised. The problem is, all words that refer to created things tend to mislead by their very context in ordinary language. Most words, including the word Persons, tend to confuse God's nature with the created order. On the other hand, all our words in one way or another refer to the created order. So it is important to know what we mean, and what we do not mean, when we use any word in reference to God.

A helpful word, and one that was used by Greek-speaking Christians in expressing the oneness and threeness of God, is found in Hebrews 1:3. This passage is helpful in several ways. It states: "The Son is the radiance of God's glory and the exact representation of his being, sustaining all things by his powerful word."

From the description of the Son as "the radiance of God's glory," we learn a number of things. The Son is not a separate Being. The Son is not less divine than the Father. The Son is eternal, just as the Father is. In other words, the Son is to the Father as radiance or brightness is to glory. One cannot have radiance without the source of radiance, or a source of radiance without the radiance itself. Yet we distinguish between God's glory and the radiance of that glory. They are distinct, without being separate.

Likewise, there is much to learn from the words "the exact representation of his being." The Son is the full and complete expression of the Father. What God is in his being, the Son also is.

Now, let's look at the Greek word translated "being" in this passage. Some versions translate it "person." The word from which "being" and "person" in this passage are translated is *hypostasis*. It comes from Greek words meaning "standing under." It refers to that which "stands under," or that which makes something what it is. Hypostasis could be defined like this: "That without which something cannot be." It could be called "the ground of being."

God is personal

Hypostasis (in plural form, hypostases) is a good word to use of the Father, the Son, and the Holy Spirit. It is a biblical term, and it does not so easily confuse God's nature with the created order.

The word Person may also be used, as long as one understands that Person must not be confused with the way humans are persons. One reason the word Person is helpful, if it is understood correctly, is that God interacts with us in a personal way. It is wrong to say that God is impersonal. We do not worship a rock or plant, or an impersonal "power that is behind the universe." Rather, we worship a "living Person."

God is personal, but he is not a person in the way humans are persons. He says, "I am God, and not man – the Holy One among you" (Hosea 11:9). God is Creator; he is not just another part of his creation. Humans have a beginning, grow up, have a body, are separate from one another, grow old, increase or decrease in size, strength, etc., and die. God has none of those characteristics, but is nonetheless personal in his relationship to humans.

God is infinitely more than any human word can convey, yet he is personal and loves us dearly. God has revealed much about himself, but he has not revealed everything about himself – some things we are simply incapable of knowing. As finite beings, we cannot totally grasp the infinite. We can know God as he reveals himself to us, but we cannot know him exhaustively, because we are finite, and he is infinite. What God has revealed to us about himself is true. It is relevant. It is intimate. It is marvelous, and it is thorough. But we must never think we know everything about God. God has revealed all we *need* to know, and what he has revealed is wonderful!

God calls on us to continue to "grow in the grace and knowledge of our Lord and Savior Jesus Christ" (2 Peter 3:18). Jesus proclaimed, "This is eternal life: that they may know you, the only true God, and Jesus Christ, whom you have sent" (John 17:3). The more we know God, the more we realize how small we are and how great he is.

HUMANITY'S RELATIONSHIP WITH GOD

In an earlier chapter, we tried to frame a question that would capture what it is that humans want to know about God. What one question would we want to ask God, if we had the chance?

To our fumbling question "Who are you?", the awesome God who made and rules the cosmos replies, "I AM WHO I AM" (Exodus 3:14). God declares himself to us in creation (Psalm 19:1). He has interacted with the human family ever since he made us. Sometimes he speaks through thunder, quaking or fire, and sometimes he speaks in a gentle whisper (Exodus 20:18; 1 Kings 19:11-12).

In the biblical record, God reveals information about himself and inspired reports of how people responded to him. God also reveals himself through Jesus Christ and the Holy Spirit.

But we want to know more than who God is, don't we? We want to know why he made us. We want to know his will for us. We want to know what he has in store for us. We want to know not just *about* him — we want to know *him*.

What is our relationship with God now? What should it be? And what will our relationship be in the future? God made us in his image (Genesis 1:26-27). The Bible reveals a far more profound future than we can now imagine.

Where we find ourselves now

Hebrews 2:6-11 tells us that we are made "a little lower than the angels." Yet God has crowned us with "glory and honor" and put everything under our rule. His future intent for humanity is to leave "nothing that is not subject to him. Yet at present we do not see everything subject to him."

God has prepared an infinitely glorious and joyous future for us. But something stands in the way. We find ourselves in a state of sin, alienated from God by our transgressions (Isaiah 59:1-2). But the breach has been healed. Jesus tasted death for us so that he might bring "many children to glory" (Hebrews 2:9-10).

Revelation 21:7 says that God desires to unite us with him in a family relationship. Because of God's love for us and what he has done for us, and what he is doing for us now as the Author of our salvation, Jesus is "not ashamed to call [us] brothers and sisters" (Hebrews 2:10-11).

So what should we be doing now?

Acts 2:38 instructs us to repent of our sins and to be baptized – to figuratively bury the old self. Those who believe that Jesus Christ is their Savior, Lord and King are led by the Spirit (Galatians 3:2-5). As he opens our minds to understand the gospel, we repent – turning to God from the selfish, worldly, sinful ways we followed in the past. In faith, we enter into a new relationship with him. We are reborn (John 3:3), given a new life in Christ through the Holy Spirit, regenerated by the Spirit through God's grace and mercy and the redemptive work of Jesus Christ.

What happens then? We "grow in the grace and knowledge of our Lord and Savior Jesus Christ" (2 Peter 3:18) for the remainder of our lives, destined to take part in the first resurrection, after which we will "be with the Lord forever" (1 Thessalonians 4:13-17).

Awesome inheritance

God "has given us new birth into a living hope through the resurrection of Jesus Christ from the dead, and into an inheritance that can never perish, spoil or fade – kept in heaven for you, who through faith are shielded by God's power until the coming of the salvation that is ready to be revealed in the last time" (1 Peter 1:3-5).

In the resurrection, we will be given immortality (1 Corinthians 15:54) and a "spiritual body" (verse 44). "As we have borne the likeness of the earthly man [Adam]," says verse 49, "so shall we bear the likeness of the man from heaven [Jesus]." As "children of the resurrection," we will no longer be subject to death (Luke 20:36).

Could anything be more wonderful than what the Bible says about God and our future relationship with him, a relationship that can begin right now? We will "be like him [Jesus], for we shall see him as he is" (1 John 3:2). Revelation 21:3 says that, in the time of the new heaven and new earth, "the dwelling of God is with humans, and he will live with them. They will be his people, and God himself will be with them and be their God."

We will be one with God in holiness, love, perfection, righteousness and spirit. As his immortal children, we will be the family of God in its fullest sense, sharing complete fellowship with him in perfect and everlasting joy. What a marvelous and inspiring message of hope and eternal salvation God has for all those who are prepared to believe!

The Name of God — YHWH

When God called to Moses out of the burning bush, telling him to free the Israelites from bondage in Egypt, Moses asked: "Suppose I go to the Israelites and say to them, 'The God of your fathers has sent me to you,' and they ask me, 'What is his name?' Then what shall I tell them?" (Exodus 3:13).

God answered Moses, "I AM WHO I AM" (verse 14). The Hebrew word for "I AM" is *ehyeh,* which comes from the verb "to be." It can also be translated as "I SHALL BE."

God further told Moses: "Say to the Israelites, 'The Lord, the God of your fathers...has sent me to you'" (verse 15). Although the Hebrew word for "Lord" is *adon,* the word translated "Lord" in verse 15 is different. It is spelled with the four Hebrew consonants YHWH – "the tetragrammaton" (Greek for "four letters"). The word is related to *ehyeh* and also comes from the verb "to be." Both words have the sense of "being actively present."

Although most scholars pronounce the tetragrammaton as Yahweh, the correct pronunciation is not known for certain. The Hebrews avoided saying the tetragrammaton because they believed that doing so might take God's name in vain. When reading a passage of the Hebrew Bible that contained it, they referred to God by another one of his names – *adonai* or "my Lord."

The oldest known manuscript fragments of the Septuagint leave the tetragrammaton untranslated. Later manuscripts, probably reflecting Christian editing, render the tetragrammaton as *kyrios,* Greek for "Lord." Later, English versions rendered the personal name YHWH as the impersonal "the LORD." They used all capital letters for "Lord" to indicate they were translating YHWH, rather than *adon* or *adonai.*

The text of the Hebrew Bible originally had only consonants. When vowels were added in the 10th century A.D., the vowels of *adonai* were also used for the tetragrammaton, reminding the readers to pronounce the word as adonai. In the 16th century, Latin translators combined the vowel points of *adonai* with the consonants of the tetragrammaton to produce the artificial form *Iehoua.* In 1530, Tyndale rendered the tetragrammaton as *Iehouah* in his translation of Exodus 6:3. Subsequently, the I became J, and the u became v, and Jehovah became the standard spelling. The King James Version uses this spelling (Psalm 83:18 is one example), but the KJV usually translates YHWH as "the Lord" and *adonai* as "the Lord."

A GOD OF CHAOS?

Do you ever feel you're in a chaotic mess? I'm spending much of my time either trying to avoid chaos or get out of it. Earlier this year—you know, New Year's resolutions—I had the bright idea to reorganize my home office. I know what, I'll (meaning my husband) build some shelves in the office closet to hold the printers and other equipment taking up my space.

Well, one thing led to another. Electrical and computer cables had to be redirected. Files had to be moved out of the closet to make space for the shelves. Everything was piling up in my office, so we could hardly get in and out.

Moving that equipment into the closet allowed us to get rid of some furniture, which meant moving around the other furniture. It was chaotic for days and it wasn't long before I was apologizing to Ed and sorrowfully regretting my bright idea.

But then, all was put back in order. I had more space. The office looked much better, and Ed didn't hurt his back. I promised him it would be years before I would change that office around again.

God likes order. It says in Genesis 1 that God created raw material out of nothing. And he took that chaotic mass of raw material and made a universe out of it. One planet he focused on in particular was our earth.

Genesis 1:1-3 (New Revised Standard Version): "In the beginning when God created the heavens and the earth, the earth was a formless void and darkness covered the face of the deep, while a wind from God swept over the face of the waters. Then God said, 'Let there be light'; and there was light." We know the rest of the story.

With the subject of this article firmly in mind, I looked at several translations. The earth was "without form and void"; "formless and empty"; "void and vacant"; "unformed and void"; and finally in the Living Bible, "a shapeless, chaotic mass."

Yes, I finally found the words I was looking for: *chaotic mass.*

God makes order out of chaos. But then, as he made everything, didn't God also make the chaos? He had to make that shapeless, chaotic mass to begin with. Who is this God we worship? What's he really like?

I know God is creative—wonderfully creative. No two snowflakes alike, no two fingerprints the same. When I watch in wonder at cloud formations swirling around changing patterns or at the ever-changing colors in a sunset, I'm looking at a moving canvas of art never to be repeated in quite the same way.

Before you scoff at abstract paintings, look at the most beautiful abstracts ever by viewing Hubble telescope's photos of the stars, nebulas and the constellations. Or look at organic structures under a microscope. No one can create abstracts as beautiful as God creates.

And what about us humans? We start out tiny as the head of a pin, then through ingesting animal and vegetable products we grow into adults. How can wheat, rice, milk, beef, green beans, or here where I live in Texas, chicken-fried steak and biscuits and gravy grow a human being? Yet here we are, made out of a mess of seeds, grasses, fish and animals.

A meteorologist studying weather patterns in the 1960s came to the conclusion that because of the endless variations in the weather, we could never accurately predict the weather. It was too chaotic. The study was famous for saying even the flutter of a butterfly's wings could change the weather—the butterfly effect. This eventually led to what is called Chaos Theory.

I won't attempt to explain that theory, but in later studies what scientists considered chaotic: how weather changes, how tree branches grow, how blood veins branch out, all individually different and unpredictable, some brainiac came up with a formula that worked across these so-called chaotic patterns. To scientists' astonishment, they found order even in chaos. There's so much we have yet to learn about the mind of God.

Our God is the greatest artist, greatest architect, scientist, biologist, zoologist, physicist—greatest everything because he created everything. I wonder how much Christ knew in his physical form about what he created. The Bible writers are more concerned with what Christ did and taught, so few are the clues to what Christ understood about the world he lived in.

He changed water into wine. Did he understand the molecular structures he was working with? Did he need to? He healed people. Again, did he know exactly how the healing took place? Not sure if it mattered to him. His purpose was not to reveal the secrets of the universe but to redeem, reconcile and save us.

We live in a chaotic world full of people living chaotic lives. Before surrendering my will to God, I could describe my life as "without form and void." Many are out there living in desperation, yearning for some kind of escape from the mess they've made of their lives. That's where Christ comes in like the conquering hero he is.

Who is this God who calls himself the Creator? Jesus came to show us. He came to reveal the sovereign God. Some say we can learn about God through looking at his creation. That may be true to a point. As 17-century

English poet John Milton wrote:

> "The planets in their stations list'ning stood,
> While the bright pomp ascended jubilant.
> Open, ye everlasting gates, they sung,
> Open, ye heavens, your living doors; let in
> The great Creator from his work return'd
> Magnificent, his six days' work, a world"
> (Paradise *Lost*).

Yes, a magnificent work indeed. But God cannot be examined through microscopes or telescopes. He is spiritual. Jesus came to let us know who God really is. Even scientific minds marvel at his creation, but only Jesus could let us know how much God loves us.

Sheila Graham

PERICHORESIS — WHAT'S THAT?

A discussion with C. Baxter Kruger, founder of Perichoresis, Inc.

Question: Most of us can't even pronounce perichoresis, much less spell it. What does it mean?

Baxter Kruger: Some years ago a woman walked into my office around Christmastime with a stack of newsletters in her hand. She was crying, and she slammed the newsletters down on my desk and said, "I just feel like a pile of junk!"

I said, "What is wrong?"

She said, "I've been reading these newsletters from these people from all over the world, and they and their children are all doing all these great things for God, and it just hit me what a worthless life I have. For Pete's sake, I'm married and I've got three kids. When I'm not grocery shopping, I'm cooking the groceries, and when I'm not cooking the groceries I'm cleaning up, and when I'm not doing that I'm trying to find clothes for my children and keep this mess of a house presentable. And sometime in there I'm trying to find time for my husband. I don't even have time to read my Bible. What do I have that I can do for God?"

I stopped her, and I said, "Wait a minute, hang on here a minute. Yesterday you spent two hours driving around Jackson searching for a coat for your daughter. A winter coat, and not just any winter coat but one she would like, one that would be large enough to put away for next year but not look like it was bought this year. And one that was on sale. And you did it, you found it, and she's thrilled."

The woman said, "What's that got to do with this?"

I said, "Where did that concern for your daughter come from? Did you wake up yesterday morning and decide you were going to be a good momma?"

She said she had been thinking about the coat for a week.

"The Triune God meets us not in the sky or in our self-generated religions, but in our 'ordinary' human existence."

I said, "Isn't Jesus the good Shepherd who cares about all his sheep? He put his concern for this sheep (your daughter) in your heart. You are participating in nothing less than Jesus' life and burden. He was tending to his sheep through you. What is greater than that?"

In the light of the fact that Jesus Christ has laid hold of the whole human race, cleansed us in his death, lifted us up in his resurrection and has given us a place in his relationship with his Father and Spirit in his Ascension, we've got to rethink everything we thought we knew about ourselves and others and our ordinary human life.

The simple truth is there is nothing at all ordinary about us and the life we live. Caring for others, from orphans to our friends and the poor, our love for our husbands and wives and children, our passion for music and beauty, for coaching, gardening and fishing; these things do not have their origin in us.

They are not something that we invented. It is all coming from the Father, Son and Spirit. When this dreadful secular/sacred divide is exploded, we can see and honor life as it truly is—the gift of participating in the life and relationship of the Father, Son and Spirit.

So we're really talking about God meeting us in our day-to-day lives?

BK: Exactly. Through the work of Jesus, we have been adopted into the Trinitarian life. The concept of perichoresis helps us understand what our adoption means for us. We could define perichoresis as "mutual indwelling without loss of personal identity." In other words, we exist in union with the Triune God, but we do not lose our distinct personhood in the process. We matter. We are real to the Triune God.

Only the Trinity could have union without loss of personal distinction. If you have union without distinction, you tumble into pantheism, and we would be united to God in such a way as to be completely absorbed into him. There would no longer be a distinct "us" to feel and taste and experience the Trinitarian life.

If you have distinction without union, you end up with deism, where God is just up there watching us from a distance, and we never see our humanity as included in the Trinitarian life. Motherhood and fatherhood, work and play and music then appear to be merely secular, non-divine aspects of our human experience. Deism leaves us with a Christ-less humanity, and forces us to search beyond our humanity for connection with God.

In Trinitarian theology we say "no" to both pantheism and deism. We have union but no loss of personal distinction, which means that we matter and that our humanity, our motherhood and fatherhood, our work and play and music form the arena for our participation in the Trinitarian life of God. The Triune God meets us not in the sky or in our self-generated religions, but in our "ordinary" human existence.

So the gospel is about God knowing us and us knowing God.

BK: Exactly. Let me give you a quick story. I like stories better than long and convoluted theological explanations. Many years ago when my son was six (he's 18 now), I was sitting on the couch in the den sorting through junk mail on a Saturday afternoon. He and his buddy came in and they were decked out in their camouflage, face paint, plastic guns and knives, the whole nine yards. My son peers around the corner of the door and looks at me, and the next thing I know, he comes flying through the air and jumps on me. We start wrestling and horsing around and we end up on the floor. Then his buddy flies into us and all three of us are just like a wad of laughter.

Right in the middle of that event the Lord spoke to me and said to pay attention. I'm thinking, it's Saturday afternoon, your son comes in and you're horsing around on the floor, it happens every day all over the world, so what's the big deal? Then it started to dawn on me that I didn't know who this other kid was. I had never met him. He had never met me. So I re-wound the story and thought about what would have happened if this little boy would have walked into my den alone. Remember, he didn't know me and I didn't know him, and he didn't know my name and I didn't know his name. So he looks over and sees me, a complete stranger, sitting on the couch. Would he fly through the air and engage me in play? Would we end up in a pile of laughter on the floor? Of course not. That is the last thing that would have happened.

Within himself, that little boy had no freedom to have a relationship with me. We were strangers. He had no right to that kind of familiarity and fellowship. But my son knows me. My son knows that I love him and that I accept him and that he's the apple of my eye. So in the knowledge of my love and affection, he did the most natural thing in the world. He dove into my lap. The miracle that happened was that my son's knowledge of my acceptance and delight, and my son's freedom for fellowship with me, rubbed off onto that other little boy. He got to experience it. That other little boy got to taste and feel and know my son's relationship with me. He participated in my son's life and communion with me.

Then it dawned on me that that's what perichoresis and our adoption in Christ mean. Jesus is the one who knows the Father. He knows the Father's love and acceptance. He sees the Father's face. Jesus has freedom for fellowship with his Father. And Jesus shares his heart with us. He puts his own freedom for relationship with his Father in us through the Spirit, and like that little boy we get to taste and feel and experience the relationship Jesus has with his Father. He shares it all with us. He unites himself with us, and we get to experience his divine life with him. He shares with us his own knowledge of his Father's heart, his own knowledge of the Father's acceptance, his own assurance of his Father's love, his own freedom in knowing the Father's passionate heart. He reaches into his own soul, as it were, and pulls out his own emotions, and then puts them inside of the whole human race. We're all included in the Son's relationship with the Father in the fellowship of the Holy Spirit.

Then we never have to worry about whether God accepts us and loves us?

BK: Never. What does the understanding that we are accepted into the mutual indwelling and communion with God remove from our hearts? Fear and hiding. So because of Jesus' knowledge of the Father's acceptance, which he shares with us, we now are free to let go of our racial and personal prejudices, and to love and accept one another, which leads to the freedom to know and be known, which leads to fellowship and mutual indwelling.

This is what the kingdom of the Triune God is all about. The kingdom is simply the life and love, the communion, the fellowship, the camaraderie and joy of the Father, Son and Spirit, being shared with us and coming to full and abiding and personal expression in us, in our relationships with one another and in our relationships with the whole creation, so that the whole earth is full of the Son's knowledge of his Father in the Spirit. As to why we don't experience our life in Christ more fully, that is a question for another day.

C. Baxter Kruger is Director of Perichoresis, Inc.— A Trinitarian Ministry. Dr. Kruger's resources can be accessed at www.perichoresis.org.

THE TRINITY: JUST A DOCTRINE?

Ask ten average Christians in ten average churches to explain the doctrine of the Trinity, and you'll probably get ten different explanations. Most Christians "accept" the Trinity as orthodox Christian doctrine. But they would be at a loss to explain why the doctrine matters, or how it affects their Christian lives.

As Catherine Mowry LaCugna explains in her introduction to *God For Us*, the Trinity is a doctrine that most people "consent to in theory but have little need for in the practice of Christian faith" (Catherine Mowry LaCugna, *God For Us*, p. ix).

LaCugna continues, "On the one hand, the doctrine of the Trinity is supposed to be the center of faith. On the other hand, as Karl Rahner [one of the most influential theologians of the 20th century] once remarked, one could dispense with the doctrine of the Trinity as false and the major part of religious literature could well remain virtually unchanged" (*ibid.,* p. 6).

Does it make any difference?

And no wonder. The doctrine is hard to understand, and most discussions about it are…well… boring. For the average Christian, the kind of people who have families to feed, jobs to get to, and lives to live, what difference does an ancient doctrine make anyway? God is God, isn't he? Isn't that enough? If he happens to be Father, Son and Spirit instead of just Father, well, fine, but that doesn't really change anything from our end, does it?

Actually, it does matter. It matters a lot, in fact—which is exactly what you'd expect us to say since, after all, why else would we be writing an article about an ancient, boring doctrine?

First, let's dispense with going through the biblical proof that the doctrine is correct. You can find that in a later chapter. Instead, let's spend some time talking about why the doctrine of the Trinity matters, and especially, why it matters to you.

Let's start by taking a look at the common idea that God is a single, solitary being "out there" somewhere, looking down on Earth, watching us, judging us. Bette Midler put it to music in the chorus to her tune "From a Distance" with the lyrics, "And God is watching us, God is watching us, God is watching us from a distance."

This God comes in three main flavors: first, vanilla, the one who just kind of wound up the universe and then stretched out in the heavenly gazebo for a few-billion-year nap. (Who knows, maybe he wakes up once in a while and does something nice, like the kind of God George Burns portrayed in the film *Oh God.*) Second, red hot cinnamon, the one who keeps careful tabs on everything everybody does, and since everybody blows it now and then, he gets madder and madder. His worshippers say he takes joy in watching people who offend him slowly roast but never quite get done. Third is apricot, the one who might or might not like you, depending on many things, none of which are all that clear to anybody. He's the one that Oakland Raiders fans pray to for touchdowns.

Sometimes this God comes in an alternate flavor, water balloon. You might think water balloon isn't a flavor, but it is. It's chewy, and the variety of colors is endless, but it always tastes watery. This God is more of an abstract principle than a supreme being, kind of a "spirit of everything" that you can try to get in touch with if you empty your head of all thoughts and sit still long enough without going to sleep. (I think that's where Burger King commercials come from.)

A God who wants to share

The God of the Bible is not like that. The God of the Bible is Father, Son and Holy Spirit—three Persons. (Keep in mind that the Father, Son, and Spirit are not "persons" in the same way we humans are. They are not three Gods, but one, and each "Person" of the Godhead is distinct, but not separate from the others.) These three divine Persons share perfect love, joy, unity, peace, and fellowship. It's important to know that because, when the Bible talks about us being "in Christ," it means that we get to take part in that divine kind of life. Just like Christ is the beloved of the Father, so we too, because we are "in him," are also the beloved of the Father.

That means that you are included in the household of God. It means you're not an outsider or a stranger. You're not even a respected guest. You're one of the kids, beloved of the Father, with free run of the house, the grounds, and the fridge.

The trouble is, you probably have a hard time believing that. You know what you're really like deep down inside, so you think God doesn't like you. How could he, you figure. You don't even like yourself. So based on your assessment of your "goodness/badness" ratio, you determine that God is more than likely mad at you, and *far* more than likely mad at all those other types you meet in traffic every day.

But the whole point of God letting us know through the Scriptures that he is Father, Son and Spirit, and not just "God out there somewhere," is so that we'd know he really does love us and we really are on the ins with him.

And again, how do we know? Because Jesus, you know, "God with us," "God in the flesh," the one the Father sent not to condemn the world but to save it (John 3:17), is the Father's Son, and that means that the Son of God is now one of us. And as one of us, but still God, only God in the flesh now, he dragged the whole bunch of us home to the Father right through the front door.

No, we didn't deserve it and no, we didn't earn it. We didn't even ask for it. But he did it anyway, because that's the exact reason he made us in the first place—so he could share with us the life he has shared eternally with the Father and the Spirit. That's why he tells us he made us in his image (Genesis 1:26).

Showing us the Father

Salvation isn't about a change of location, floating off to some secret set of coordinates in the Delta Quadrant called heaven, as if that would solve all our problems. And it's not about a new super government patrolled by angelic cops who never miss an infraction of the divine penal code.

Salvation is about getting adopted into God's family—and learning how to live in it. And the Trinity is at the heart of it: The Father (Let's get technical—the First Person of the Godhead) loves us so much, in spite of our screw-ups, that he sent the Son (the Second Person of the Godhead) to do everything it took to bring us home (John 1:1, 14), and the Father and the Son sent the Spirit (the Third Person of the Godhead) to live in us, teach us and strengthen us in how to live in God's family so we can enjoy it like we were created to do, instead of being screw-ups forever.

In other words, the God of the Bible is not three separate Gods, where one, the temper-challenged, unpredictable Father, is so furious at humans that he just has to kill somebody in order to calm down, so the sweet, loving Son, seeing Dad about to lose it, steps up and says, "Okay, if you've got to kill someone, then kill me, but spare these people." The doctrine of the Trinity is important precisely because it keeps us from seeing God in such a ridiculous way, and yet, that is how a whole lot of people *do* see God.

If you want to know what the Father is like, just look at Jesus, because Jesus is the perfect revelation of the Father. Jesus told Philip, "Anyone who has seen me has seen the Father" (John 14:9). He told the crowd, "I and the Father are one." We know how the Father feels about us because we know how Jesus feels about us.

To summarize, God is not some isolated cosmic bean counter "out there" keeping tabs on us in preparation for Judgment Day, nor is he three Gods with very different ideas about how to deal with humanity. The God of the Bible is one God who is three divine Persons, in perfect unity and accord, who love each other in perfect love and dwell in indescribable joy, and who created us for the express purpose of sharing that life with them through our adoption into Christ, who is eternally the beloved of his Father.

That's why the doctrine of the Trinity matters. If we don't understand God the way he reveals himself in the Bible, then we wind up with all kinds of messed up, funky and scary ideas about who God is and what he might be cooking up to do to us some day.

Reconciliation for everyone

You're still not convinced, are you? Well, try reading this one again: "…while we were yet sinners Christ died for us" (Romans 5:8). God did not wait for you to get good enough to bring you into his household. You can't get good enough, which is the reason he went after you to bring you home in the first place. When Paul says God saves sinners, he's talking about everybody, since that's what everybody is—a sinner. (By the way, if you're worried God might find out how rotten you really are and send a lightning bolt your way, take heart, he's known all along and loves you anyway.)

Paul makes the point even stronger in verse 10: "For if, when we were God's enemies, we were reconciled to him through the death of his Son, how much more, having been reconciled, shall we be saved through his life!"

Did you notice how Paul puts that reconciliation with God in the past tense? Jesus died for our sins—*past tense*. God does not count our sins against us—*period*. They've already been paid for. Jesus has already put us in good standing with God. All that remains for us now is to turn to God (repent), believe the good news (have faith), and follow Jesus (let the Holy Spirit teach us how to enjoy life in the new creation).

Jesus said, "If anyone would come after me, he must deny himself and take up his cross and follow me." When we think of God in any other way than the way he revealed himself in the Bible—as the Father, Son, and Spirit who created us and redeemed us and have made us to share their joy though union with Jesus Christ—we're going to find these words of Jesus daunting and discouraging.

But when we know God the way he reveals himself, we can say with all assurance of joy, "Therefore, there is no condemnation for those who are in Christ Jesus…" (Romans 8:1). "For God," Paul wrote to the Colossian church, "was pleased to have all his fullness dwell in him [Jesus], and through him to reconcile to himself all things, whether things on earth or things in heaven, by making peace through his blood, shed on the cross" (Colossians 1:19-20).

All humanity is included in that reconciliation, according to Paul. In the doctrine of the Trinity, God has shown himself to be the God who loves the world and who beckons every person to come to Christ and take part in the joy of life in the household of God. There is no person whom God does not want, whom God does not include, whom God does not love. And in Christ, following the Spirit's lead, we are all freed from the chains of sin to come to the Father whose arms are open wide to receive us, if only we will.

That's why the doctrine of the Trinity matters. Without it, we might as well join the Canaanites wondering whether Baal will flood out the crops with storms this year or burn them out with lightning. In Jesus Christ, God has taken up our cause as his own. God has, through the atoning work of Jesus, healed us from head to toe, mind and heart, and made us the Father's Son's best friends, no, much more than that; made us adopted children of the Father, brothers and sisters of our older Brother and full members of the household of God.

With Paul, we can only say, "Thanks be to God for his indescribable gift!"

Key points

1. God created all humans in his image, and he wants all people to share in the love shared by the Father, the Son and the Holy Spirit.
2. The Son became a human, the man Jesus Christ, to reconcile all humanity to God through his birth, life, death and resurrection and ascension. In Christ, humanity is loved and accepted by the Father.
3. Jesus Christ has already paid for our sins, and there is no longer any debt to pay. The Father has already forgiven us, and he eagerly desires that we turn to him.
4. We cannot enjoy the blessing of his love if we don't believe he loves us. We cannot enjoy his forgiveness unless we believe he has forgiven us.
5. When we respond to the Spirit by turning to God, believing the good news, and picking up our cross and following Jesus, the Spirit leads us into the transformed life of the kingdom of God.

J. Michael Feazell

DON'T JUST ACCEPT THE TRINITY

Many years ago, when my denomination was correcting certain longstanding doctrinal errors, I was asked to supervise our churches in Britain. Since we had decided to publish the denominational magazine, we applied to take a display stand at the Christian Resources Exhibition. The prestigious CRE is open to all legitimate churches, charities and distributors of religious products. On the first morning of the conference, a tall, thin, rather severe-looking clergyman made a beeline for us.

"I must say," he said pompously, "that I am surprised to see you people here."

"I don't see why you should be," I answered, "This is the Christian Resources Exhibition and our magazine is a Christian resource. Why shouldn't we be here?"

"Because you're not orthodox," he said imperiously.

"Yes we are," I replied, and reached for a copy of our *Statement of Beliefs*. I had some on hand, suspecting this objection might come up.

"No you are not," he insisted. "You do not accept the Trinity."

"Yes we do — read this." Reluctantly he read the relevant paragraph. It seemed to take the wind out of his sails. But only temporarily.

He handed the document back to me, and said, "That is all very well. But do your people *understand* the Trinity?"

"Do yours?" I asked.

"My people" he said, with a rather smug smile, "don't need to understand it, because we never rejected it." Then he stalked off. I think my comments upset him, but his comments made me think.

Most Christians do not give the Trinity a second thought. It is one of the "givens" of their faith. If you have believed something all your life, you probably take it for granted. But when you come to a belief later, you have to think it through carefully. I had spent many years rejecting the doctrine of the Trinity as an explanation of God's being. It was difficult to abandon my suspicion about it, even though I had to accept that my reasons for rejecting it had no basis in Scripture. I had been taught that it was an idea that had been injected into Christianity by pagans who wanted to distort a true understanding of God. It was humbling to see that, far from trying to hide the truth, the doctrine was formulated in technically precise theological language by devoted Christian scholars who were striving to combat and eliminate some corrosive ideas that could undermine the role of Jesus as Savior.

Okay, so I could see why Trinitarian theology was a litmus test for being accepted as a "legitimate." But it was a fearfully difficult doctrine to use. I am a practical person, and I find analogies helpful. But I could not come up with the perfect analogy that would clarify things sufficiently to put the Trinity to practical use in preaching and teaching.

As the combatant vicar pointed out, most Christians, including many learned and scholarly theologians, haven't needed to do this. They have just accepted the Trinity as part of the historical backdrop of their faith. In doing so, they may have short-changed themselves. Through the ages, however, some prominent theologians have gone beyond just an acceptance of the doctrine, and asked searching questions about what the tri-unity of God *means*. They realized that the doctrine is more than just a useful barrier erected to keep the faith safe from dangerous heresies. They have seen that it highlights foundational biblical concepts that are very exciting and, indeed, quite important for our Christian faith. These are not new ideas, but they have been somewhat neglected, and as such, they are sometimes looked on with suspicion.

They needn't be, for they pose no threat. What they can do is confront you with the real Jesus of the Bible, who is the perfect revelation of his Father, and show you how knowing the Father, the Son and Spirit can blow fresh air through your faith, removing the stale smell of guilt and fear, and transform your everyday life. We have been exploring these ideas. We hope you will share our enthusiasm — and see how the good news of the gospel is even more exciting than you may have thought.

John Halford

IS THE DOCTRINE OF THE TRINITY
IN THE BIBLE?

Some people who reject the Trinity doctrine often claim that the word "Trinity" is not found in Scripture. Of course, there is no verse that says "God is three Persons" or "God is a Trinity." This is all evident and true, but it proves nothing. There are many words and phrases that Christians use, which are not found in the Bible. For example, the word "Bible" is not found in the Bible.

More to the point, opponents of the Trinity doctrine claim that a Trinitarian view of God's nature and being can't be proven from the Bible. Since the books of the Bible are not written as theological tracts, this may seem on the surface to be true. There is no statement in Scripture that says, "God is three Persons in one being, and here is the proof. . ."

However, the New Testament does bring God (Father), the Son (Jesus Christ) and the Holy Spirit together in such a way as to strongly imply the Trinitarian nature of God. Three Scriptures are quoted below as a summary of the various other biblical passages that bring together the three Persons of the Godhead. One Scripture is from the Gospels, another is from the apostle Paul and a third is from the apostle Peter. The words in each passage referring to each of the three Persons are italicized to emphasize their Trinitarian implication:

- All authority in heaven and on earth has been given to me. Therefore go and make disciples of all nations, baptizing them in the name [singular] of the *Father* and of the *Son* and of the *Holy Spirit* [Matthew 28:19].

- May the grace of the *Lord Jesus Christ*, and the love of *God*, and the fellowship of the *Holy Spirit* be with you all [2 Corinthians 13:14].

- To God's elect. . .who have been chosen according to the foreknowledge of *God the Father*, through the sanctifying work of *the Spirit*, for obedience to *Jesus Christ* and sprinkling by his blood [1 Peter 1:1-2].

Here are three passages in Scripture, one on the lips of Jesus, and the other two from leading apostles, each bringing together the three Persons of the Godhead in an unmistakable way. But these are only a sampling of other similar passages. Among others are the following: Romans 14:17-18; 15:16;1 Corinthians 2:2-5; 6:11; 12:4-6; 2 Corinthians 1:21-22; Galatians 4:6;

Ephesians 2:18-22; 3:14-19; Ephesians 4:4-6; Colossians 1:6-8; 1Thessa-
lonians 1:3-5; 2 Thessalonians 2:13-14; Titus 3:4-6. The reader is encouraged
to read each of these passages and note how God (Father), Son (Jesus Christ)
and the Holy Spirit are brought together as instruments of our salvation.

Such passages show that the New Testament faith is implicitly Trinitarian.
It's true that none of these passages say directly that "God is a Trinity. . ." or
"This is the Trinitarian doctrine. . ." But they don't need to. As mentioned
above, the books of the New Testament are not formal, point-by-point
treatises of doctrine. Nonetheless, these and other Scriptures speak easily and
without any self-consciousness of God (Father), Son (Jesus) and Holy Spirit
working together as one. The writers show no feeling of strangeness in
joining these divine Persons together as a unity in their salvific work.
Systematic theologian Alister E. McGrath makes this point in his book
Christian Theology:

> The foundations of the doctrine of the Trinity are to be found in
> the pervasive pattern of divine activity to which the New Testament
> bears witness…. There is the closest of connections between the
> Father, Son, and Spirit in the New Testament writings. Time after
> time, New Testament passages link together these three elements as
> part of a greater whole. The totality of God's saving presence and
> power can only, it would seem, be expressed by involving all three
> elements…[page 248].

Such New Testament Scriptures answer the charge that the Trinity
doctrine was only developed well into the church age and that it reflects
"pagan" ideas, and not biblical ones. If we look at Scripture with an open
mind regarding what it says about the being we call God, it's clear that he is
shown to be Triune in nature. The Bible reveals that the Father is God, Jesus
the Son is God, and the Holy Spirit is God, and yet the Bible also insists that
this is only one God. These biblical teachings led the early church to
formulate the doctrine of the Trinity.

We can confidently say that the Trinity, as a truth regarding God's
essential being, has always been a reality. Perhaps it was not completely clear
in antiquity, including even in the Old Testament. But the Incarnation of the
Son of God and the coming of the Holy Spirit revealed that God was Triune.
This revelation was made in *concrete fact*, in that the Son and the Holy Spirit
broke into our world at definite points in history. The fact of the Triune
revelation of God in historical time was only later described in the word of
God we call the New Testament.

James R. White, a Christian apologist, says in his book *The Forgotten Trinity*:

"The Trinity is a doctrine not revealed merely in words but instead in the very action of the Triune God in redemption itself! We know who God *is* by what He has *done* in bringing us to himself!" (page 167).

Paul Kroll

DOES THE DOCTRINE OF THE TRINITY TEACH THREE GODS?

Some people take issue with the use of the word "Person" in the doctrine of the Trinity when the word is applied to the Father, Son and Holy Spirit. They wrongly assume that the doctrine of the Trinity inadvertently teaches that three Gods exist. Their reasoning goes something like this: If God the Father is a "Person," then he is a God in his own right (having the characteristics of being divine). He would count as "one" God. The same could be said about the Son and Holy Spirit. Thus, there would be three separate Gods.

The Trinity doctrine has the opposite intent – to preserve the biblical witness to the oneness of God's Being, yet at the same time accounting for the divinity of the Father, Son and the Spirit. When we speak of God's divine nature, we must not confuse tritheism with the Trinity or think of "persons" as we do in the human sphere. What the Trinity says is that God is one with respect to his essence but is three with respect to the internal distinctions within his Triunity.

Here is how Christian scholar Emery Bancroft described it in his book *Christian Theology*, pages 87-88:

> The Father is not God as such; for God is not only Father, but also Son and Holy Spirit. The term Father designates that personal distinction in the divine nature in virtue of which God is related to the Son and, through the Son and the Spirit, to the church.
>
> The Son is not God as such; for God is not only Son, but also Father and Holy Spirit. The Son designates that distinction in virtue of which God is related to the Father, and is sent by the Father to redeem the world, and with the Father sends the Holy Spirit.
>
> The Holy Spirit is not God as such; for God is not only Holy Spirit, but also Father and Son. The Holy Spirit designates that distinction in virtue of which God is related to the Father and the Son, and is sent by them to accomplish the work of renewing the ungodly and sanctifying the church.

When we are seeking to understand the Trinity doctrine, we need to be careful how we use and understand the word "God." For example, whatever the New Testament says about the oneness of God, it also draws a distinction between Jesus Christ and God the Father. This is where the above formula from Bancroft is helpful. To be precise, we should speak of "God the

Father," "God the Son" and "God the Holy Spirit" when we are referring to each hypostasis or "Person" of the one God.

There are limitations of using the word "person" when explaining the nature of God. Do we really understand how God can be one in Being and three in Person? We have no experiential knowledge of God as he is. Not only is our experience limited, but so is our language. Using the word "Persons" for each of the three hypostases of God is in some ways a compromise. But, when speaking of God's nature, we need a word that emphasizes his personalness in relationship to us human creatures and within himself, and yet carries with it the concept of distinctiveness. "Person" is the most appropriate word we have in the English language to do this.

Unfortunately, the word "person" also contains the notion of separateness when used of human persons. How can we deal with this? We understand that God does not consist of the kind of persons that a group of human beings do. Human persons are separate from each other and have separate wills because they only have external relations with each other, while the Persons of God have internal relations and share the same essence.

The Trinity doctrine uses the word "Person" for each hypostasis of God because it is a personal word, and God is a personal being in his dealings with us. Only a personal being can love, and love is the defining essence of God, according to the biblical witness (1 John 4:8; John 3:16; 15:9-10)

The word "persons" distinguishes between the three Persons of God and the one Being of God in the sense that the three Persons constitute his one Being. Thus, the doctrine preserves both the biblical revelation that there is but one God and no other, as well as its testimony that the Father, the Son and the Spirit are all equally divine and true God of true God.

Those who reject the Trinitarian explanation of God's nature are in a quandary. If they reject the theology of the Trinity, they have no explanation that preserves two biblical truths about God's Being: God is One Being and also he is plural in his Being. If they accept the biblical fact that Jesus is divine, they need some way of explaining that God is one, yet has more than one Person.

That is why Christians formulated the doctrine in precise technical language – so that we could rightly speak of God, according to the witness he has left us of himself through Christ and in the Spirit, as attested to by the New Testament. The church confesses the biblical testimony that God is one divine Being. But Christians also confess that Jesus Christ and the Holy Spirit are divine, true God of true God, according to the New Testament.

The Trinity doctrine was developed with the intent of explaining, as well as human words and thought would allow, the reality that God has existed from eternity both as One Being and yet as three Persons. The Trinity doctrine says that God is one and that in his oneness he is Triune.

Explanations of the nature of God other than the Trinity have been put forth throughout the history of the Church. Arianism is one example. This theory claimed that the Son was a created being. The Arians thought they had preserved the oneness of God in their explanation, but created a heresy that did not rightly speak of God's nature. The Arian conclusion was fundamentally flawed in that if the Son was a created being, he would not be divine, of the same essence of God, and therefore, could not be our Savior and could not be worshipped. Only God can save us and make us new creations. All other theories advanced to explain God's nature in terms of the revelation of the Son and Holy Spirit have proved equally unfaithful to the gospel and the nature of God.

On the other hand, the Trinitarian explanation takes into consideration the divinity of the Father, the Son and Holy Spirit – and the biblical truth that there is only one God. That's why the doctrine of the Trinity has survived for centuries as the explanation of God's nature that preserves the truth of the biblical witness of who God is – and that he has saved us in himself through the Son and in the Spirit.

Paul Kroll

THE TRINITY: 1 + 1 + 1 = 1 ?

It Just Doesn't Add Up

The Father is God, and the Son is God, and the Holy Spirit is God, but there is only one God. "Wait a minute," some people say. "One plus one plus one equals one? This can't be right. It just doesn't add up."

True, it doesn't add up—and it's not supposed to. God isn't a thing that can be added. There can be only one all-powerful, all-wise, everywhere-present being, so there can be only one God. In the world of spirit, the Father, Son, and Holy Spirit are God, unified in a way that material objects cannot be. Our math is based on material things; it does not always work in the infinite, spiritual realm.

The Father is God and the Son is God, but there is only one God being. This is not a family or committee of divine beings—a group cannot say, "There is none like me" (Isaiah 43:10; 44:6; 45:5). God is only one divine being—more than one Person, but only one God. The early Christians did not get this idea from paganism or philosophy—they were led to it by statements in Scripture.

Just as Scripture teaches that Jesus Christ is divine, it also teaches that the Holy Spirit is divine and personal. Whatever the Holy Spirit does, God does. The Holy Spirit, like the Son and the Father, is God—three Persons perfectly united in one God: the Trinity.

Michael Morrison

HOW MANY GODS DOES GOD SAY THERE ARE?

Scriptures that show there is only one God

Some Bible passages are difficult to understand. Others are easy. The Bible has many plain, simple, straightforward, unambiguous verses, and these are the verses we should study first when we want to understand what the Bible teaches. Understanding the plain, straightforward verses then becomes our basis for understanding the more difficult verses. The plain verses become the foundation for the rest of our biblical understanding. We build on those.

By building such a foundation, we have something to go back to when we have difficulty understanding other verses. We can take the "difficult" verses and explain them within the context of the plain, straightforward ones. This assures us that our explanations and understanding conform with the foundational verses.

Rather than throw out or ignore those simple, straightforward verses, we should throw out the explanations that contradict them. In theological terms, this is the correct exegetical approach.

The Bible proclaims plainly and clearly that there is one and only one God. When the Bible says that God is one, the word *one* does not refer to a "God Family," but to one God. Let's begin by looking at passages in the Old Testament.

Old Testament verses

Deuteronomy 4:35: "You were shown these things so that you might know that the Lord is God; besides him there is no other."

Deuteronomy 4:39: "Acknowledge and take to heart this day that the Lord is God in heaven above and on the earth below. There is no other."

Deuteronomy 6:4-5: "Hear, O Israel: The Lord our God, the Lord is one. Love the Lord your God with all your heart and with all your soul and with all your strength."

Deuteronomy 32:39: "See now that I myself am He! There is no god besides me."

1 Samuel 2:1-2: "There is no one holy like the Lord; there is no one besides you; there is no Rock like our God."

2 Samuel 7:22: "How great you are, O Sovereign Lord! There is no one like you, and there is no God but you, as we have heard with our own ears."

2 Samuel 22:32: "For who is God besides the Lord? And who is the Rock except our God?"

1 Kings 8:60: "So that all the peoples of the earth may know that the Lord is God and that there is no other."

2 Kings 19:15-19: "Hezekiah prayed to the Lord: 'O Lord, God of Israel, enthroned between the cherubim, you alone are God over all the kingdoms of the earth. You have made heaven and earth. Give ear, O Lord, and hear; open your eyes, O Lord, and see; listen to the words Sennacherib has sent to insult the living God. It is true, O Lord, that the Assyrian kings have laid waste these nations and their lands. They have thrown their gods into the fire and destroyed them, for they were not gods but only wood and stone, fashioned by men's hands. Now, O Lord our God, deliver us from his hand, so that all kingdoms on earth may know that you alone, O Lord, are God.'...''

Psalm 18:30-31: "As for God, his way is perfect; the word of the Lord is flawless.... For who is God besides the Lord? And who is the Rock except our God?"

Psalm 83:18: "Let them know that you, whose name is the Lord — that you alone are the Most High over all the earth."

Isaiah 43:10, 13: "'You are my witnesses,' declares the Lord, 'and my servant whom I have chosen, so that you may know and believe me and understand that I am he. Before me no god was formed, nor will there be one after me. I, even I, am the Lord, and apart from me there is no savior.... Yes, and from ancient days I am he. No one can deliver out of my hand. When I act, who can reverse it?'"

Isaiah 44:6-8: "This is what the Lord says — Israel's King and Redeemer, the Lord Almighty: I am the first and I am the last; apart from me there is no God. Who then is like me? Let him proclaim it. Let him declare and lay out before me what has happened since I established my ancient people, and what is yet to come — yes, let him foretell what will come. Do not tremble, do not be afraid. Did I not proclaim this and foretell it long ago? You are my witnesses. Is there any God besides me? No, there is no other Rock; I know not one."

Isaiah 45:5-6: "I am the Lord, and there is no other; apart from me there is no God. I will strengthen you, though you have not acknowledged me, so that from the rising of the sun to the place of its setting men may know there is none besides me. I am the Lord, and there is no other."

Isaiah 45:18: "This is what the Lord says — he who created the heavens, he is God; he who fashioned and made the earth, he founded it; he did not create it to be empty, but formed it to be inhabited — he says: 'I am the Lord, and there is no other.'"

Isaiah 45:21-22: "Declare what is to be, present it — let them take counsel together. Who foretold this long ago, who declared it from the distant past? Was it not I, the Lord? And there is no God apart from me, a righteous God and a Savior; there is none but me."

Isaiah 46:9: "Remember the former things, those of long ago; I am God, and there is no other; I am God, and there is none like me."

As you can see, there is no question about the biblical fact that there is one and only one God, not two or more "Gods." God speaks in the singular, as "I," saying that he is the only God, and there is no other being that is even like him. That's why God commands us, "You shall have no other gods before me" (Exodus 20:3).

The idea of more than one being in a family of gods is condemned throughout the Scriptures. That was precisely the concept that the polytheistic nations surrounding Israel taught. Polytheistic is a word that refers to a belief in more than one god (*poly* = many; *theos* = god). The Bible teaches that there is only one God, a belief called monotheism, from *mono* (one) and *theos* (God).

A family is made up of more than one being. The pagan hierarchies of gods were made up of more than one "god being," and at the top of the hierarchy were usually a father god, a mother god and one or more son and daughter gods. The Bible condemns the concept of a family of gods.

New Testament

The Bible does not allow for the existence of two God Beings. It categorically denies it. Let's take a look at some New Testament passages.

Matthew 19:17: "'Why do you ask me about what is good?' Jesus replied. 'There is only One who is good.'" The parallel verse in Mark is 10:18: "'Why do you call me good?' Jesus answered. 'No one is good — except God alone.'"

Jesus quoted Deuteronomy 6:4 when he affirmed that there is one God. Answering the question about what is the greatest commandment, he said: "The most important one...is this: 'Hear, O Israel, the Lord our God, the Lord is one'" (Mark 12:29).

Mark 12:32-34: "'Well said, teacher,' the man replied. 'You are right in saying that God is one and there is no other but him. To love him with all your heart, with all your understanding and with all your strength, and to love your neighbor as yourself is more important than all burnt offerings and sacrifices.' When Jesus saw that he had answered wisely, he said to him, 'You are not far from the kingdom of God.'"

There is no other being that is worthy of worship (Matthew 4:10).

John 5:42-44: "I have come in my Father's name, and you do not accept me: but if someone else comes in his own name, you will accept him. How can you believe if you accept praise from one another, yet make no effort to obtain the praise that comes from the only God?"

John 17:3: "This is eternal life: that they may know you, the only true God, and Jesus Christ, whom you have sent."

Likewise, Paul taught that there is one God. He wrote:

Romans 3:29-30: "Is God the God of Jews only? Is he not the God of Gentiles too? Yes, of Gentiles too, since there is only one God."

Romans 16:27: "To the only wise God be glory forever through Jesus Christ! Amen."

1 Corinthians 8:4-6: "So then, about eating food sacrificed to idols: We know that an idol is nothing at all in the world, and that there is no God but one. For even if there are so-called gods, whether in heaven or on earth (as indeed there are many 'gods' and many 'lords'), yet for us there is but one God, the Father, from whom all things came and for whom we live; and there is but one Lord, Jesus Christ, through whom all things came and through whom we live."

Galatians 3:19-20: "The law was put into effect through angels by a mediator. A mediator, however, does not represent just one party; but God is one."

Ephesians 4:6: "One God and Father of all, who is over all and through all and in all."

1 Timothy 1:17: "Now to the King eternal, immortal, invisible, the only God, be honor and glory for ever and ever. Amen."

1 Timothy 2:5: "For there is one God and one mediator between God and men, the man Christ Jesus." Even while describing the role of Jesus Christ, who was God in the flesh, Paul still affirmed that there is only one God. When the Son became flesh, he did not cease to be God — he was God in the flesh (John 1:1, 14). But there was not, never has been, never will be, two Gods.

1 Timothy 6:13-16: "In the sight of God, who gives life to everything, and of Christ Jesus, who while testifying before Pontius Pilate made the good confession, I charge you to keep this commandment without spot or blame until the appearing of our Lord Jesus Christ, which God will bring about in his own time — God, the blessed and only Ruler, the King of kings and Lord of lords, who alone is immortal and who lives in unapproachable light, whom

no one has seen or can see."

James wrote: "You believe that there is one God. Good! Even the demons believe that — and shudder" (2:19).

James 4:12: "There is only one Lawgiver and Judge, the one who is able to save and destroy."

Jude 25: "To the only God our Savior be glory, majesty, power and authority, through Jesus Christ our Lord, before all ages, now and forevermore!"

Contradictory truths?

The Bible gives us two facts that (on the surface) look contradictory. But they only *appear* to be contradictory because our minds are finite and limited, while God, our Creator, is infinite and unlimited. The Bible tells us there is one God. The Father is God. The Son is also God (John 20:28-29). He was eternally with God and also was God (John 1:1-2). The Father is God and the Son is God, but there is only one God. God is one in one respect, but plural in another respect.

The early church explained this by saying that God is one in *being,* but plural in *persons.* This is part of the Christian doctrine usually called the doctrine of the Trinity. This doctrine does not teach plural Gods, but only one. They are distinct, but not separate. There is no "family" of Gods.

God *has* a family (we are his children), but he is not a family in himself. People cannot be born into the "God family," because there is no such thing. We will never be God in the same way that God is God. Rather, we are partakers of the divine nature (2 Peter 1:4) — children of God, but never Gods. We are children by adoption, but in essence or being. We will always remain created beings. There can be only one God. We are born into God's family, but not the God family. We belong to God, but we will never be God,

This is not a matter of confusion, as some say. It is a matter of believing the Bible and realizing that God is greater than our finite imaginations can perceive. It is a matter of faith, because we believe the Bible.

The "average" Protestant or Catholic cannot explain God's nature. Some may even think that there are three God Beings in one Godhead, or a three-headed Being of some sort. But their misunderstandings do not affect the truth of the teaching. The Bible teaching is that there is one God who is the Father, the Son, and the Holy Spirit. It is not my idea, nor is it the idea of some fourth-century theologians. It is the teaching of the Bible.

The fourth-century theologians formulated a doctrine that denies certain unbiblical teachings about God that were in vogue at the time. One such teaching was the idea that the Son was a created being. Another heresy is the idea that the Father, the Son, and the Holy Spirit are not distinct but are really all the same — in other words, the idea that the one God is sometimes the Father, sometimes the Son, and sometimes the Holy Spirit, but not all three all the time. This was declared to be false.

God is not like a human

God transcends our world of time and space. He created time and space. He appears in it when he desires, but he is in no way limited to time and space. He does not need time and space to exist. However, we are able to think only in terms of creation, in terms of time and space. God is everything we can conceive of, but much more! He uses all sorts of concepts in the Bible to reveal himself to us, and he does it in terms we can understand — like King, Redeemer, Shepherd, Defender, Fire, Rock, Shelter. He is all those and more, and not just like any of them, because they are all part of the created world.

God does not have or need a "mighty arm," for example. God uses the human term, "mighty arm," because it is one we can understand, one that helps us understand something important about the power of God. But it is not a literal description of God. It is a metaphor.

God also speaks of his "right hand." Is that because his "right hand" is stronger or more skilled than his "left hand"? Of course not. He is conveying the fact that he is powerful, that he intends to do a particular thing, and that he is going to do it in a powerful way. Bible-believers should not take such descriptions literally and think of God as subject to time and space like ourselves.

This brings to mind Paul's statement in Romans 1:22-23: "Although they claimed to be wise, they became fools and exchanged the glory of the immortal God for images made to look like mortal man and birds and animals and reptiles." There are stone images, and there are mental images.

None of us would want to make God like a created thing, but if we think that God has a body (a male body, some will attest), or is subject to time and space (who can only be in only one place at one time), and needs to have something in order to create (that he needs a preexisting "substance"), just like we need physical matter to fashion things, then we have inadvertently reduced God to an "image made to look like mortal man."

God is not created. He does not have a body. Bodies are put together or composed, and God is neither put together nor composed of anything. He is the Creator, not the created. Until God created, there was nothing. Only God is eternal. Only God is uncreated. There is no eternal matter or "spiritual substance" that co-existed with God. That would mean that God did not create everything, and such a God is not the God of the Bible. Such a God is a limited God, a less-than-supreme God, a God who needs something beside himself to act as God.

One other important point. God is personal — and he relates to us in a personal way. We should never think of God as so transcendent, so unlike us, that we cannot relate to him in a personal way. That is precisely why he reveals himself to us in the Bible in human terms, in terms we can understand. That is why the Son of God became human to reconcile us to God. God wants a close and personal relationship with us. He wants fellowship with us. That is the reason he made us, and he has made it possible (despite our sin) through our mediator, the God-made-human Jesus Christ.

Ralph Orr and Paul Kroll

IS GOD A FAMILY?

I'm sometimes asked why we do not refer to God as a "family." Isn't that term appropriate, given that there is a Father and a Son who are bringing "many sons to glory"? My answer is that whereas the analogy of God as a family works at some levels, we must be very careful because it can lead in directions that distort the biblical revelation of the one God who is Father, Son and Holy Spirit.

The analogy of God as a family can be used in a limited way to indicate that just as there are relationships between family members, there are relationships in the triune God. However this analogy is easily misunderstood as indicating that just as in a family there are separate persons who each have their own being, so God is made up of persons with separate beings.

But that is not the case. What is true of human relationships in families is not necessarily true of God, who is not a creature. While there is a triune relationship within God's one being, that relationship is not between separate beings. The three "persons" of the Trinity, through their absolutely unique relationships, constitute the one being of God in a way that is quite unlike a human family.

The uncreated God cannot be explained in terms of a created human family. Trying to do so amounts to mythology and even idolatry.

Most of us probably are familiar with the Hebrew word *Elohim*. It is one of several names used for God in the Old Testament. Some people claim that *Elohim* is a "uniplural" noun—like the noun "family." Following this line of reasoning, they erroneously conclude that there are two separate Gods (Father and Son), comprising a "God family."

From the Akkadians and Egyptians to the Greeks and Romans, pagan religions have taught a plurality (pantheon or family) of gods. The Greeks even constructed a family tree for their pantheon.[1] This pagan conception is known as polytheism (many gods, like the pantheon of Egyptian gods pictured below), or bitheism or ditheism in the case of two gods.

In contrast to the polytheistic misconceptions of paganism, God revealed himself to Israel as one (single, exclusive) God. He commanded his people: "You shall have no other gods before me" (Exodus 20:3). "Before me" is literally, "before my face"—a Hebrew idiom meaning "beside me" or "in addition to me."[2] Though *Elohim* is a plural noun, it was never understood as a reference to many gods, and certainly not a reference to a family of gods.

The pantheon of gods in pagan religions ruled the realm of the gods, the supernatural and, ultimately, the human world. Typically one of these gods was designated head of the pantheon and, like the other gods, would have at least one consort (female partner). But God forbade Israel to think of him in these polytheistic and sexual terms. Yahweh definitely is not the head of a pantheon. He has no consort. There are no other gods in his presence.[3] Therefore, Moses proclaimed: "Hear, O Israel, the LORD [*Yahweh*] our God [*Elohim*], the LORD [*Yahweh*] is one" (Deuteronomy 6:4).

Old Testament Hebrew does not support the idea of a "God family." The nouns used for God's names and titles are coupled with singular verbs. For example, it is said in Genesis 2:7 that "the Lord [*Yahweh*—a singular noun] God [*Elohim*—a plural noun] formed [a singular verb] a man from the dust of the ground." Though *Elohim* is a plural noun, the Bible almost always couples it with a singular verb.

Note, however, that while emphasizing the unity and uniqueness of one God, *Elohim* does allow for the idea of a plurality of persons in the one Godhead. We see this hinted at in Genesis 1:2, 26: "Now the earth was formless and empty, darkness was over the surface of the deep, and the Spirit of God was hovering over the waters…. Then God said, 'Let us make mankind in our image, in our likeness…'" This rich linguistic character of *Elohim* is found only in Hebrew and in no other Semitic languages—not even in Biblical Aramaic.[4]

Note also that, as is true in the English language, Hebrew has both singular and plural nouns. However, quite unlike English, Hebrew is able to specify singular, dual and plural meanings for nouns. [5] For example, in the Old Testament, God is named *Eloah* (a singular noun) 57 times; he is named *Elohim* (a plural noun referring to three or more) 2570 times; and he is named *Elohiam* (a plural noun referring to two) exactly zero times.

The nature and usage of the plural noun *Elohim* in biblical Hebrew, taken together with the singular verbs that are coupled with it, while allowing for the possibility of some kind of plurality in God, does not allow for separate beings who make up a pantheon (family) of gods. When we add to this the Old Testament's emphatic teaching that there is only one God, it becomes clear that our former teaching that God is a family of two separate Gods is not biblical. Even though the Hebrew Scriptures hint at a plurality of persons in the Godhead, the notion of there being two separate "god beings" is ditheism (a form of polytheism)—a belief expressly prohibited by God himself.

God is one being with a plurality of what we refer to as divine "persons." This is why I say we should be very careful in saying that "God is a family." The truth about the nature of God, which is only hinted at in the Old

Testament, is revealed to us fully by Jesus Christ. Given that revelation, we can say with confidence that the Father, Son and Holy Spirit live in a loving, eternal relationship as one Triune God—a relationship in which, by grace, we have been included.

1 See chart at en.wikipedia.org/wiki/Family_tree_of_the_Greek_gods.

2 H.D. Spence. *The Pulpit Commentary: Exodus Vol. II.* Logos Systems, S. 131.

3 Victor H. Matthews; Mark W. Chavalas; John H. Walton. *The IVP Bible Background Commentary: Old Testament.* Ex 20:3.

4 Gustav Oehler, *Theology of the Old Testament,* 88.

5 E. Kautzch, ed., *Gesenius' Hebrew Grammar*, 244.

Joseph Tkach

DOES ELOHIM REFER TO A FAMILY OF DIVINE BEINGS?

The word *elohim* can refer to the true God, to a false god, to angels, and to human beings. In its wide application, this name is unusual and difficult to translate into English. The ability of this word to refer correctly to God, angels, humans, and false gods can be understood only if the root of the word is kept in mind. The root means somewhat like the "powers that be," whether they are human or divine, singular or plural. In this light, it becomes clear that the Hebrews applied the name *elohim* to the true God because it conveyed one of his attributes – that of power.

When *elohim* refers to a singular being (the true God or a false god), it takes a singular verb. When it refers to more than one being, as in the heavenly powers (the angels or God and the angels) or in the human powers (the judges), it takes a plural verb. The one form can be either singular or plural, and its meaning is indicated by whether the verb is in a singular or a plural form. In no case does the word *elohim* refer to a family of beings, whether they are human or divine. The following passages are sufficient to make the use of this word clear.

God (*elohim*) created

In Genesis 1:1 *elohim* takes the singular verb *bara,* which means "he created." The verb tells us what was done by the one God. Even with this point in mind, the objection can be raised that collective nouns in English (church, nation, etc.) take singular verbs. That answer will not do, in this case, because one needs to ascertain first that *elohim* is such a word. It cannot simply be assumed to be so. It is not obvious in Hebrew, and no authority on the Hebrew language has ever said such a thing. The voice of scholarship has been united on this point, that *elohim,* when speaking of the Creator, refers to a single deity. The use of the word in the Old Testament is ample testimony of this truth, as the following examples show.

Greater than all the gods (*elohim*)

Exodus 18:11 compares the true God with all the false gods (*elohim*) and says that none of them is like him. This is clearly a plural reference, yet it does not refer to a family of beings. The false gods to which Exodus refers were not considered to be members of one family.

Ashtoreth the goddess (*elohim*)

1 Kings 11:5 is one of the clearest examples of the singular use of *elohim* in which it cannot possibly be construed to refer to a family of divine beings. "Ashtoreth the goddess (*elohim*) of the Sidonians" was but only one deity, not a family of such beings.

Lower than the angels (*elohim*)

Psalm 8:5 says that God made humans a little lower than the angels (*elohim*). Since all the angels were created beings, there are no father angels, mother angels, or offspring angels. Angels do not marry. This use of *elohim* is not in the context of a family.

Bring him to the judges (*elohim*)

Exodus 21:6 is a law regarding Hebrew slaves. If freed slaves expressed a desire to continue to serve their masters, they were to be brought before "the judges [*elohim*]," who would make it official. The judges were an institution of Israel and did not constitute a family.

The above passages may be enough to indicate that the word *elohim* – in its reference to God, angels, judges, and false gods – is not a collective noun; it is not like "church," "nation," etc. The concept of a divine family of beings is not applicable to the true God, and did not arise out of the Holy Scriptures. It may be helpful to note some reasons why this concept is inappropriate.

The names "Father" and "Son" indicate a family relationship. (We can omit reference to the Holy Spirit, in this light, because the name "Holy Spirit" does not immediately suggest a family relationship.) This is acceptable – and biblically sound. The error creeps into the concept when the relationship is understood in terms of separate beings. The following explanation will make this easier to understand.

In a human family, a father and a son are two beings. One is the father because he existed while the son was not yet born. The father provides for the son, because the son needs his help. Human beings are limited beings. They have a beginning, they have needs, and the father-son relationship is meaningful in light of these limitations.

It is a gross misunderstanding to think of God in such terms. God is spirit. He has no limitations in space or time. The Son did not have a beginning, and at no time did the Father exist while the Son did not. Neither is it true that the Father looked after a young Son during some childhood, or provided for the Son's "needs." We should not form our concepts of God based on what human fathers and sons are.

The book of Hebrews speaks of the Son in various ways. He is referred to as a Son, as the "brightness of his glory," and as the "express image of his person." These are three ways of expressing the same idea. As the Son is God, he has no needs, and he is not in the same relationship to the Father that a human son is to his parent.

The names "Father" and "Son" are applied to God by analogy, without the limitations that hold true in a human family. This is another way of saying that God is not a family (for that word has meaning only in the context of limited human beings). God is infinite, eternal, and in all ways unlimited. The attempt to make *elohim* refer to a family of divine beings is not only impossible historically, linguistically and culturally; it is theologically wrong and inappropriate in the discussion of the true God.

IS ELOHIM A PLURAL WORD?

People will occasionally read statements to the effect that the Hebrew word *elohim* is plural, as can be seen from the ending *-im*. The thought behind this claim is that this plural form indicates that there is plurality in the Godhead. Some conclude that the biblical references to a Father and a Son are a biblical way of supporting the idea that God is a family of divine beings headed by the Father.

Is the form *elohim* plural? So long as the question is about the *form,* the answer is yes. That, however, does not mark the end of the relevant questions that should be asked. There is a second important question to be answered, about the meaning of the word. Is the *sense* of the word *elohim* plural? The answer is that it is not.

All languages make a distinction between the form and the sense of a word. In English, the word "put" has one form. This form is made up of three specific letters laid out in a particular order, but the senses or meanings of that form are many. "Put" may mean the act of placing something in a particular location (in the present tense). It may mean the act of having already placed something in a particular location (in the past tense). It may mean an entirely different kind of act, such as a ship's sailing into a port or harbor. Moreover, "put" can take a singular construction or a plural one (he put, or they put). The person who knows English is not confused when the same form is used with different senses. Neither is the Hebrew speaker confused by the one form and the different senses of *elohim.*

Those who argue the nature of God from the fact that *elohim* is a plural form make a fundamental mistake. They are under the impression that it is the form of this word that determines its sense! No English speaker would insist that the form of "put" be the guideline in determining its sense. Neither is that possible in Hebrew. That would generate confusion. In Genesis 1:1, for example, to take *elohim* as plural in sense would distort the Hebrew text for the following reason:

The English verb "created" has the same form in the singular and in the plural. The sense, however, is clearly seen when a pronoun is attached (he created, or they created). In Hebrew, the singular and plural of this verb are two different forms. Genesis 1:1 uses the singular form (*bara,* "he created"). This verb, then, prevents the interpreter from considering only the form of Hebrew noun. The noun is plural in form, but the verb is singular in form, telling the reader that both the noun and the verb are singular in meaning.

One must look at the sense, or else a wrong interpretation will be attached to the verse. In the Hebrew text of Genesis 1:1, both the form and the sense of the verb "created" are singular. There is no possibility of a different understanding of that verb. By itself, it means "he created."

Those who propose the idea of a family of divine beings acknowledge that the verb is in the singular number and that its form and sense are singular. But they dismiss this detail by saying that there are instances (in English, for example) in which a singular verb accompanies a collective noun (a family is, a nation is, etc.). This move is in error, because it presupposes (it starts with the premise) that the name "God" stands for a group of beings. Thus a new, third, relevant question must be asked: Does the word "God" refer to a group of divine beings? The Jews say, "Of course not. That is preposterous." The Muslims say the same, and the Christians traditionally have held the same view as the Jews and Muslims.

The advocates of "family of divine beings" acknowledge that such a concept is preposterous to Jews, Muslims, and Christians, but they see that as an indication of the error in which these religions are steeped. For traditional Christianity, the attack is leveled at the church councils. The claim is made that such councils were the devil's playground, because the only thing that seemed to matter was what people thought, not what God's word teaches.

This approach to the subject invites a fourth relevant question regarding the family of God. How do the advocates of a family of God beings proceed to establish that God's word, the Bible, means a group of divine beings when it uses the word *elohim*? Their answer is that this is a plural form. But, as explained above, a plural form does not necessarily suggest a plural sense. This is where the fundamental mistake lies.

There is one more question: How did a reference to the true God end up as a plural form? Since the question is about the form, it is a question about the Hebrew language. It is not about the nature of God. Even so, the answer is not difficult to understand. Hebrew has its own characteristics as a language. Among these is the way in which it expresses might, authority, and reverence. An example from the Old Testament may make the point clear.

In Exodus 4:16, Moses is told that Aaron would be to him for a mouth, while he would be for a god (*elohim*) to Aaron. The form of *elohim* is plural, yet Moses was clearly one person — not a group or family of beings. This is sufficient to indicate that a distinction that must be drawn between the form and the sense of a word. Second, Moses was to be like *elohim* to Aaron only in the sense that he would be in a position of more authority and respect. The same expression is used in 7:1, where Moses is told that he would be like *elohim* to Pharaoh.

These examples show that *elohim* has a singular sense, despite its form. In order to understand how the form arose, one needs to examine the development of linguistic forms that the Israelites inherited from those who spoke Semitic languages before them. In polytheistic societies such as those of the Canaanites, Amorites, Egyptians, etc., a plural reference to the gods would be standard, and hardly out of place. As the language undergoes changes in a monotheistic society such as Israel, it is natural that older forms would be used with new senses.

For example, in English, the form of the word "conversation" has remained unchanged since the days of the King James Bible, but the sense of this word has changed to suggest speaking, rather than conduct. The reasons for the semantic shift are to be found in a detailed study of the way the language developed under certain internal and external influences. This is a linguistic project, whether the focus is on an English word like "conversation," or a Hebrew word like *elohim*. Just as the form of the word "conversation" does not bring to mind a person's conduct, so with *elohim;* it does not bring to mind any concept of polytheism, and there is no discrepancy with the consistent rejection of polytheism throughout the Scriptures.

YOU CAN PROVE WHAT ELOHIM MEANS

In Genesis 1:26, God says, "Let us make man in our image." "Let us...." Does this mean that there is more than one God? Some say yes. They say that the Hebrew word *elohim* is a plural noun, showing that there is more than one God. Yet the Hebrew Bible plainly quotes God as saying that there is only one God. "I am God," he says, "and there is no other" (Isaiah 45:22). God does not say, "we are God."

So what does the Hebrew word *elohim* mean? Is it plural? Does it prove there is one God or many? If we can't read Hebrew, how can we find out?

You can prove it yourself

You may already have some Bible-study tools that can help you learn what *elohim* means. We do not have to be Hebrew scholars, but we will need to do some study.

We should begin with prayer, to ask God to give us understanding. Tell him of our willingness to give up old cherished ideas if he shows us that they are wrong. Confess any pride, vanity or anger that might inhibit our understanding. Express faith in Christ's leadership. Admit to him that our humanity sometimes limits our vision and distorts our thinking. Pray in faith that God will teach us and that he will grant us ears that hear and a heart that responds.

Having done that, we'll be ready to study. We'll be like the Bereans, who "received the message with great eagerness and examined the Scriptures every day to see if what Paul said was true" (Acts 17:11).

To help us know the truth about the word *elohim*, we should be aware of one important concept: To know what any word means, we need to observe how it is used. We need to note whether the word is used as a noun, verb, pronoun, adverb or another part of speech. If the word is used as a noun, we should see if it is a singular, plural or proper noun. We should analyze how the word is used.

We should note the words that are used with it, too. For example, if we are uncertain if the noun is plural or singular, are there any pronouns associated with it that could help us find out? The more examples that we have of its use in context, the more certain we can be of its definition. We might even discover that a word has different meanings in different contexts. Some words are verbs in one context but nouns in another. The English word "saw" is an example of this.

A study in Strong's concordance

Our study can begin with Strong's *Exhaustive Concordance*. Those who own other concordances or computer Bible programs can apply the same principles with slight modifications for their situation. Some resources will make the job easier than Strong's does.

Look up the English word "God" in Strong's concordance. Under that heading we'll find a list of all the verses where we can find the word *God* in the King James Version. The verse list begins with Genesis 1:1, "God made the heaven and the earth." To the right of that verse is the number 430. If we turn to the Hebrew and Chaldee dictionary in the back of the concordance and look up word number 430, we'll find that this word is *elohim*. Genesis 1:1 is the first place in the Bible where the word *elohim* occurs.

You can now read elohim in Genesis 1:1 by reading the text like this. "In the beginning *elohim* made the heaven and the earth." If we read Strong's definition of *elohim,* we will notice that it has several definitions and that it is a plural noun. By this, Strong means that *elohim* is plural in form. However, we should not assume in advance that it is always plural in meaning. The context tells us the meaning.

Returning to the verse list for God, notice that for the vast majority of times that we read "God" in the Old Testament, it corresponds to the Hebrew word *elohim*. The *NIV Exhaustive Concordance* claims that one can find *elohim* 2,602 times in the Old Testament. The New International Version translates it 2,242 times as "God." It's the most common word in the Old Testament translated as "God." We have more than 2,200 verses that can help us understand what *elohim* means. If we want to be convinced what *elohim* means, then we can start reading those verses.

It may help to take Strong's verse list of "God" and to read each verse aloud, substituting *elohim* for "God" at the appropriate places. Substituting *elohim* into the text is probably the closest we will ever come to reading the Hebrew Bible. Yet it's a simple way of cementing the true meaning of *elohim* in our minds. But don't just read the verse by itself — read it in its broader context.

Substituting *elohim* for God in Genesis 1:1 can change our perspective of that verse and it can begin to help us understand this subject. Let's notice that applying this principle affects the reading of other verses in that same chapter. Genesis 1:2-5 will read:

Now the earth was formless and empty, darkness was over the surface of the deep, and the Spirit of *elohim* was hovering over the waters. And *elohim* said, "Let there be light," and there was light. Elohim saw that the light was good, and he separated the light from the darkness. Elohim called the light "day," and the darkness he called "night." And there was evening, and there was morning — the first day.

Notice that shortly after *elohim* is used, singular pronouns are used to refer to it: "he separated...he called." These reflect the fact that in Hebrew, these verbs are in the singular form.

Genesis 1:26 reads, "Then God [*elohim*] said, 'Let us make man in our image, in our likeness.'" I don't know Hebrew, so I can't tell if the verb "said" is singular or plural. But I do read English, and the pronouns here are plural. But does it automatically follow that *elohim* is plural? Before answering the question, I will ask another. Should we base our theology on one unusual verse or on more than 2,000 clear verses? What would lead to sound doctrine — 2,000 sure witnesses or one aberrant witness?

Genesis 1:26 is an enigmatic witness. It does not tell us why *or to whom* God is speaking. It does not say, "The Father said to the Son" or "God said to God" or "God said to the angels" or any other combination. Because the Bible remains silent as to whom and why God said this, any conclusions about these points would be conjectures, and therefore not a solid basis for doctrine. Note that there are several possibilities that do not require the existence of more than one God for them. Many commentaries will give us those explanations. You might think of some yourself.

Second, this is not the only verse that quotes God. Many of the later verses are God's revelation of himself to us in which he unambiguously says that there is but one God. Those other verses are the verses that should decide our doctrine — the verses that address the question directly and clearly.

Singular pronouns for *elohim*

Third, the context of the verse proves the plurality theory wrong. Genesis 1:27, the very next verse, reads: "So *elohim* created man in his own image, in the image of God [*elohim*] he created him; male and female he created them." Just as they are in the rest of the chapter, the pronouns here are singular. When *elohim* creates humanity, God reveals himself to be but one God.

As we continue our study, we'll notice several other interesting facts about *elohim*. For example, it was *elohim* who said "I give you every seed-bearing plant" (verse 29). It was *elohim* who said, "I will make a helper suitable for him" (Genesis 2:18). Later *elohim* told Noah, "I am going to put an end to all people" and "This is the sign of the covenant I am establishing between me and you" (Genesis 6:13; 9:12). God refers to himself with singular pronouns.

A beautiful trait of *elohim* is that he never lies. He thundered to Israel, "I am the Lord your *elohim*.... You shall have no other gods before me" (Exodus 20:2-3). Moses, the prophet of The God Who Does Not Lie, encouraged the Israelites to "acknowledge and take to heart this day that the Lord is *elohim* in heaven above and on the earth below. There is no other" (Deuteronomy 4:39).

In the Bible, it was *elohim* who walked in the Garden, made a covenant with Abraham, wrestled with Jacob and spoke out of the burning bush. There was only one. It was *elohim* who thundered from Sinai, gave victory to Joshua, sanctified the Temple and spoke to the prophets. This God, The God Who Does Not Lie, reveals himself to be the only God there is. "Turn to me and be saved, all you ends of the earth; for I am *elohim,* and there is no other" (Isaiah 45:22). The God of truth says, "See now that I myself am he! There is no *elohim* besides me" (Deuteronomy 32:39).

Elohim is not the only word
plural in form but singular in meaning

Elohim is not the only Hebrew noun that can be plural in form but singular in meaning. Such Hebrew noun forms are sometimes used for abstract nouns and as intensifiers. Gesenius' *Hebrew Grammar* devotes several pages to this subject. The following list is not exhaustive, but it illustrates the point. The masculine plural ending is *-im; -oth* is the feminine plural ending.

zequnim — old age (Gen. 21:2, 7; 37:3; 44:20).

ne'urim — youth. David was only a boy (*na'ar*), but Goliath "has been a fighting man from his youth [*ne'urim*]" (1 Sam. 17:33).

chayyim — life. (This is used in the song "To life, to life, *lechayyim*" in Fiddler on the Roof.)

gebhuroth — strength. The singular form *gebhurah* is the usual word for strength, but the plural form is used in Job 41:12.

tsedaqoth — righteousness. The singular form *tsedaqah* is the usual word, but *tsedaqoth* is used in Isaiah 33:15 — "he who walks righteously [or "in righteousness"]."

chokmoth — wisdom. *Chokmah* is the usual form, but *chokmoth* is used in Prov. 1:20.

'adonim — lord. *'adon* means "lord," and *'adonim* normally means "lords," but Isaiah 19:4 says, "I will hand the Egyptians over to the power of a cruel master ['adonim]."

behemoth. This word normally means beasts, but in Job 40:15 it refers to one animal.

Specifically discussing *elohim*, Gesenius observes: "The language has entirely rejected the idea of numerical plurality in *'elohim* (whenever it denotes one God).... [This] is proved especially by its being almost invariably joined with a singular attribute" (such as a singular adjective or verb). For more information on the subject, consult Gesenius' *Hebrew Grammar*, pages 396-401, 1909 edition.

WHAT DOES DEUTERONOMY 6:4 MEAN?

"Hear, O Israel: The Lord our God,
the Lord is one" (Deuteronomy 6:4, NIV).

The problem in translating this verse is not the meaning of the Hebrew term for "one," but the division of the sentence *"Yahweh Elohim Yahweh echad."* Since the Hebrew text has no punctuation, various renderings are possible, all requiring the addition of the verb "is." The four most important possibilities can be found in the New Revised Standard Version and its footnote on this verse:

Yahweh (is) our God, Yahweh alone.
Yahweh our God (is) one Yahweh.
Yahweh our God, Yahweh (is) one.
Yahweh (is) our God, Yahweh (is) one.

These versions have major differences in emphasis. The question here is not about the psychological effect created by each possibility, but the meaning of the passage for its theological import.

The King James Version of 1611 and the Revised Version took option 2, probably because the repetition of the subject of the sentence ("Yahweh") in 3 and 4 seems forced, unnatural. Option 1 has the disadvantage of using *"echad"* (one) in a sense that is unusual and unexpected. In other passages, a different word is used for "alone."

Theological importance

The theological possibilities behind Deuteronomy 6:4 are two. The first is that this verse stresses God's unity, and the second is that it stresses God's uniqueness. "Unity" means oneness (a state of being single). In a theological context, it does not mean harmony among people (unity of mind, etc.) – it means that there is only one God. "Uniqueness" means a state in which there is no equal. Although many gods may exist, only one is to be Israel's God.

This passage, then, is announcing either that there is only one single being in the Godhead, or that Israel is not to worship any of the other (existing) gods. A possibility of the combination of the two need not concern us, because it does not alter anything significant, as will become clear below.

In determining which of these meanings is correct, it is necessary to give some thought to the second possibility, the notion that the Israelites are to accept Yahweh as their national God (rather than any other existing deity). This can be held by those who take Deuteronomy to be an anthropological account (one that explains the ideas current in a polytheistic Israel) rather than an actual revelation from the true God. Or it can be held by those who believe that God limited his self-revelation to accommodate the polytheistic ideas of the day. Both of these approaches clash with Deut. 4:35 and 39, which assert that only the Lord is God, and there is none other besides him. Deut. 6:4 should not be interpreted to imply that the people thought that other gods might exist, but that only Yahweh should be worshiped.

Although God is unique, Deut. 6:4 is not about his uniqueness. It is about God's unity. This is not to assert that the Israelites totally understood the true God, or that they abstained from the worship of other (false, non-existing) gods – far from it; the record indicates the opposite. It would be equally wrong to assume that Deuteronomy 6:4 says that God is pure spirit. This concept is the result of abstract reasoning concerning God, which was foreign to the society that received and read the Torah.

Irrespective of what Israel thought about God (or about Deuteronomy), Deut. 6:4 is a divine revelation. It proceeds from the true God. The meaning is that there is no other divine being in existence, and that Yahweh is that being, a single being, whom we should worship.

GOD'S NAMES AND TITLES

The names of God and the words used for God found in the Old Testament reflect a Semitic world's commitment to the relationship between the nature of anything and the name of that thing. The name could not be divorced from the nature of the actual being of the thing. The revelation of God belongs to the divine freedom of the Self-Naming God. The various names of God in his acts with his people in the world cannot be divorced from his actual nature and being. All the names of God must refer to who he truly is with Israel and the world.

The most common name of God found in the Old Testament – YHWH (used 6823 times) – refers to the great I-AM of God, established in his divine freedom to be present with Israel in the Exodus tradition. The fundamental assertion of the five books of Moses or the Pentateuch is that YHWH is none other than the Elohim (used 2550 times) of the world.

It is the nature and being of this one that would establish both the redemption of his people and the creation of the world. Deuteronomy 32:3, in the Song of Moses, the poet declares that he will proclaim the name of YHWH, he will praise the greatness of "our" Elohim. There is a strong polemic inherent in the use of these names that demythologizes the world of the ancient deities. With the use of these names, Israel confessed the unique power of the oneness of the "Lord our God" (Deuteronomy 6:4).

The names YHWH and Elohim are usually translated by the English words LORD and GOD. We should understand these names as referring at once both to the Deliverer of Israel and the Creator of the universe – the heavens and the earth.

In a few places, the King James Version translated the consonants YHWH with the vowels from the word *Adonai;* the resulting hybrid was "Jehovah." The four consonants of the name that the Jews would not pronounce in the synagogues of Judaism were read aloud as "Adonai," and the scribes recorded the practice in a conflation of the consonants from YHWH and the vowels of Adonai. Transliterated in the King James Bible, the word Jehovah was produced.

Modern scholars believe that in some sense YHWH is to be associated with the verb "to be" in Hebrew, and may have been pronounced something like "Yahweh." That is the way the name is sounded among most scholars today. Many Jews cling to their reverence for the name and in their congregations, when they see the Tetragrammaton (YHWH) in the texts, they say, "Ha Shem," meaning "the Name."

The important thing to understand is that "Lord God" refers us to the actual nature and being of the actual existence of his deity with us in the world. Because of his actions in delivering Israel from Egypt, YHWH is the name confessed by the people of God, and Elohim, the name associated with his creation in the beginning of the world, is affirmed as being none other than YHWH. We do not exhaust the ways the Lord God in his divine freedom chose to interact in covenant with his people. There are many other names of God in the Old Testament.

Associated directly with the Lord God (*YHWH Elohim*) is the name *Elohim* in construct form with the fathers of Israel. He is the God of Abraham, Isaac, and Jacob/Israel (Exodus 3:13-15). Other forms of *YHWH* may be observed: *YHWH Yireh* (Genesis 22:14, "He sees"), *YHWH Rophekah* (Exodus 15:26, "He heals"), *YHWH Nissiy* (Exodus 17:15, "My Banner"), *YHWH Meqaddishkem* (Exodus 31:13, "He makes you holy"), *YHWH Shalom* (Judges 6:24, "Lord of peace"), *YHWH Tseba'oth* (1 Samuel 1:3, "Lord of hosts"), *YHWH Tsidqenuh* (Jeremiah 23:6, "Lord, our righteousness"), *YHWH Shammah* (Ezekiel 48:35, "He is there"), *YHWH Elyon* (Psalm 7:17, "He is most high"), *YHWH Ro'iy* (Psalm 23:1, "He is my shepherd"), and others.

The book of Ezekiel may be understood as a prophecy that shows that God does not name himself in vain: "I am YHWH" is announced over and over again throughout the book. The rhetoric is clearly that, when the prophecy is fulfilled, the whole world will know him for who he truly is.

Combinations of terms with *El* or *Elohim* are also frequent in the Old Testament. Genesis 14:18-22 possesses a play on the names for the Lord God, and it claims the *El Elyon* (God Most High) as the begetter (*Qoneh*) of the heavens and the earth is the one who is Abram's Shield or Protector. *El Shadday* (God of Provision, Genesis 17:1) was known among the ancestors of Israel (Exodus 6:3), long before the great I-AM had given Moses the name YHWH, with which Moses could confront Pharaoh.

El in certain combinations can refer to angels, mighty heroes or humans, as well as the supreme God. *El Olam* (God of Forever, Genesis 21:33) bears the interaction of God's eternity with created time. *El Rachum* (God of Compassion, Exodus 34:6) signifies the way God is in the conception of Israel, even in spite of Israel's opposition to who he truly is. *El Emunah* (God of Faithfulness, Deuteronomy 32:4) refers to the God whom Israel can trust with her future.

The confession in Exodus 34:6-7 shapes a "credo" that forms much of Israel's understanding of the Lord God in covenant with her and the development of her history in the world. Here *YHWH* is the *El* of that compassion, favor, patience, and great grace and truth that is inherent in the way the great I-AM has chosen in his divine freedom to be present with Israel's past, present and future.

Besides these combinations of names with *YHWH* and *El* or *Elohim,* the term *Adonay* can be employed in the superlative to refer to the Lord of Lords (Deuteronomy 10:17). In Genesis 15:1, the Word of YHWH calls himself for Abram a *Megen* (Shield). In Exodus 31:13, YHWH calls himself the one who makes Israel holy (*Meqadish*), a name especially important in the Levitical law (Leviticus 20:8; 21:8; 22:32). In his interaction with his people, he is of a dynamic nature and being.

YH and a shortened form *YHu* can be found throughout the ancient Near East to signify a deity in the pantheons of some city-states as well as the God of the Old Testament (Exodus 15:2 and with many names of places and people). *El* and *Elohim* are commonly found among the mythologies and cosmogonies of the ancient civilizations. These names for the gods of the temples and palaces in the city-states of the ancient civilizations are also reflected in the pantheons of the Greek gods. The Canaanite *Baal,* Mesopotamia's *Marduk,* and the Greek *Zeus* may all be understood as storm-gods bound up with the fertility myths of these peoples.

These gods are the background for the names of the Lord God that we find in use in ancient Israel. But Israel employs what was common in this background with unique significance. The names of the Lord God in the biblical usage could never be understood free from the actual being and nature of the one true Creator and Redeemer of the world in opposition to the other gods. He is to be known in Israel as the great I-AM, the one who makes Israel the people of God (cf. Hosea 1:9). She is to know this one for who he truly is in the world (cf. the "I am YHWH" of the book of Ezekiel). This is the prophetic power of the self-revelation of the self-naming God that lies behind the use of the divine names and titles in the Old Testament.

Thus, the use of the words Greek *Kyrios* and *Theos* in the New Testament resounds in the Greco-Roman world the names of *YHWH* and *Elohim* in the Old Testament.

John McKenna

QUESTIONS & ANSWERS

Let's address several questions and objections.

Are you saying there is no difference between a Christian and a non-Christian?

No. We are saying that because of who Jesus is and what he has done, all humans—believers and non-believers—are joined to God in and through Jesus, through his human nature. As a result, God is reconciled to all people. All have been adopted as his dearly loved children. All, in and through Jesus, are included in the Triune love and life of God: Father, Son and Spirit.

However, not all people acknowledge who Christ is and therefore the truth of who they are in Christ. Those who have not yet repented and put their trust exclusively in Christ are not believers. They are not living in relationship with him and receiving the abundant life he gives.

One way to speak of the distinction between believers and non-believers is to say that all people are included in Christ (objectively) but only believers are actively participating in that inclusion.

We see these distinctions throughout the New Testament, and they are important. However, we must not take these distinctions too far, creating some kind of separation or opposition, and think of non-believers as not accepted by and not loved by God. To see them in this way would be to overlook the great truth of who Jesus Christ is and what he has already done for all humanity. It would be to turn the "good news" into "bad news."

When we see all humanity joined to Christ, some of the categories we might have held in our thinking fall away. We no longer see non-believers as "outsiders" but as children of God in need of personally acknowledging how much their Father loves them, likes them, and wants them. We approach them as brothers and sisters. Do they know who they are in Christ? Do they live in personal communion with Christ, No—and it is our privilege to tell them of God's love for them that they might do so.

If all are reconciled already to God in Christ, why does Scripture say so much about repentance and faith?

In the New Testament, the Greek word translated "repentance" is *metanoia,* which means "change of mind." All humanity is invited and enabled by the Spirit to experience a radical change of mind away from sinful egoistic self-centeredness and toward God and his love experienced in union with

Jesus Christ through the Holy Spirit.

Notice Peter's invitation to this change of mind in Acts 2:38-39:

> Repent and be baptized, every one of you, in the name of Jesus
> Christ for the forgiveness of your sins. And you will receive the gift of
> the Holy Spirit. The promise is for you and your children and for all
> who are far off—for all whom the Lord our God will call.

God does not forgive people in exchange for their repentance and belief.
As Scripture proclaims, forgiveness is an unconditional free gift that is
entirely of grace. It is a reality that exists for us even before we enter into it
in our experience. We repent because we are forgiven.

The gospel truth—the truth about Jesus and about all humanity joined
with God in Jesus—is that God has already forgiven all humanity with a
forgiveness that is unconditional and free: "Therefore," invites Peter, "repent
and believe this truth—and be baptized by the Spirit with the mind of Jesus—
which involves supernatural assurance that we truly are the children of God."

Repentance is a change of mind and heart; it involves coming to
acknowledge who Jesus is for us and who we are in him, apart from anything
we have done or will yet do. Through repentance, which is God's gift to us
through the Spirit, our minds are renewed in Jesus and we turn to him and
begin to trust him.

The Spirit moves us to repent because our forgiveness has already been
accomplished in Christ, not in order to be forgiven. We repent because we
know that, in Jesus, our sins have already been forgiven, and that, in Jesus,
we are already a new creation. In this repentance, we turn away from the
alienation within us as the Spirit baptizes our minds in Jesus' acceptance and
in the assurance that comes with it.

Why does Paul say that if you don't have the Spirit, you don't belong to Christ?

Romans 8:9 says, "You, however, are not in the realm of the flesh but are
in the realm of the Spirit, if indeed the Spirit of God lives in you. And if
anyone does not have the Spirit of Christ, they do not belong to Christ."

The sentence "And if anyone does not have the Spirit of Christ, they do
not belong to Christ" is not meant to be lifted out of context and turned into
a proof that some people do not belong to God. In the context of this
passage, Paul is addressing believers; he is not making a statement here about
non-believers. He is warning disobedient believers who are refusing to
submit to the Holy Spirit in their lives. In effect, he is saying, "You say that

the Spirit of God is in you, and you are right. However, your life should be reflecting the presence of the Spirit of Christ. Your actions do not demonstrate that you really do belong to Christ as you claim to. I don't dispute that you belong to Christ. But if you do, then on that very basis act in accordance with that reality."

As Paul says to believers in verse 12, "We have an obligation—but it is not to the flesh…" We have an obligation to live in the light of who Christ has made us be.

If the world is reconciled, why would Jesus say that he doesn't pray for the world?

In John 17:9, Jesus says: "I pray for them [his disciples]. I am not praying for the world, but for those you have given me, for they are yours."

Just because Jesus said in one instance that he was not praying for the world, but instead for his disciples, does not imply that he never prayed for the world. It is just that right then, his emphasis was on his disciples. He is praying in particular for them, focusing on them.

It is important to understand how John uses the word "world" (*kosmos* in Greek) in the flow of his Gospel. At times the word can refer to all people (who are all loved by God; see John 3:16) while at other times it can refer to the worldly "system" that is fallen and hostile toward God.

It is apparently this system that Jesus has in mind in John 17. Since this fallen system or world resists God, Jesus' prayer does not include it. He is not praying for the world in its current fallen form, rather, he is praying for a group of people whom he can use to declare his love in this fallen world.

Later on in his prayer, Jesus turns his attention to those who are not yet his disciples. He prays "also for those who will believe in me through their message." He prays for them that they, along with those who are already believing, "may be one, Father…so that the world may believe that you have sent me" (John 17:21). This aligns with the Gospel of John's message (3:16): God loves the whole world and wants to save everyone.

If all are reconciled already to God, why does Scripture speak of hell?

Scripture speaks of hell because it is the natural consequence of rebellion against God. When we cut ourselves off from God and refuse his mercy, grace and forgiveness, we are rejecting communion with him and cutting ourselves off from the very source of our life. Christ came to prevent that from happening. Grace enters in and disrupts the natural course of a fallen creation. Being created for personal communion with God means we must be receptive to what he has done for us in Christ. All are included in what Christ intends for everyone, but we can refuse our inclusion. We are reconciled to the Father, but we can refuse to receive that reconciliation and live as if God had not reconciled us to himself.

However, such refusal does not negate what God has done for all humanity in Christ.

In *The Great Divorce,* C.S. Lewis wrote:

> There are only two kinds of people in the end; those who say to God, "Thy will be done," and those to whom God says, in the end, "Thy will be done." All that are in hell, choose it. Without that self-choice there could be no hell. No soul that seriously and constantly desires joy will ever miss it. Those who seek find. To those who knock it is opened.

Why does the Bible talk about people whose names are not in the book of life?

Revelation 13:8 says, "All inhabitants of the earth will worship the beast— all whose names have not been written in the Lamb's book of life, the Lamb who was slain from the creation of the world."

Revelation 17:8 says, "The inhabitants of the earth whose names have not been written in the book of life from the creation of the world will be astonished when they see the beast."

We need to consider the literary context of these statements in Revelation. John writes using a literary genre (style) known as apocalyptic. This genre, which was commonly used by Jewish writers in John's day, is highly symbolic. There is not a literal "book of life." The "book of life" is a figure of speech, a symbolic way of referring to those who are in allegiance with the Lamb. These verses in Revelation refer to people who reject the new life that Christ has already secured for them.

Why does Peter say it is hard to be saved?

First Peter 4:17-18 says: "It is time for judgment to begin with God's household; and if it begins with us, what will the outcome be for those who do not obey the gospel of God? And, 'If it is hard for the righteous to be saved, what will become of the ungodly and the sinner?'"

The point of verses 17-18 is found in verse 19: "So then, those who suffer according to God's will should commit themselves to their faithful Creator and continue to do good."

Peter has been encouraging persecuted believers to live in accord with their identity as children of God and not like those who live in debauchery and idolatry (verses 1-5). The difficulty is not in Jesus' power to save but for those believing to live faithfully through times of the suffering of persecution. The difficulties involved in being saved call for perseverance. Peter does not say that salvation is impossible for anyone. (See also Mark 10:25-27, where Jesus replies to his disciples' query as to how anyone could be saved if it was difficult for the wealthy. Jesus answered, "For mortals it is impossible, but not for God; for God all things are possible," NRSV).

As part of his argument, he points out that persecution is participation in the suffering of Christ, and therefore if believers are to suffer, they should suffer for their faith and godly behavior instead of suffering for sinful and ungodly behavior (verses 12-16). His point is that believers, who know that Jesus, the Savior, is the merciful Judge of all, should not be living in the same base and evil ways as those who oppose Christ even under the threat of persecution.

It is actually impossible for anyone to be saved—were it not for Christ. Christ has done what is impossible for humans to do for themselves. But those who reject Christ are not participating in Christ's suffering; they participate in their own suffering as they reap what they sow. That experience is a far more difficult path to be on than the narrow one of those who know Christ and can have fellowship with him even in their sufferings.

What is everlasting contempt and destruction?

Daniel 12:2 reads, "Multitudes who sleep in the dust of the earth will awake: some to everlasting life, others to shame and everlasting contempt."

2 Thessalonians 1:6-9 says,

> God is just: He will pay back trouble to those who trouble you and give relief to you who are troubled, and to us as well. This will happen when the Lord Jesus is revealed from heaven in blazing fire with his powerful angels. He will punish those who do not know God and do not obey the gospel of our Lord Jesus. They will be punished with everlasting destruction and shut out from the presence of the Lord and from the glory of his might.

Both of these passages refer to the time of the final judgment when Jesus is "revealed" (sometimes referred to as the Second Coming or Jesus' "return in glory"). All humans will then see clearly who Jesus is and thus who they are because of who he is and what he has done. This "revealing" presents to them a choice—will they say "yes" to their belonging to Christ, or will they say "no"?

Their decision neither creates nor destroys their inclusion, but it does determine their attitude toward it—whether they will accept God's love for them and enter the joy of the Lord, or continue in alienation and frustration (and thus in shame and everlasting contempt and destruction). The destruction is a self-destruction as they refuse the purpose for which they have been made, and the redemption that has already been given to them. They refuse to submit to God's righteousness through repentance and so refuse to receive his life, effectively cutting themselves off from it.

In the Judgment, everyone will face Jesus, the Judge who died for all, and they will have to decide whether they will trust him and count on his being judged in their place. Those who trust their Savior agree with the judgment of God as to what is evil and must be done away with. They humbly receive the joy of the life God has given them in Christ. Those who reject him continue in their hostility and the hell that goes with denying the truth and reality of their sin and Christ's salvation for them.

What about the "narrow gate"?

Jesus says in Matthew 7:13-14: "Enter through the narrow gate. For wide is the gate and broad is the road that leads to destruction, and many enter through it. But small is the gate and narrow the road that leads to life, and only a few find it."

Jesus describing what is happing in the present. A clearer translation is: "many are entering" and "only a few are finding it." In his day, at that time, most were living on the "broad road" of destruction. What Jesus offers here is descriptive, not prescriptive. It does not say what Jesus wants nor what God intends. This is a warning, and warnings are given to prevent the negative outcome from occurring. No parent says to their child, "Watch out, a car is coming!" because they hope the child gets run over! Jesus gives the reason for the need to be warned: under fallen conditions the way to destruction is wide, inviting and easy to follow, or we can simply be swept along into it. The narrow way to life can be easy to miss, may seem difficult to follow and takes our being deliberate and intentional. There were only a "few" who had at that time embraced the truth that is in Jesus—and it is he who is "the narrow gate." But Jesus wants to turn that around so that there are many, not a few, who enter into the life that Jesus has for them. So he gives this warning out of his love for them.

Jesus addresses a similar issue in Matthew 7:21-23:

Not everyone who says to me, "Lord, Lord," will enter the kingdom of heaven, but only the one who does the will of my Father who is in heaven. Many will say to me on that day, "Lord, Lord, did we not prophesy in your name, and in your name drive out demons and in your name perform many miracles?" Then I will tell them plainly, "I never knew you. Away from me, you evildoers!"

These people have done miracles, and in doing so have deceived many. They claim to know Jesus. Although Jesus knows them (he is omniscient), he does not see himself in them with regard to their actual faith or behavior, and so he proclaims, "I never knew you." That is, I don't recognize you as a follower of mine. We haven't been in relationship, in communion with one another despite what you were doing.

Don't we become God's children only at the point of belief?

John 1:12-13 says, "Yet to all who did receive him, to those who believed in his name, he gave the right to become children of God—children born neither of natural descent, nor of human decision or a husband's will, but born of God."

We have seen in Scripture that God has provided for everyone in the vicarious humanity of Jesus. When he died, we all died; when he rose, we rose. Our human natures have been regenerated in him. Therefore all humans are, from God's perspective, already adopted into his family. In Jesus, God gives people that "right" long before they accept it and live in it. They have an inheritance, as Paul puts it.

If we say that we don't have a right to become the children of God until after and unless we believe, then we end up denying what John goes on to say: that it doesn't come from natural descent or from human decision. Such an understanding would make our having the right depend on our decision!

Those who believe in and accept Jesus as their Lord and elder brother enter into and begin to experience the new life as children of God. But that place in God's family has been theirs all along. It is the new life that has been "hidden with Christ in God" (Colossians 3:3). In other words, what has been objectively true for them all along in Jesus, becomes subjectively and personally experienced by them when they become believers. They begin taking up their right and living as the children of God.

Is this universalism?

No, not in the sense that every person ultimately will be saved (or enter into or receive their salvation) regardless of whether they ever trust in Christ. There is no salvation outside of Jesus Christ (Acts 4:12). Those who absolutely refuse to enter into their salvation, or to receive it by repentance and faith in what Christ their Savior has done for them, have refused the benefits of their salvation, refused their inheritance, and repudiated the "hope laid up for [them] in heaven" (Colossians 1:5).

Jesus' atonement has universal intent (Romans 5:18). He died for all and he was raised for all because God so loved the world. He is the "Lamb of God, who takes away the sin of the world" (John 1:29). Scripture shows that God, in Christ, has reconciled all humans to himself (Colossians 1:20; 2 Corinthians 5:19), but he will never force any person to embrace that reconciliation. Love cannot be coerced.

A relationship of love as the children of God could never be the result of a cause-effect mechanism. God wants sons and daughters who love him out of a joyful response to his love, not people who have no mind or choice of their own. As has been revealed in Jesus Christ, God is love in his innermost being, and in God the Persons of the Trinity relate to one another in the truth and freedom of love. That same love is extended to us in Christ that we might share in it, and in nothing less.

To hope that all people will finally come to Christ is not universalism—it is simply Christian and reflects the heart of God (1 Timothy 2:3-6; 2 Peter 3:9). If God calls us to love our enemies, does God himself do less? If God desires that all turn and be saved, can we do anything less?

This does not mean we can proclaim that every person will finally come to faith and receive their salvation. However, it means that, given who God is and what he has done for us in Christ, we ought to be more surprised that some may somehow come to reject the truth and reality of their salvation than to find many in the end turning to Christ to receive his forgiveness and eternal life as his beloved children.

If we are reconciled already, why struggle to live the Christian life?

Some people do not like the idea that others who do not work as hard as they do will end up with the same reward as they (see parable of the laborers in the vineyard, Matthew 20:12-15). But this concern overlooks the truth that no one, no matter how hard they work, deserves salvation. That is why it is, for everyone, a free gift.

However, in Scripture we learn that is why God doesn't want us to live that way. Consider the following passages:

No one can lay any foundation other than the one already laid, which is Jesus Christ. If anyone builds on this foundation using gold, silver, costly stones, wood, hay or straw, their work will be shown for what it is, because the Day will bring it to light. It will be revealed with fire, and the fire will test the quality of each person's work. If what has been built survives, the builder will receive a reward. If it is burned up, the builder will suffer loss but yet will be saved—even though only as one escaping through the flames. (1 Corinthians 3:11-15)

Do not be deceived: God cannot be mocked. People reap what they sow. Whoever sows to please their flesh, from the flesh will reap destruction; whoever sows to please the Spirit, from the Spirit will reap eternal life. (Galatians 6:7-8)

We are joined to Christ in order to live in fellowship with Christ. We are united to Christ in order to participate with him in all he does. It makes no more sense to say that since we belong to Christ there is no point in living the Christian life, than to say, since a man and woman are married, there is no point to them living together. No. They are married in order to live together. We are joined to Christ in order to live with him. Similarly, it makes no sense to say that we want to experience the life of Christ in eternity if we refuse to experience it now.

How do we explain John 6:44?

John 6:44 says, "No one can come to me unless the Father who sent me draws them."

The Jewish religious leaders were seeking to deflect Jesus' seemingly outrageous claim: "I am the bread of life that came down from heaven" (John 6:41). This statement was practically the same thing as claiming divine status.

Jesus' reply to the Jewish leaders' complaint concerning this claim was that they "stop grumbling" (verse 43) and realize that "no one can come to me [the bread of heaven] unless the Father who sent me draws them…" (verse 44). Jesus' point is that the people would not be responding to him, except that God was making it possible for them to do so. If they really knew God, they should recognize that people were coming to the Son according to the will and purpose of the Father. What they see happening in Jesus' ministry is not evidence that Jesus is a blasphemer, disobeying the will of God, but rather that God the Father is accomplishing his will through Jesus, his faithful Son.

In this passage, Jesus is not limiting the number of people who are drawn to him; he is showing that he is doing the Father's work. Elsewhere he says: "When I am lifted up, I will draw all people to myself" (John 12:32). Since

Jesus does only what his Father wants, John 12:32 shows that the Father indeed draws all people to Jesus.

How does this theology compare to Calvinism and Arminianism?

In comparing and contrasting Christian theologies, we are talking about different approaches or understandings among Christian brothers and sisters who seek to serve the same Lord and thus share the same faith. Thus, our discussion should reflect respect and gentleness, not arrogance or hostility.

Calvinism is a theology that developed from the teachings of the Protestant reformer John Calvin (1509-1564). Calvinism emphasizes the sovereignty of God's will in election and salvation. Most Calvinists define God's "elect" as a subset of the human race; Christ died for only some people ("limited" or "particular" atonement"). Those elect for whom he did die were truly and effectively saved in the finished work of Christ, long before they became aware of it and accepted it. According to Calvinist doctrine, it is inevitable that those Christ died for will come to faith in him at some point. This is called "irresistible grace."

Trinitarian theology's main disagreement with Calvinism is over the scope of reconciliation. Its objection is based on the fundamental fact of who Jesus is and that he is one in will, purpose, mind, authority and act with the Father in the Spirit. The whole God is Savior, and Jesus is the new Adam who died for all. The Bible asserts that Christ made atonement "not only for our sins, but for the sins of the whole world" (1 John 2:2). While Trinitarian theology rejects the restrictive extent of "limited atonement" and the determinism of "irresistible grace," it agrees with Calvinism that forgiveness, reconciliation, redemption, justification, etc. were all accomplished effectively by what Christ did, and these gospel truths have been secured for us irrespective of our response to them.

Arminianism derives from the teachings of another Protestant reformer, Jacob Arminius (1560-1609). Arminius insisted that Jesus died for all humanity, and that all people can be saved if they take personal action, which is enabled by the Spirit. This theology, while not ignoring God's sovereignty, gives a more central or key role to human decision and free will. Its premise is that salvation, forgiveness, reconciliation, redemption, justification, etc., are not actually effective unless a person has faith. Only if God foresees a person using their free choice to receive Christ, does he then elect them. Those whom he foresees rejecting his salvation, he condemns. So like the Calvinist, in the end God wills the salvation of some and the condemnation of others.

Trinitarian theology differs from Arminianism over the effectiveness of the reconciliation. Atonement, or at-one-ment between God and humanity, is only a hypothetical possibility for Arminians; it does not become an actuality unless God foresees someone's decision of faith. In this view, God, on the basis of his foreknowledge of an individual's acceptance or rejection, then accepts or rejects that person. Trinitarian theology, however, teaches that the atonement and reconciliation represents the heart and mind of God towards all and is objectively true in Christ, even before it has been subjectively accepted and experienced. It remains true even if some deny it. God has one ultimate will or purpose for all, realized from the Father, through the Son and in the Spirit.

While Calvinism and Arminianism emphasize different aspects of salvation theology, Trinitarian theology has attempted, as did early church leaders Irenaeus, Athanasius, and Gregory, to maintain in harmony the wideness of God's love emphasized by Arminians with the unconditioned faithfulness of God emphasized by Calvinists. The Incarnational and Trinitarian theology of GCI aligns neither with traditional Calvinism nor Arminianism. It emphasizes the sovereignty of God's Triune holy love that calls for our response. His sovereign will is expressed in accord with God being a fellowship of holy love. Its center is the heart, mind, character and nature of God revealed in the person and work of Jesus Christ, the Incarnate Savior and Redeemer. God's sovereignty is most clearly and profoundly shown in Jesus Christ. The place and importance of human response to God's grace is also shown in Jesus Christ, who makes a perfect and free response to God in our place and on our behalf as our Great High Priest. Our response then is a gift given by the Holy Spirit by which we share in Christ's perfect response for us in our place and on our behalf.

What is perichoresis?

The eternal communion of love that Father, Son and Spirit share as the Trinity involves a mystery of inter-relationship and interpenetration of the divine Persons, a mutual indwelling without loss of personal identity. As Jesus said, "the Father is in me, and I in the Father" (John 10:38). Early Greek-speaking Christian theologians described this relationship with the word *perichoresis,* which is derived from root words meaning "around" and "contain." Each person of the Trinity is contained within the others; they dwell in one another, they envelop one another.

Tips on Biblical Exegesis

We have sought to address typical questions and objections that arise as people consider Trinitarian theology. Other verses bring similar questions or objections. We have sought to demonstrate a Trinitarian, Christ-centered approach to reading and interpreting all passages of Holy Scripture.

Some object to the idea of interpreting Scripture. They say, "I just let the Bible say what it means." This idea, though admirable, is not accurate, nor possible. The act of reading is, necessarily, an act of interpretation. The issue is not whether to interpret; it is this: What criteria do we use in interpreting as we read?

We always bring to Scripture certain ideas and advance assumptions. What we are urging here is that we come to Scripture with the truth of who Jesus Christ is as the beginning point and the ongoing criterion by which we read and interpret the Holy Scriptures. Jesus must be the "lens" through which all Scripture is read.

Therefore, in reading Scripture, we recommend thinking about the following questions:

- How does this passage line up with the gospel, which answers its central question, "Who is Jesus?"

- Is this passage referring to the universal, objective salvation of all humanity in Jesus, or is it referring to the personal, subjective experience of accepting or rejecting that salvation?

- What is the historical, cultural, and literary context?

- How is this passage worded in other translations? Other translations can sometimes help us see passages from different perspectives. It's also helpful to check Greek lexicons and other translation helps, because some of the richness and subtleties of the Greek New Testament are lost in translations into other languages.

For a guide to biblical exegesis, you may find it helpful to consult *How to Read the Bible for All Its Worth,* by Gordon D. Fee and Douglas Stuart (Zondervan, 2014) or *Elements of Biblical Exegesis: A Basic Guide for Students and Ministers,* by Michael J. Gorman (Baker, 2010). See also the book *A Guided Tour of the Bible,* by John Halford, Michael Morrison, and Gary Deddo.

ABOUT THE AUTHORS

This book is a collaborative effort. Some chapters give the name of the author at the end. Other articles are corporate products, perhaps drafted by one person but extensively edited by others. All of the authors were, at the time of writing, employed by Grace Communion International.

Terry Akers worked in the letter-answering department for Grace Communion International.

Gary Deddo has a PhD in theology from the University of Aberdeen and is Professor of Theology at Grace Communion Seminary.

Neil Earle is a retired GCI pastor, and an instructor in church history for Grace Communion Seminary.

J. Michael Feazell has a D.Min. degree from Azusa Pacific Seminary. Dr. Feazell was Vice President of Grace Communion International.

Sheila Graham worked in the GCI editorial department for many years; she is retired.

John Halford was editor of *Christian Odyssey* magazine; he died in 2014.

Paul Kroll worked in the GCI Personal Correspondence Department for many years, and is now retired.

Michael Morrison has a Ph.D. in New Testament from Fuller Theological Seminary. He is Professor of New Testament at Grace Communion Seminary, and the editor of this compilation.

Ralph Orr was a pastor, research, and writer for Grace Communion International.

Dan Rogers was the superintendent of U.S. ministers for GCI. He has a PhD from Union Institute and University. He has retired, but teaches for Grace Communion Seminary.

Joseph Tkach has a D.Min. degree from Azusa Pacific Seminary. He was president and chairman of the board of Grace Communion International.

ABOUT THE PUBLISHER...

Grace Communion International is a Christian denomination with about 30,000 members, worshiping in about 550 congregations in almost 70 nations and territories. We began in 1934 and our main office is in North Carolina. In the United States, we are members of the National Association of Evangelicals and similar organizations in other nations. We welcome you to visit our website at www.gci.org.

If you want to know more about the gospel of Jesus Christ, we offer help. First, we offer weekly worship services in hundreds of congregations worldwide. Perhaps you'd like to visit us. A typical worship service includes songs of praise, a message based on the Bible, and opportunity to meet people who have found Jesus Christ to be the answer to their spiritual quest. We try to be friendly, but without putting you on the spot. We do not expect visitors to give offerings – there's no obligation. You are a guest.

To find a congregation, write to one of our offices, phone us or visit our website. If we do not have a congregation near you, we encourage you to find another Christian church that teaches the gospel of grace.

We also offer personal counsel. If you have questions about the Bible, salvation or Christian living, we are happy to talk. If you want to discuss faith, baptism or other matters, a pastor near you can discuss these on the phone or set up an appointment for a longer discussion. We are convinced that Jesus offers what people need most, and we are happy to share the good news of what he has done for all humanity. We like to help people find new life in Christ, and to grow in that life. Come and see why we believe it's the best news there could be!

Our work is funded by members of the church who donate part of their income to support the gospel. Jesus told his disciples to share the good news, and that is what we strive to do in our writings, our worship services, and our day-to-day lives.

If this book has helped you and you want to pay some expenses, all donations are gratefully welcomed, and in several nations, are tax-deductible. If you can't afford to give anything, don't worry about it. It is our gift to you. To donate online, go to www.gci.org/participate/donate.

Thank you for letting us share what we value most – Jesus Christ. The good news is too good to keep it to ourselves.

See our website for hundreds of articles, locations of our churches, addresses in various nations, audio and video messages, and much more.

www.gci.org
Grace Communion International
3120 Whitehall Park Dr.
Charlotte, NC 28273
800-423-4444

You're Included...

Dr. J. Michael Feazell talks to leading Trinitarian theologians about the good news that God loves you, wants you, and includes you in Jesus Christ. Most programs are about 28 minutes long. Our guests have included:

Ray Anderson, Fuller Theological Seminary
Douglas A. Campbell, Duke Divinity School
Gordon Fee, Regent College
Jeannine Graham, George Fox University
Trevor Hart, University of St. Andrews
George Hunsinger, Princeton Theological Seminary
C. Baxter Kruger, Perichoresis
Jeff McSwain, Reality Ministries
Paul Louis Metzger, Multnomah University
Paul Molnar, St. John's University
Cherith Fee Nordling, Antioch Leadership Network
Andrew Root, Luther Seminary
Alan Torrance, University of St. Andrews
Robert T. Walker, Edinburgh University
N.T. Wright, University of St. Andrews
William P. Young, author of *The Shack*

Programs are free for viewing and downloading at https://learn.gcs.edu/course/view.php?id=58

GRACE COMMUNION
SEMINARY

GRACE COMMUNION SEMINARY

Ministry based on the life and love of the Father, Son, and Spirit

Grace Communion Seminary serves the needs of people engaged in Christian service who want to grow deeper in relationship with our Triune God and to be able to more effectively serve in the church. We offer three degrees: Master of Pastoral Studies, Master of Theological Studies, and Master of Divinity.

Why study at Grace Communion Seminary?

- Worship: to love God with all your mind.
- Service: to help others apply truth to life.
- Practical: a balanced range of useful topics for ministry.
- Trinitarian theology: a survey of Bible, theology and ministry with the merits of a Trinitarian perspective. We begin with the question, "Who is God?" Then, "Who are we in relationship to God?" In this context, "How then do we live and serve?"
- Part-time study: designed to help people who are already serving in local congregations. There is no need to leave your current ministry. Full-time students are also welcome.
- Flexibility: take your choice of courses or pursue a degree.
- Affordable, accredited study: Everything can be done online.

For more information, go to www.gcs.edu.

Grace Communion Seminary is accredited by the Distance Education Accrediting Commission, www.deac.org. The Accrediting Commission is listed by the U.S. Department of Education as a nationally recognized accrediting agency.

216

Made in the USA
Columbia, SC
27 August 2024

41237728R00124